The Gifford Lectures, 1952, Second Series

NATURAL RELIGION
AND
CHRISTIAN THEOLOGY

This book follows

NATURAL RELIGION AND CHRISTIAN THEOLOGY

FIRST SERIES: *Science and Religion*

Cambridge University Press, 1953

NATURAL RELIGION

AND

CHRISTIAN THEOLOGY

THE GIFFORD LECTURES 1952

SECOND SERIES:
Experience and Interpretation

BY

CHARLES E. RAVEN
D.D., D.Sc., F.B.A.

Regius Professor Emeritus of Divinity,
University of Cambridge

CAMBRIDGE
AT THE UNIVERSITY PRESS
1953

PUBLISHED BY

THE SYNDICS OF THE CAMBRIDGE UNIVERSITY PRESS

London Office: Bentley House, N.W. 1
American Branch: New York

Agents for Canada, India, and Pakistan: Macmillan

Printed in Great Britain at the University Press, Cambridge
(Brooke Crutchley, University Printer)

CONTENTS

PREFACE

THE second series of these lectures attempting to set out a modern *Religio Medici* was delivered in May 1952; and the friendship already shown to me in Edinburgh was continued and deepened. Obviously in attempting to cover so large a field my inadequacies were even more evident; and lack of space sharpened controversial issues and left small opportunity for adequate discussion of them.

One point requires explanation. Certain pages of these lectures contain illustrations and phrases employed in the broadcast talks delivered by me in the Home Service in June and July 1951 and published by the Student Christian Movement as *Science and the Christian Man* in 1952. When invited to give these talks I warned the authorities that as I was to touch upon ground similar to that of my Gifford lectures I should wish to use material which I must be free to print hereafter. It did not seem necessary in view of the very different scope of the work to avoid a small amount of overlap and repetition.

My gratitude to my Scottish hosts and audience must be gladly acknowledged once more. To my oldest friends in America, Mr and Mrs John F. Moors of Brookline, in whose home much of this volume was written and all of it revised, I owe the increase of a debt which goes back to 1926.

C. E. R.

I

INTRODUCTORY: THE NEW REFORMATION

W HEN the Churches in spite of a larger measure of sympathy than he had expected failed to adjust their doctrine of Creation to the requirements of the post-Darwinian age, Thomas Henry Huxley was not alone in taking up John Milton's summons[1] of near two hundred years ago and proclaiming the need for a new Reformation. It had long been evident, as we have seen, that traditional orthodoxy was no longer consonant with educated knowledge or adequate to meet the moral needs of the social order then coming to birth. As in the sixteenth century so now Christianity was in the main allied with and represented by habits of thought and life and, indeed, definite convictions and policies which affronted the intelligence and scandalized the conscience of the age. Then, as now, there were groups and individuals within the Churches eager for reform: Cardinal Quignon and Desiderius Erasmus had plenty of followers; and among them were men of singular wisdom and devotion. But the temper both of the official leaders and of the rank and file in Christendom was against them—more so, as it transpired, in the nineteenth century than previously. It seemed plain that change by consent could hardly be accomplished in time to avert disaster. The new Reformation, like its predecessor, would involve the rending of Christendom—and as such might well prove beyond the strength of the institutions that required it. So at least it appeared to Huxley and those who shared his appreciation of the achievements of science and his genuine desire to see religion able once more to satisfy the aspirations and guide the conduct of mankind. This Reformation is in

---

[1] Cf. the magnificent passage in *Areopagitica* predicting 'The approaching Reformation'.

fact taking place—though its progress is not what he hoped or expected.

That the situation is more difficult for the would-be Reformers now than in Luther's day might well be admitted. Both in the scale and in the speed of their reforms they must face a more exacting task. Industrialism and the hungry forties had produced revolutions in most European countries, and in many of them a complete estrangement between Christianity and any form of liberal or socialist policy. If in Britain, thanks to a handful of pioneers and one or two men of prophetic quality, no final break had occurred, there was a strong tendency to regard the Churches as always obstructive and if established as definitely reactionary. Frederic Denison Maurice had been deprived of his chair at King's College nominally on theological grounds but actually because of his advocacy of Christian Socialism; and Shaftesbury, aristocrat though he was, in his campaign against the exploitation of women and children in mines and factories never found clergy or ministers ready to support him on a public platform. Dread of reform was accompanied by alarm at the spread of liberalism in theology. Critical studies, first of the Old and then of the New Testament, could no longer be dismissed as atheism or ascribed only to a few blasphemous Germans. If Britain had been able to ignore the Tübingen school and had produced no Strauss or Renan, yet as Browning confessed in *Gold Hair*

> Our Essays-and-Reviews debate
> Begins to tell on the public mind
> And Colenso's words have weight.

Uneasiness amounting almost to terror was widespread. Robertson Smith, a more learned reformer than the Bishop of Natal, had been driven from his own university. Herbert Spencer, appropriate exponent of contemporary agnosticism, had won his way to Oxford. *Robert Elsmere* had become 'the most effective and popular novel since *Uncle Tom's Cabin*'.[1] There were plenty to

---

[1] So Oliver Wendell Holmes; see M. H. Watt, *The History of the Parson's Wife*, p. 130.

advocate safe paths in perilous times: but to meet the real issues demanded not only learning but insight and courage.

Darwinism, then, coming at a time of general tension and in a form exaggerated by Wilberforce's intervention, served as the spark in the powder magazine. Under the circumstances a new Reformation might well seem the least that could be expected. For the situation plainly called for radical remedy, not only in regard to the specific problems, practical and doctrinal, already mentioned, but because behind them lay the basic issue of the relation of the world of nature to the world of religion, or more specifically of the principles and discipline of the sciences to the study and formulation of theology.

In Britain—more easily perhaps than anywhere else—the response of Christians to the new social order was sufficient to prevent the sheer antagonism universal in the Catholic countries of the Continent. The work of F. D. Maurice and the Christian Socialists, of E. V. Neale, Thomas Hughes and above all J. M. Ludlow in the Co-operative Movement, the Friendly Societies, the Working Men's College and all that accompanied these developments; the similar work of Stewart Headlam, Charles Marson and the Anglican priests who created the famous parishes in east and south London, in Leeds and Portsmouth and many other poverty-stricken areas; the example set by the great Quaker firms in improving conditions and humanizing relationships in industry; and the long tradition of public service among the Free Churches and of evangelism among the Methodists; these kept the young labour organizations from breaking away from Christianity—indeed, in very many directions supplied them with protection and leadership.

In the general relationship of sacred to secular studies Britain owes its unique opportunity largely to the tradition and personnel of the Church and universities of Scotland. Robertson Smith might have to be sacrificed; but the intimate relationship of Church and State and the great inheritance of a religious education were preserved and splendidly employed. To pay homage to the succession of thinkers and teachers who held together the worlds of science and theology through the dark days of the opening century down to the present would be to recite a long list of names in almost every department of intellectual activity. To single out any in particular is invidious; but 'as in private duty bound' it may be allowable to express special obligation to Henry Drummond, to whom all Christendom is in debt, to J. Y. Simpson, whose two books, *The Conflict between Religion and Science* and *The Spiritual Interpretation of Nature*, were most timely and valuable, to Sir D'Arcy Thompson, last of the great omniscients, to the ever-loved and revered David Cairns, and among many other philosophers to Archibald Allan Bowman, greatest of our prophets in the years after the First World War. To these must be added by any Cambridge man the great teachers and leaders whom Scotland sent to us, and especially James Adam, Peter Giles, John Oman and Alexander Wood.

For discussing the problems that arose out of the critical study of the Scriptures, Britain also was fortunately placed. There was no such taboo upon scholarship as was imposed by the College of Propaganda in Catholic countries; nor was there the unchecked speculation which amid much that was suggestive and valuable easily ran to exaggerated extremes in Germany and France. Our tradition of classical scholarship, narrow as it certainly was, gave us a sound technique in linguistic studies combined with a sense of history in general and a knowledge of the Graeco-Roman world in particular. Men like the great Cambridge trio, J. B. Lightfoot, B. F. Westcott and F. J. A. Hort, or their successors at Oxford, W. Sanday, B. H. Streeter and their colleagues,[1] were admirably qualified for the special work which had first to be undertaken, the discovery and interpretation of the authentic text of the New Testament by the application to it of tests which the most sceptical investigator would approve. They did not make the mistake so common in biblical scholarship of divorcing the text from its background and ignoring its place in history. They

[1] It is a joy to an Englishman to read the glowing testimony to the sincerity and scholarship of Sanday's seminar on the Synoptic Gospels by Dean W. L. Sperry of Harvard in *Jesus Then and Now* (New York, 1949), pp. 191–4: his account of the contrast between their work and that of the neo-orthodox is highly significant.

realized and were competent to deal with the importance not only of the small details of textual variations but of the large questions of date, provenance and authorship. In consequence their work has a soundness of scholarship and a broad-based wisdom to which few of their successors have attained. They vindicated the ability of theologians to hold a high place in the academic world and laid a sound foundation for the exegetical and doctrinal studies of the next generation. With these we shall be concerned hereafter.

Meanwhile, and in a sense prior to all other enquiries, there is the question how far theological studies, being concerned with religion and so with the most intimate and personal of human interests, are amenable to the same kind of treatment as is appropriate to scientific or historical research. In this matter there has been a considerable change of outlook in the past thirty years, parallel to the similar change in regard to science[1] and to history, and due to the realization that in no field of knowledge can absolute objectivity be attained. At present this change has, in theology, been carried to lengths which threaten to discredit the claim of Christianity to be in any real sense historic. If it is successfully pressed, a radical transformation of the faith will have been effected; and Modernism in the Roman Catholic sense of the word will have gained acceptance. The issue is plainly one that requires full consideration: it is, indeed, one of the most important with which Christian scholarship is at present concerned. It will be well to begin with a brief sketch of the development of the problem in recent years.

As a prelude and to avoid misunderstanding it is necessary to explain two points on which British theologians have been often and naturally misinterpreted at home, on the Continent and in America.[2]

These concern the terms 'liberal' and 'modernist'.

In Britain theological liberalism derives not from the 'enlightenment' of the eighteenth century, from Voltaire and his disciples,

---

[1] Due in the first place to the principle of relativity; cf. Vol. I of this book, pp. 189–97.
[2] A typical instance is Canon R. Lloyd's two volumes, *The Church of England in the Twentieth Century*; see Note at the end of Vol. I of this book, pp. 212–15.

but from an older and more august ancestry, the Cambridge Platonists or 'Latitude-men' of the seventeenth century, who broke away from the Calvinism of the Puritans and the Catholicism of Archbishop Laud and appealed to the Fourth Gospel and the Greek theologians of Alexandria on behalf of a reasonable faith. S. T. Coleridge, Thomas Erskine of Linlathen, F. D. Maurice and the liberal or broad-church movement in England and Scotland carried on this tradition which has always been independent of Continental liberalism even when it has owed much to it.

In 'modernism' the two principal claimants to the title are less easily contrasted. The proper use of the word should apply it to the movement within Roman Catholicism, associated with George Tyrrell, Baron F. von Hügel and others in this country and with A. Loisy and a small group of French scholars.[1] They were united in their acceptance of historical criticism for the study of Scripture, found themselves constrained by it to accept opinions widely different from those imposed by authority, and sought a solution by contrasting the verifiable facts of the historian with the differently verifiable experiences of the believer, and maintaining that facts of faith need not necessarily be such as a secular historian would accept as having actually happened. Their views were condemned in 1907 in the Papal Encyclical *Pascendi*. In Britain the same title has been given to the group of 'Modern Churchmen' initiated by Bishop Boyd Carpenter and Dr H. D. A. Major, and including Bishop E. W. Barnes, Dean W. R. Inge, J. F. Bethune-Baker, Hastings Rashdall, William Sanday, B. H. Streeter and others, and represented by a periodical and an annual conference. These, although as liberals they would admit a wide divergence of individual opinion, yet had in common an insistence upon a reasonable faith, a regard for scientific studies and an emphasis upon history; and in this last respect were almost exactly the opposite of Continental Modernists. They were and are convinced that scholarship and all the resources proper to science, history and philosophy must be applied to the study of theology,

---

[1] Tyrrell's own definition treats it as simply the opposite of medievalism (cf. his *Medievalism*, pp. 143–4); obviously this is only appropriate in a Roman Catholic context.

since, if truth be one and Christ be the truth, anything less is dishonest and dishonouring. They have therefore felt obliged to examine and test the historicity of the Scriptures and to reject, or reserve judgment upon, the records in accordance with the evidence. Insisting that the basic message of Christianity proclaimed the actual occurrence at a certain time and place of certain momentous and revelatory events, they insisted that if this occurrence were abandoned the Christian claim could not be sustained, and so regarded Continental modernism as a surrender of it: if facts of faith had no factual origin except in human imagination, then Christianity did not differ from an enlightened Mithraism. In their contention they may have been mistaken; if this tendency in neo-orthodoxy prevails,[1] we may find that some sort of Christianity can still survive. But at least it is unfortunate that 'Modernist' should be a term applied to two movements which in their essentials proceed from similar starting-points but in different directions.

These explanations account for the concern of progressive theologians at the turn of the century with the scrutiny of the Gospels and the analysis and comparison of their sources. The historicity of 'the things concerning Jesus' was plainly the crux of the Christian position as they understood it; and now that the text of the documents had been securely determined the interpretation of their relationship to one another and thence to the facts could be investigated. The patient persistence with which the task was fulfilled and the value of the results obtained can hardly be appreciated by those who only know the story at second hand: to those who took part in the work its thoroughness compares very favourably with the relatively superficial and speculative studies which succeeded it. Its chief defect was that it was too narrowly concerned with the documents, treating them without due regard to the nature of their sources or the circumstances of their

[1] It is difficult to foresee the effect of the recent protests against mythologizing by Dr R. Bultmann and his colleagues. Their value will probably depend upon the quality of their historical researches; and for this, Bultmann's work on Form-criticism is not a very encouraging preparation. But he is certainly right in warning us against the danger of suggesting that Christianity is a myth.

composition. But when this was recognized by the form-criticism school, the reaction, in some cases at least, clearly went too far. A more serious but cognate weakness was the tendency to ignore the subjectivity inherent in every record of human happenings and to ascribe to the evidence an almost scientific precision. In their zeal for historical accuracy they fell into the error, common at this time to most secular historians, of expecting history to yield a complete and objective rendering of the facts. They thus tended to define theology as if it were an exact science capable of an academic, indeed mathematical, precision, and this invariably led to disappointment.[1]

The consequent failure of the attempt to apply the scientific method, as then understood, to the field of theology led to an emphasis, first, upon the difference in the data to be studied as between science and theology and then, less justifiably, upon the contrast between their respective methods. Theology, it was urged, dealt with facts which, though they happened at particular times and places and in connexion with special individuals, yet were in character experiential, intimate, personal, indeed internal, such that only the person experiencing them could record and describe. For such events the ordinary criteria of historical investigation are inappropriate; even the tests of analogy and probability cannot apply to what, if true at all, is unique and unprecedented. We can only take them in relation to the whole Christian claim in itself and in its effects and, if we make the venture of faith, accept these data as part of it. Moreover, this experiential element enters into the whole evidence; for the New Testament in all its various parts is the product of men who had shared and believed and been converted by the 'fact' of Christ. To disentangle the fact from its impact, the event from their response and interpretation of it, is an impossible proposal: inspiration, the revealing experience which illuminates and transforms, cannot be weighed and measured by any application of the scientific method: it belongs to a different category and can only be examined by those who have themselves a first-hand acquaintance with it. Only Christians living

[1] For a further and similar source of difficulty, cf. Note 1 below, p. 204.

in the community of the Church can understand and expound theology.[1]

This claim, unsound though it plainly proves to be, is yet obviously arguable. It has been expanded by some recent apologists into the statement that as the New Testament deals with a unique event, only appreciable at its true value by those who experienced and recorded it, their testimony is beyond criticism and must be accepted or rejected as it stands. This, if we agree to it, would imply that in fact the whole study of theology would be reduced to an exegesis of the Scriptures—if, indeed, exegesis could properly be applied to a theme which had been thus removed from the categories of human understanding. We should be driven, as fundamentalists have in fact been driven, to the segregation of the Bible to a realm apart so that only its language remains for our study, and this can only be understood by cross-references within the inspired volume. No one who appreciates the need for an exact interpretation of the text and has fully realized the difficulty of defining the great words of the New Testament will lightly criticize the insistence expressed so strongly by Sir Edwyn Hoskyns, that religion has a language of its own and that the Jewish-Christian experience charged with new significance the terms of common speech. But here we touch a problem which we shall meet continually in each phase of Christian doctrine and particularly in Christology. Granted the uniqueness of Christ and of the records of His coming, it still remains that unless His language and the language of His disciples had been intelligible without special vocabularies to contemporary hearers and readers, the Christian religion could not have been founded or propagated. 'Speaking in a tongue' had to be interpreted in order that the casual listener (ἰδιώτης) might be seised of its meaning. Incarnation if it is to be real must involve the acceptance and use of language 'understanded of the people'. Much of the current insistence upon the esoteric meaning of

[1] This seems to be the contention of Dr Paul Tillich, *Systematic Theology*, I, pp. 22–8. But his dialectic method of making one elaborate and exaggerated generalization, following it by another on the opposite side, and then producing a sort of synthesis makes it sometimes difficult to be sure of his own real meaning.

Scripture is appropriate only to a divine intruder, a Gnostic or Apollinarian Christ.

The same objection is relevant to those who insist upon the contrast between scientific and theological methods. So long as scientists restricted their researches to data only amenable to quantitative treatment it was plain that their method of study could only be slightly and indirectly relevant to the subject-matter of theology. But as we have seen with the coming of the new physics, of the new concepts in regard to natural law, and of psychology and kindred sciences, the restrictions have been relaxed and new lines of investigation are being explored. Indeed, whatever may have been claimed for it in the past, the method of science has in fact never been so peculiar as laymen have supposed. It consists in the assembling, testing, sifting and classifying of data and the formulating by induction of an hypothesis, in testing it by comparison with possible alternatives, in revising it in the light of analogies and of its bearing upon cognate problems, and so in relating it to the whole body of relevant knowledge. Such a method is merely that which every branch of enquiry pursues: the field of research will differ; the particular means of obtaining and testing data will differ; the technique appropriate to the formulation of results will differ; but the main process is the same whether we are investigating the structure of an atom or a problem in animal evolution, a period of history or the religious experience of a saint. The field differs; yet even so in the last resort every problem, like that of the 'flower in the crannied wall', only becomes fully answered as it is related to the whole body of knowledge.

In point of fact the changes thus outlined, as they win recognition, will in themselves amount to a New Reformation attained not by the breach with the past that tore Christendom asunder in the sixteenth century but by the gradual acceptance of a new outlook such as seems now to be gaining ground. At present the air is still heavy with controversy: liberals and neo-orthodox, immanentists and transcendentalists, not to mention the representatives of the traditional schools, Platonists, Thomists, Lutherans, Calvinists and the followers of Kierkegaard, create a superficial appearance of continuing disruption: but behind the conflicts those who are most evidently aware of the needs and opportunity of the time seem to be reaching a measure of agreement in regard to the broad principles which must underlie their interpretation of the faith and a temper less exclusive in its general and less provocative in its particular claims. It is the intention of the chapters that follow to examine some aspects of the task of interpreting the Christian experience in such terms as the outlook of our time and the conditions of this lectureship make appropriate.

With this in mind we are in a position to consider more closely the special conditions and issues which make the present time so opportune.

First there arises the criticism, glibly accepted of old and now still repeated with a reference to the work of Wilhelm Dilthey,[1] that science deals only with the general and has no room for the unique, whereas history and, still more, theology treat of the individual and particular. With the extension of the field of science, this is in fact a false distinction. When dealing with inanimate objects where variability if existent is not yet perceptible, the findings with regard to any one example are valid for all similar cases: if I drop two pebbles, their descent to the ground can be expressed under a general law. In the case of two starfish or even two ants, the behaviour patterns can easily be interpreted under general headings, though, even here, there seems to be room for trial and error and thus for some measure of variation. When we get to the bird level, there is, as any observer knows, definite individuality: Wrens build their nests with different materials in different parts of the country; the final phrases of the Chaffinch's song vary both locally and individually.[2] When we get higher,

---

[1] Dilthey's view of science is that of a previous age; he limits it to the mechanistic study of the inanimate. Therefore to him the study of science demands no imagination or sympathy, and its method is in contrast with that of history.

[2] That birds vary individually and to a high degree is maintained by Miss L. Howard, *Birds as Individuals* (London, 1951) and in America by Mrs A. C. Govan, *Wings at my Window* (New York, 1947), or perhaps most clearly by K. Z. Lorenz, *King Solomon's Ring* (London, 1952). It is worth stating that such records and interpretations are fully supported by my friend Mr T. C. Wyatt, Fellow and Bursar of Christ's College, who has the gift of taming wild birds and for many years has known his Robins, Tits and Finches individually.

individuals differ profoundly: the student of dogs can only deal with 'my dog Tony' and 'your dog Bess'.[1] The passage from such diversity to the shape of Cleopatra's nose and its effect upon history may be the opening of a new chapter; but it is all in the same volume. Science must particularize as soon as it deals with individuals as its data. Moreover, if science has broken loose in one direction, history has done so in the other. When Carlyle wrote *Heroes and Hero-worship*, history (or at least his kind of history) was merely the record of great men. Since Marx we have learnt to look also at the collective and generalized behaviour of men in the mass, and to realize that human aggregates are not just the instruments and background of the heroes' lives, but that the hero is only one trifling variant among a mass of largely homogeneous kindred. The fact is, of course, as we shall consider later, that the whole story of our universe is a serial and that the volume dealing with the evolution and character of life on this planet begins (perhaps) with the amoeba and ends (at present) with the saint.

If history is thus the completion of the story unfolded in its earlier stages by biology and psychology, theology, whose primary data are the lives and experience of the saints through whom God most fully reveals Himself to us,[2] should be at once the culmination and the integration of the whole. Science has indeed, ever since the days of alchemy, 'begun with the egg'; and on occasion its followers have thought to explain the end in terms of the beginning. But if, as most scientists and all Christians would surely agree, the creative process in nature and history shows not only continuity but the emergence of real novelty, there is more in the saint than in the amoeba; and we shall form a truer concept of the process if we study it from its end rather than from its beginning. In that case a special effort to understand and appreciate

---

[1] Cf., for instance, C. Lloyd Morgan, *The Animal Mind*, pp. 5–39.

[2] Those theologians who insist that theology is ultimately concerned with God but that God is always subject and never object would (I presume) deny this. It is not easy to see how they would replace it. Dr W. R. Matthews, in *The Purpose of God* (London, 1935), pp. 173–4, argues that 'the doctrine of the self-sufficiency of God should be rejected'.

the perfect Son of Man might well prove to be of the highest value for the scientist and the historian; and theology, for which such an effort is of basic importance, would find their contributions to it of singular worth.

It is, indeed, not absurd to suggest that we should combine to tell the story of evolution first in the traditional manner from its beginning in radiant energy and then in reverse starting from the highest human level and tracing back the qualities there displayed to their origins at earlier phases of the tale. At present we are all familiar with the interpretation of human events by the analogy of the inanimate and in terms of physical-chemical reactions or by reference to the psychic processes of animals, infants and invalids. Nor shall we deny that there is much, very much, to be learned by this road, even if we are bold enough to insist that it inevitably leaves out of account almost all that is characteristic of mature humanity at its best.[1] It would be a novel experience for most of us to take our start from the mature human and to see how far we can trace back the qualities that distinguish it, the conditions under which they are developed, and the elements out of which they emerge. It would not be so easy to get back to the beginning that way; but the attempt, even if not completed, would give us a more interesting and adequate view of the road. Some of our younger theologians might try out such a course: if they take the work of Professor Gilbert Ryle[2] seriously and accept the belief that the dualism of body and mind is a myth, they will plainly be encouraged to do so. For they will have abandoned the idea of two worlds and be ready to attempt the task of telling a single tale which shall treat the whole universe of our experience as ultimately one and indivisible.[3]

[1] Cf. G. Ryle, *The Concept of Mind*, p. 328: 'Man need not be degraded to a machine by being denied to be a ghost in a machine. He might, after all, be a sort of animal, namely, a higher mammal. There has yet to be ventured the hazardous leap to the hypothesis that perhaps he is a man.'

[2] Cf. *op. cit.* pp. 11–24 etc.; it is possible to accept his starting-point without agreeing with the details of his position; cf. the criticisms by S. Hampshire in *Mind*, LIX, no. 234, pp. 237–55 and F. Sibley, *Review of Metaphysics*, IV, no. 2, pp. 259–78.

[3] William Blake had of course insisted in *The Marriage of Heaven and Hell* that 'Man has no Body distinct from his Soul; for that call'd Body is a portion of Soul discern'd by the five Senses'.

The challenge to the Cartesian dualism of body and mind from the standpoint of an integrative or holistic philosophy has been accompanied by a widespread, and at present hardly recognized change of opinion as to the relationship of experience to interpretation. Until quite recently, unformulated experience was regarded as the primitive and preliminary phase of the human adventure out of which it was man's special task to define his concepts, to shape them into hypotheses and so to build up a logical structure which would constitute his wisdom and orthodoxy and be at its best the supreme achievement of the race.[1] We have seen how in the heyday of scientific self-confidence such an orthodoxy was acclaimed as giving us a complete, objective and accurate picture of the universe as a closed system—a picture by the aid of which this sorry scheme of things could be grasped and reconstituted. Today the position has been turned round. In addition to the area usually defined as the subconscious and thereby regarded as primitive and debasing, we see man's apprehension as giving him awareness of experiences that are not originated by sense-perceptions and cannot be fully comprehended or defined:[2] if primitive they are also primary—in importance and reality; the reach of man's personality in its encounter with the universe exceeds and will always exceed his grasp. To interpret and communicate he must use all the means at his disposal, art and music action and conduct, not less than science and learning. In each field there will be a scaling down of experiences: however full the presentation, something will be missed; the interpretation will always be an abstraction, and to that extent incomplete. To identify the picture with its original, or the formula with reality

[1] The behaviourists (and, I fear, Prof. J. Z. Young, *Doubt and Certainty in Science*, in spite of the admission on p. 10) still maintain the supremacy of interpretation over experience.

[2] Those who reject the evidence of the mystics may be referred to the proofs of extra-sensory perception by Professor J. B. Rhine, *New Frontiers of the Mind*, G. N. M. Tyrrell, *Science and Psychical Phenomena*, etc.—proofs which cannot be ignored even if the attempts to define the data in terms of telepathy, clairvoyance or even extra-sensory perception be regarded as premature. The relation of this realm to the familiar subconscious as described by psychologists from F. W. H. Myers to C. G. Jung has not yet been fully investigated. There is an interesting enquiry into this problem in Dr W. R. Matthews's *The Problem of Christ in the Twentieth Century*, pp. 41–60.

is to ascribe infallibility to human wisdom and to identify the idol with God. But that does not justify us in irrationalism, or prove that a paradox is a solution, or excuse us if we throw away or misuse the instruments at our disposal. If we cannot grasp the scheme entire, yet our life and growth depend upon the energy and integrity with which we strive to understand and appreciate and express it. Only we must be constantly aware lest we fall into the error of making the part the equal of the whole.

Yet while maintaining the subordinate status of interpretation this must not lead to any underestimate of its importance. It is as interpreted that experience becomes comprehensible: only so can we appreciate, understand and communicate it; only so does it find concrete expression in individual action and in the shaping of communal life. If, as we may well admit, men's basic experience is similar, indeed identical, their interpretations vary widely and create profound differences in aesthetic, intellectual and moral performance. To ignore or diminish these differences as is done by many of the advocates of religious syncretism is to promote confusion. It is simply not the case, in spite of Mr Aldous Huxley, that non-attachment is the same as agapé or an impersonal deity identical with a super-personal, or that Nirvana, however defined, is a synonym for what Jesus called the Kingdom of heaven. In our very praiseworthy attempts to remove barriers and promote better understanding, we darken counsel by assuming that a few verbal adjustments and the substitution of vagueness for clarity are all that is needed.[1]

Theology rightly understood must always testify to the essentially holistic and personal character of the universe as man perceives it—that it is indeed a cosmos and that it cannot be properly interpreted in less than personal terms. On the former of these convictions scientists will be in full agreement: they have abandoned the idea of a closed system; they are ready to accept an element of indeterminacy; they no longer speak as if the laws formulated by them could be imposed upon or were necessarily endorsed by the Deity; but that it is a universe of order in which

[1] Cf. below pp. 54–6; compare Note v below, p. 209.

patient research can attain verifiable results, this they most assuredly believe. Historians are perhaps less confident: they have lost the Victorian belief that man was always better than his ancestors by virtue of standing upon their shoulders, and with it the idea (if, indeed, any of the best of them ever held it) that progress is as automatic as growing older; but these changes and particularly the recognition of the personal equation, the prejudices, imagination, experience and defects of the historian, have fostered a stress upon subjectivity which has on occasion threatened to reduce history to myth. Yet even so they have not destroyed the sense that in the records of the past, historically interpreted, we have not the outpoured wallet of an academic Kai-lung or the rhapsodies of a prosaic ballad-monger, but discernible, authentic and objective events constituting, if we could see it, the serial story of man's life on the earth. Only among the less judicious of the neo-orthodox is it assumed that, since all history is interpretation and all interpretation subjective, we need not hesitate to accept the legend of the Magi or to regard the Fourth Gospel as equally historical with St Mark. If we accept these modern apologists we shall soon be forced to suppose that the Napoleon of Austerlitz is no more 'historical' than the 'Napoleon of Notting Hill'.

On the latter conviction agreement will be less general. Scientists have been for so long conditioned to their prison-house of weight and measurement and to a phobia at any suggestion of teleology that their immediate reaction to the claim that the cosmos cannot be explained in subpersonal terms may well be a statement that such an affirmation lies beyond their purview. One who has shared their outlook and still shares their dislike of being pushed into assertions that go beyond his reading of the evidence will not condemn their caution: the eagerness with which popular religion fastens upon any statement by a scientist that seems to leave room for orthodoxy is almost as disturbing as the consequences which are too often said to follow from it. But if the new trends in biology, the development of comparative psychology and the consequent belief that the study of evolution cannot stop short of anthropology and of history prevail, then it will be easier to recognize that we are concerned with a process which includes individuation and personality and which therefore cannot be explained in lower than personal categories—since the whole cannot be less or lower than its parts. So far as the record of evolution is concerned it ought not to be difficult for them to return to the interpretations in organic terms such as Ralph Cudworth and John Ray advocated in the seventeenth century, and a number of eminent biologists, E. S. Russell, W. E. Agar and others, have been recently restating.[1] Historians, who have seen the extent to which their subject has been exploited by propagandists[2] and who have had to abandon the belief in a strictly impartial objectivity, have not yet been very successful in defining their own criteria. It is evident that standards other than the idiosyncrasies of the author or the dictates of partisanship should be chosen; and that these should be the highest that we know. It is perhaps permissible to repeat the observation made some ten years ago[3] that the biblical method of writing history in terms of 'the Acts of the living God'—the last example of which is to be seen in the Acts of the Apostles—though it could hardly be followed in its simple anthropomorphism, yet contains a suggestion which we should do well to ponder. The historian must in fact be, as Dr G. M. Trevelyan has put it,[4] a philosopher as well as a scientist and an artist. That many historians follow some such principle is a proper inference from their scrupulous desire to deal fairly with their theme and to have due regard for the personalities of their subjects.

Theology would be benefited in the whole character and scope of its work by the extension and integration which we have been considering: this will be obvious to anyone familiar with its present trends. It was plainly right to protest against any separation

---

[1] For these see below pp. 139–42.

[2] The Marxist and the 'British patriot' type are familiar; but a student of the recent contributions to the history of science can parallel these by noting the ardour with which both Communists and Roman Catholics are exploiting this relatively new field.

[3] In my book *The Gospel and the Church*, pp. 213–18.

[4] Cf. his paper 'Bias in History' in *An Autobiography and other Essays*, pp. 68–81.

of theology from religion other than that which must exist between an experience and its interpretation. If the adoration of the ineffable and the essentially personal exaltations and agonies of religion which symbolize it, its moments of mystic union, of abasement and the dark night of the soul, its vision of God, its sense of moral constraint, of guidance and of forgiveness, are to be defined and explained, they must be 'scaled down' into the imagery that mind and speech can employ. The theologian, like any other artist or thinker, must devise the appropriate means to convey to others an experience of his whole self. That poetry and drama are better media for such transmission may be inferred from the teaching method of Jesus and from the value of sacramental acts like baptism and the eucharist. But theology, the translation of religion into an intellectual version, has a place, a high and essential place, to fill.

Such considerations would be too commonplace to deserve statement, were it not that certain recent advocates of 'the revolt against reason' have limited the scope of theology to the statement of the belief and practice of the Christian Church,[1] and indicated that since religion transcends reason therefore theology need not submit itself to the criteria of rationality. If Christians are also men and if men are reasonable animals, such restrictions can only be justified on the ground that Christianity belongs to a sphere of absolute being whose sanctity has no points of contact with the world of ordinary folk; in which case an Incarnation is impossible and we are back in the theophany of a divine intruder and the Gnostic and Apollinarian heresies, or else in the Arian belief that Christ is essentially different from God.

Here is, indeed, one of the crucial issues of our time. In the desire to safeguard the uniqueness of Christianity and to counteract the tendency to syncretism manifested when the Churches come into contact with Hinduism and Buddhism, there has recently been a revival of the tendency besetting all strongly held convic-

[1] So apparently Canon A. Richardson in *Apologetics*, pp. 51–3. For a protest that the condemnations and definitions of the Church restrict, if they do not destroy, the possibility of a scientific theology, cf. J. L. Stocks, *Reason and Intuition*, pp. 218–26.

tions, to magnify our own beliefs by decrying all others or, in this case, to emphasize the sanctity of the Christian mystery by claiming for it an exclusive and solitary status. Such a procedure is so common a human failing, and in this particular case Christ's condemnation of the practice of thanking God that we are not as other men is so explicit and oft-repeated, that it should suffice to give a bare warning against it. But the alternative—a uniqueness which is not exclusive but representative and illuminative—is not so familiar as it would be if we saw the field of theology in relation to the fields of science and of history. To trace, as Clement of Alexandria or our own John Ray loved to do, the 'many-coloured wisdom' of God in His works, to catch glimpses and foreshadowings of the way of Christ in the order of nature or the records of secular history, to find points of contact with Christian doctrine and experience in the writings of the sages of India and China, of Persia and Arabia, this is not to diminish the unique significance of the Christ but to magnify His glory and confirm His claim. We cannot serve God or advance Christendom today by going back to the ancient lie which denies all virtue to the virtuous acts of the heathen or to its modern version that because God is the ground of all being therefore He cannot be in any sense an object of our thought. If love, joy, peace, fortitude and the rest are the fruit of the Spirit of God, it is difficult for an honest man to deny that where these are present the same Spirit is manifested—even though it be outside the Churches; or, alternatively, that if this Spirit is God's Spirit, then God can be in some sense known to, accepted by and even incarnate in us.

Moreover, and most importantly, this integration of the whole field will have the effect of bringing the three aspects of the divine activity—in creation, redemption and sanctification—into a closer and more evident harmony. We shall examine the problems involved in these changes at greater length in subsequent chapters. Here it is sufficient to say that the segregation of natural religion from Christian theology has involved a contrast between the First and Second Persons of the Trinity almost amounting to heresy, and a restriction of the work of the Third Person such as to sunder it from the pre-Christian dispensation and thus to contradict the definition in the Nicene Creed[1] and to foster a Montanist doctrine of a successively graded Trinity. Tritheism is so common and the danger of an Arian contrast between Creator and Redeemer so evidently present in much of the recent theology of crisis that an incentive towards the affirmation of the essential unity of the Godhead is especially timely. To see life steadily and whole in the light of Christ's revelation is surely the first business of the Christian theologian.

It is an impossible task—manifestly. If science can only comprehend the physical universe in terms of mathematical formulae that cannot be fully translated into speech, we cannot expect theology to give an easy account of man's freedom and God's foreknowledge, or of progress and eschatology, or of sin and death. When, beyond these two fields, we realize that there exists a third and eternal sphere of which these are in some degree presentations, and that if we are to make sense of them it must be in relation to the abiding spiritual reality, then the hopelessness of our undertaking is indisputable. We can hesitantly portray the story in terms of the creativity of the organism (or perhaps, indeed, of the atom) operated upon by the selective power of its environment and producing at intervals and from causes at present unknown simultaneous modifications of structure or behaviour which constitute new levels of capacity. We can more tentatively sketch some such outline of creative purpose as St Paul proposes in Romans viii, amplified in the light of our fuller understanding of nature and history. But the spiritual significance of it all, the quality of life and relationship that it expresses and enables, and the means by which humanity can apprehend and disclose and practise an abiding awareness of the eternal—this is beyond our grasp, even if not wholly beyond our reach. For the threefold interpretation thus indicated, it may well be that at present no adequate synopsis is possible; the records may well have to be preserved, as it were, in parallel columns. The first business is to

[1] Popularly so-called. The clause 'Who spake by the Prophets' was added later than A.D. 325.

compile them as concomitant accounts of a single experience, taking care that contradictions, if such occur, are noted, and neither evaded nor accepted as necessarily final—since a paradox is never a solution or more than a challenge to further research. As we ponder upon their contents, and submit them to expert scrutiny, and compare them continually with one another and give effect to them in our conduct and contacts, we may hope to find them if not producing a coalesced picture, at least promoting a consistent and integrated way of life. Few descriptions of it are so simple and yet so searching as that which Oliver Cromwell sent to his son in his letter from Ireland on 2 April 1650: 'The true knowledge is not literal or speculative, but inward, transforming the mind to it.'[1] For, indeed, it is only in the quality of our whole personality that we can approximate to the business of living eternally. Only the perfect man can, for us men, be in any real sense the image of God. By such image the eternal can be shown to us, and as so shown be imitated, interpreted and in some measure defined.

[1] Cf. G. M. Trevelyan, *An Autobiography and other Essays*, p. 170.

II

RELIGIOUS EXPERIENCE: ITS ORIGIN
AND CHARACTER

IF we are right in contending that to anyone who takes the scientific developments of the past three centuries seriously human history is continuous with the whole record of evolution, then a question immediately arises concerning the status and peculiarity of mankind. Descartes, when he denied that animals were more than automata,[1] was merely echoing Catholic tradition which then as now affirmed that they had no souls and therefore no rights:[2] Darwin's *Descent of Man*, underlining the most unpopular element in his *Origin of Species*, was attacked as depriving humanity of its special and God-given element. Recent studies alike in biology and in psychology have done much to affirm the homogeneity between man and the animals, and to trace back into the behaviour of the higher apes, if not further, qualities previously regarded as our particular prerogative. Indeed, in the last few years when research into the evolution of psychic life has been vigorously pursued, evidence at the insect level bearing upon the perception of different tones of colour and particularly upon methods of orientation and communication in honey bees involves conclusions quite revolutionary.[3] At the bird level, where still more work has been done, there is clear evidence of ability to learn and in some

---

[1] So also did Spinoza (*Ethics*, IV, prop. 37).

[2] This is one chief cause for the relative lack of interest in birds and animals in all Catholic countries and for the brutality of their treatment in too many of them; cf. the letter by J. and J. Tharaud prefixed to J. Delamain, *Why Birds Sing* (Eng. trans.).

[3] Cf. K. von Frisch, *Bees, their Vision, Chemical Senses and Language* and 'Solved and unsolved problems of bee language' in *Bulletin of Animal Behaviour*, IX, pp. 1–33, and Dr W. H. Thorpe in *Nature*, CLXIV, p. 11.

species even to count,[1] and of a code of conduct in species that live and nest in communities.[2] If it is difficult to find proof of ratiocination below the level of the apes, the intelligence of young chimpanzees is not much different from that of human infants up to the age of eighteen months and definite reasoning is not beyond their powers.[3] So far as a sense of values has been used to distinguish man from his forbears, the distinction has become precarious.[4] It is almost as absurd to suggest that morality came into existence with the placental mammals as to maintain that purpose is nowhere manifested in the universe except in 'the uniqueness of man'.[5]

In the days when it was obligatory for the Christian to believe that man possessed a distinctive spiritual nature, 'the soul', and that this conferred immortality in the hereafter and a relationship with God enabling special emotional, intellectual and moral capacities here and now, such admissions as we have made were thought to be atheistic. We have nowadays, and for the most part, come to realize that our human responsibilities and opportunities are not impaired even if our privileges are not exclusively peculiar to mankind; and that, even if the most characteristic of them, the sense of wonder at the mystery of the universe and of self-consciousness[6] at our isolation from it, should be traceable in some degree back into the anthropoids, nothing of religious significance would have been altered. But at present it still seems that here in the basic religious experience rather than in our wisdom or our

[1] Cf. the full record and bibliography by W. H. Thorpe in *Ibis*, XCIII, pp. 1–52, 252–96; T. O. Koehler in *Bulletin of Animal Behaviour*, IX, pp. 41–5.
[2] Cf. for example, G. K. Yeates, *The Life of the Rook*; F. B. Kirkman, *Bird Behaviour* (the Black-headed Gull).
[3] Cf. R. M. and A. L. Yerkes, *The Great Apes* (New Haven, 1929); and W. N. and L. A. Kellogg, *The Ape and the Child* (New York, 1933).
[4] It is interesting to note that twenty years ago J. Oman, *The Natural and the Supernatural*, p. 141, refused to limit this sense of values to man.
[5] Cf. F. Wood Jones, *Design and Purpose*, pp. 17, 69–72.
[6] Cf. the interesting distinction between 'primary' and 'secondary' self-consciousness in A. A. Bowman, *A Sacramental Universe*, pp. 253–86: he confines the secondary or introspective form almost entirely to mankind (p. 283). It is part of the loss occasioned by its author's early death that this book was never fully completed by him: starting from the duality of physical and spiritual he indicated an ultimate resolution; but the precise nature of their relationship is not fully stated (cf. the hints as to the nature of life, p. 363).

technical skills is the criterion of our distinctness. Man at least (whatever may or may not be the case with monkeys) has the capacity to realize his own existence as in some sense a separate centre of consciousness and to recollect and contemplate and compare his past sensations, ideas and actions; and at the same time the capacity to realize his environment as a world detached from himself, and to regard it not only with fascination and curiosity but with awe and dread: and these two, self-consciousness and contemplation, though seemingly different, are in fact complementary and correlated. That man in attaining his self-consciousness encounters the universe and recognizes it as other and alien and that his awareness of the mystery and the wonder and fear associated with it disclose to him his individuality, these are alternative methods of stating the characteristic experience which constitutes his human status. So with him the process of individuation characteristic of evolution reaches a new level.

The correlation of these twin experiences, not only in their origin but in their subsequent development, is a point of importance which is often forgotten. When, for example, Professor B. Willey says that the first step to becoming a Christian is self-knowledge,[1] or when the traditional evangelist insists that he must start his message with the fact of sin, they can quote good precedent for so doing. But a close analysis of their procedure suggests that in fact, as St Augustine claimed,[2] knowledge of self and of sin springs from a divine discontent due to an awareness, in however vague a form, of the presence of God. Unless we have the challenge of such awareness, our self-criticism cannot be aroused; until we have become conscious of the obligation occasioned by it, sin can have no meaning. For the man of the nineteen-twenties who is offended by the word *God* and accustomed to regard his encounter with the ineffable as a primitive or even illusory fancy, it may be easier to start on this business of religion from his sense of frustration and guilt: but the existence of such feelings implies

[1] Cf. his valuable and impressive lectures, *Christianity Past and Present* (Cambridge, 1952).

[2] Cf. *De Trin.* IV, 1, for a profound treatment of self-knowledge.

a criterion which they do not originate or explain; and many of us would agree with G. K. Chesterton that, although it is possible to break a drunkard of his habit by showing him the condition of his liver, it is both more wholesome and more effective to do so by confronting him with the purity of Christ.[1] But our present point is that in any case wonder and shame, the sense of self and of 'other', belong together. The evidence for the original quality of this experience can be gathered from the relics and records of the remote past of humanity, from the researches of anthropologists into the behaviour and ideas of primitive peoples, by the detailed observation of young children and by introspection from our own recollections.[2] Its character can then be tested and explained by reference to the testimony of men and women of special religious attainment, the mystics and saints of all ages and of many faiths. Finally, the thinkers who have given special attention to this subject, Plato, Augustine and Spinoza being the chief among them, may be introduced as corroboration; and their evidence can be extended to include some of the best philosophers of today.

At its lowest accessible level humanity discloses an elementary and undeveloped, but universal, reaction to a world as yet unknown. Man like his immediate forbears has intense awareness of the particular details and characteristics of each object with which he is in contact and a keen curiosity urging him to adventure and discovery and appreciation; but he can no longer accept his environment with the naïve immediacy of the animal. He becomes aware of it as akin to, yet in the last resort independent of, himself and sees particular objects in the setting of an infinity of space and time. In it, being himself alive, he ascribes life to all his surroundings: though not yet in any full sense self-conscious, he recognizes the distinction between himself and others, as is evident from his applying to them the analogy of living creatures: soon he begins to sense a power which he cannot understand or evade or control, a power which increasingly fills him with awe,

---

[1] Cf. *Heretics*, p. 27.
[2] For a valuable record of his childhood's developing awareness, cf. J. Oman, *The Natural and the Supernatural* (1st ed. Cambridge, 1931), pp. 133–7.

convicts him of his own solitariness and challenges his courage, ingenuity and imagination.[1] He is constrained to assume that the world is alive and that, if in one aspect it ministers to his wants and responds to his efforts, it is also dangerous, capricious and incalculable. He and his tribe must discover their affinities in relation to the life that surrounds and threatens them, must devise means to influence and placate it, must observe and fulfil the correct responses in ritual, folk-tale and taboo. Out of the impulses of his physical structure, the behaviour-patterns imparted to him by the community, and the notions arising from his own observation and exploits he must fashion his adjustment to the unknown. In so doing his art, his knowledge, his character are originated and developed. So, as it appears, the human adventure opens.

For the scientist, especially in these days when the evolution of behaviour is attracting the attention both of biologists and psychologists, the study of this passage from the animal to the human is plainly of the greatest importance. Unfortunately, although a considerable mass of material has been gathered both from study of living organisms in their natural surroundings and from observation of their reactions to a variety of ingeniously planned tests, the results have not yet found the Newton or Darwin who can correlate and interpret them coherently. The study of comparative psychology is still in the stage in which rival hypotheses based upon data selected for that purpose present interpretations whose objectivity is far from obvious:[2] such failure can plead manifest excuses. A thousand years of Aesop and sermons have stereotyped an impression which has hardly yet been erased. The anthropomorphism of popular natural history has till recently accepted the emblematic character of lion and eagle, of fox and serpent, and given us life stories of birds and beasts hardly less human than those of the Jungle Books. It was natural that the 'School of the Woods' should be countered by the mechanisms of the Behaviourists, and

---

[1] A valuable and beautiful account of this encounter with the 'ineffable' is given by Dr A. J. Heschel, *Man is Not Alone* (New York, 1951).

[2] Sufficient evidence is given, for example, by L. D. Weatherhead in his account of Freud, Adler, Jung, McDougall and J. B. Watson, *Psychology, Religion and Healing*, pp. 255–300.

that the sub-human and even the human should be depicted in terms of physics and chemistry and represented as on the same level as the electronic robot. We have traced and explained the steps by which this strange result was attained.[1]

In the more abstract sciences such clashes of interpretation may well generate light. In problems where human values and convictions are at stake, heat is a more evident product of controversy. Manifestly this subject is one that demands for its treatment qualities of sympathy, insight and imagination: the detached approach of the abstract mathematical mind may preserve an equable temperature at the expense of a real understanding of the issues. Human beings are not robots;[2] to regard them so, though permissible for the anatomist and perhaps for the physiologist, is fatal for the psychologist and the philosopher. Christendom has received an unfortunate heritage from medievalism in this respect; but the student of humanity must recognize that the reaction against it has gone and may easily go too far.

In spite of these difficulties inherent in the subject itself, in spite of the unjustifiable and unfulfilled claims made on its behalf thirty years ago, in spite of some charlatanry and much ill-qualified assertion, psychology has unquestionably proved its right to a place among the sciences and demonstrated the value of its contributions, actual and potential, to human welfare, and indeed to our present enquiry. It has been largely responsible for that reversal of our general estimate of the relationship between experience and interpretation which we have already noted as an important characteristic of our time.[3] For it has shown, by its emphasis upon what lies beyond the region of man's logical intellect, how large is the area of his individual and racial self, of which he is not normally aware and can give no conscious or formulated account. When Frederic Myers first drew attention to what he called the subliminal self he used the term to describe the whole area beyond the range of the conscious intelligence, the

[1] Cf. Vol. I of this book *passim*.

[2] For those (if such there be) who disagree, it is sufficient to enquire whether they or any others could endure to be treated as such.

[3] Cf. the previous chapter, pp. 14, 15.

area from which came alike 'pulses of nobleness and aches of shame'. So free was it from any idea of repression or disgust that William Sanday in his notable book *Christologies Ancient and Modern* (Oxford, 1910) suggested that this area is 'the proper seat or locus of whatever there is of divine in man' (p. 163) and therefore of the union of Godhead and manhood in Christ. Later, Sigmund Freud narrowed its meaning and defined its contents in terms of the repressed impulses and memories repugnant to the conscious mind and thus separated it not only from the racial unconscious to which Dr C. G. Jung attached importance but from those experiences of the ineffable with which religion is primarily concerned. Indeed, the very term 'subconscious', more strongly than its predecessor 'subliminal', implied that it was the primitive and animal substratum of our selfhood; the figure of the iceberg by which it was familiarly explained illustrated the same belief; and Freud's record of its contents, derived as it was from the analysis of psychopathic material, underlined their sexual and unsavoury character. Even now when the unconscious is given a much wider scope there has hardly yet been any general recognition that this whole region of uncomprehended and unformulated experience represents the peripheral range of our personality, and that in it certain elements have broken through into full consciousness and to a less or greater degree found expression in intellectual, aesthetic or practical symbols.

Those of us who have been disappointed at the small progress made towards an adequate exposition of the character and evolution of our psychic life, and who feel that human psychology cannot be properly understood so long as it is based chiefly upon evidence obtained from clinics and asylums supplemented by answers to questionnaires,[1] must realize that the researches which we assumed would lead to speedy and important results have in fact proved exceedingly complicated both for investigation and for interpretation. Capabilities plainly possessed by birds and

---

[1] In America, as the literature demonstrates, this method seems general: thus G. W. Allport, *The Individual and his Religion*, p. 40, describes it as 'traditional but far from perfect'. As a basis for scientific study it would seem highly precarious.

animals and therefore present vestigially at least in ourselves; telepathic and telaesthetic perception, the evidence for which is strong both at the subhuman and the human level;[1] problems such as have been examined now for half a century by the Society for Psychic Research; these though they have demonstrated the range of the necessary knowledge and the defects of our present equipment have not yet yielded more than hints and suggestions mostly of a negative kind. Much good work has been done both in the exploration and closing of blind alleys and in the opening up of new and important methods of research. But it is clear that, while the dogmatism and speculations of a generation ago have been largely abandoned, we are a long way from any fully coherent and integrative understanding of matters such as this which we are considering.

It is not necessary, even if within our limits it were possible, to give any detailed account of the attitudes towards religion of the various practitioners who became famous in the decade after the First World War when the New Psychology swept over the platforms and bookstalls of the world. It is a strange experience to look back at the literature of that period when Sigmund Freud was hailed as a scientist of the class of Newton and Darwin and Einstein;[2] and when the rival attempts to assign human achievements and diseases to a single source, to sex or the will to power, to a bundle of separate instincts or to a collective unconscious or to imperceptible visceral and laryngeal movements, were regarded by their several adherents as the gospels of the new age. If proof were needed of the extent to which Western man was bled white in the holocaust of war and frenzied by the scale of its terrors, the failure to recognize the exaggerations and dogmatism or even the absurdities and illogicalities of that neurotic literature would be sufficient. That such tentative and self-contradictory material

[1] The most notable examples of this are set out in the researches of Professor J. B. Rhine; cf. his *New Frontiers of Mind* (1937), and *The Reach of the Mind* (1948).

[2] These three each introduced a great generalizing principle which interpreted a whole aspect of nature. Freud did nothing of the sort. He did not 'discover' the subconscious self, but only a technique for analysing it; and this has proved of dubious validity. He was not a great scientist or a great thinker—though he may perhaps deserve the title of 'a man of genius'.

should have been so exploited and popularized is a further comment upon the mentality of the decade. No one would deny that the various theories contained elements of value or were even appropriate to particular types of abnormality: to treat them as universal truths or to suppose that any or all of them constitute an adequate psychology would be equivalent to identifying the practice of a dermatologist with the whole content of physiology.[1]

After these attempts to dispose of religious experience by ascribing it to some particular psychic mechanism and when it was freely assumed that psychology had somehow undermined the foundations of religion there came a period of anxious expectation on one side and of increasing hesitation on the other. The crisis did not develop; the onslaught announced in the later twenties did not take place; the nerves of the young, and of their teachers, overstrained by the assaults upon moral restraint and rational behaviour, began to recover; psychologists, misled by their easy success in dealing with the traumas of war-time, began to discover that techniques appropriate to them were ineffective for the deep-seated troubles of the mature; a halt was called while the wiser and less sensational students of mental health strove to underpin the improvised structures erected for dealing with 'shell-shock'. In consequence the belief that personality could be easily split up into a few basic 'instincts' or explained by still fewer simple mechanisms began to be discredited. The work of the various schools had thrown light upon certain types of ill-health, had provided data which revealed the errors and limitations of existing theories and had made it plain that normal psychology could not be satisfactorily studied by mere observation of infants and invalids. A general movement towards insistence upon wholeness similar to that which had already transformed physiology showed itself first in the academic and then in the clinical fields.

The result of this upon religion was to produce a period of silence. Professor Allport is justified in saying that 'during the

---

[1] I cannot but refer to the article 'Psychiatry' by Dr Desmond Curran in *Proc. of the Royal Society of Medicine*, XIV, pp. 105–8, a wise and brief survey of the claims and value of modern psychotherapy.

past fifty years religion and sex seem to have reversed their positions.... Today psychologists write with the frankness of Freud or Kinsey on the sexual passions of mankind but blush and grow silent when the religious passions come into view...even though religion is an almost universal interest of the human race.'[1] The reason for this is not obscure. As psychologists have plainly demonstrated, religion cannot be explained in terms of a single religious emotion or instinct, projection or psychic mechanism: it is an activity of the whole self, 'an indistinguishable blend of emotion and reason, of feeling and meaning',[2] or rather a primary reaction to the unknown, the infinite, the ineffable.[3] But to acknowledge it as such would be to give it an importance which would at once involve the discussion of a large range of theological and even ecclesiastical problems. The relation of religion to religions, and of religious experience to its expression in cultus, creed and code; the comparison of one religion with another and the psychological significance of their differences; the influence of religion and religions upon the whole range of human life, individual and collective; such questions would inevitably arise; and as their past excursions into such fields have demonstrated, few psychologists are qualified to deal with them. It is, of course, as absurd to discuss psychology without giving full attention to religion as it is to consider education and culture under a similar limitation: yet in view of the divergencies and the sensitiveness of the religions both psychologists and U.N.E.S.C.O.[4] may be forgiven for their hesitation to do so. If religion were identical with religions they would perhaps be justified. If it is in its fundamental form the universal reaction of man to his

---

[1] *The Individual and his Religion*, p. 1.

[2] G. W. Allport, *ibid.* p. 18. His belief that religion is many-rooted need not lead to his conclusion 'That there are as many varieties of religious experience as there are religiously inclined mortals upon the earth' (p. 30), which looks like individualism run wild; it can more easily demonstrate that religion is simple and universal, the white light capable of yielding all the colours of the spectrum—a metaphor which Allport himself uses (p. 9).

[3] Such a conclusion represents something like a return to the position of earlier students, e.g. R. R. Marett, *The Threshold of Religion*, pp. 10–15.

[4] The reports of speeches at its conferences and its refusal to give recognition to religion although it claims to deal with education and culture fully bear out its prudishness.

environment, it cannot be omitted from any study of personal or social health.

Before we examine it in detail it may be well to interpolate a definition which expresses in its full development the religious experience already described at a primitive level. It is appropriate to do so in the words of one whom my generation regarded with a special reverence, John L. Stocks, of Oxford, sometime Vice-Chancellor of Liverpool University. In his lectures on Religious Belief[1] he defined it as follows:

(1) It is a total assertion which has for its subject the whole world order.

(2) It asserts this world order to be the expression of infinite Wisdom and Love.

(3) This Love and Wisdom is conceived as the endorsement equally of every feature of the world process, of what seems to us bad as well as of what we think good. (God is the cause not of all things but only of the good, said Plato, but wrongly: his God was not a God of Love.)

(4) The religious life is the attempt to realize this divine and all-embracing Love in the person of the believer.

In view of the fact that so many attempts to explain away religious experience have been refuted and the further fact of an increasing insistence upon the wholeness and correlation of the normal personality, such conclusions as we have outlined at their primitive level seem much more secure and more evidently important now than a generation ago.[2] A great mass of converging evidence from the sources that we have named gives us a similar picture. Man is not 'that great and true Amphibium',[3] a soul, or mind, in a body, an inhabitant of two worlds; nor is he either a superior kind of machine whose selfhood and aspirations are a fantasy, the by-product of physical-chemical processes, or a purely spiritual being whose material environment is a prison-

---

[1] *Reason and Intuition*, p. 43. The significance of 'total assertion' is explained on pp. 38 ff.

[2] It is perhaps permissible for me to express satisfaction that my own first treatment of the subject has been endorsed by Dr D. L. Scudder in his critical examination of Dr F. R. Tennant's rejection of religious experience; cf. *Tennant's Philosophical Theology* (Yale, 1940), pp. 214–19.

[3] So Sir T. Browne, *Religio Medici*, § 34.

house or an 'illusion of mortal mind'. We see him as a person in the making, conscious of relationships, ultimately and in essence infinite, which are disclosed by, and become intelligible in terms of, the spatio-temporal imagery furnished to him through his sense perceptions. To appreciate and analyse and explain the infinity is his primary and inescapable task. He lives the more fully as he succeeds in it and by adjustment to the ephemeral becomes increasingly reconciled to the eternal,[1] correlating his experience of the mystery with his emotional, cognitive and conative interpretation of it.

Man's encounter with the infinite is characterized on his side by a response of amazement, quickened for some of us into adoration. This when analysed is found to consist at once of rapture and of dread, a rapture which often amounts to ecstasy and a sense of communion, a dread which involves abasement and a consciousness of need and of obligation. This encounter has (for the majority of Western men at least) the distinctive quality of contact with a personal or super-personal reality: to describe such a reality as inanimate would be impossible; and 'impersonal', unless used to mean unindividual,[2] would be wholly misleading.[3] Hence for such experience theistic language is natural and appropriate. The classic example of it is that of the 'great god Pan', the 'All' to whom belong the music of the pan-pipes and the blind terror which we still call panic. In the Old Testament examples are familiar: Adam and Eve heard the Lord walking in the garden in the cool of the day and they hid themselves for they knew that they were naked[4]—a more significant symbol of the origin of religion than the story of the apple and the serpent: Jacob flees from his home; 'Surely the Lord is in this place; and I knew it not';[5] and he set up a stone and called the place Beth-el: Moses in

---

[1] Cf. the sentence in which J. Oman sums up the findings of his great book, *The Natural and the Supernatural* (1st ed.), p. 470: 'If reconciliation to the evanescent is revelation of the eternal, and revelation of the eternal a higher reconciliation to the evanescent, that is only as we know all environment, which is by living in accord with it.'

[2] This seems to be the sense in which it is maintained that God is impersonal: but authors who write thus often go on to give to impersonal its proper meaning of sub-personal or even inanimate as indicating a force not a Being.

[3] The most familiar recent exposition of this 'encounter' is M. Buber, *I and Thou* (Eng. trans., 1937).   [4] Gen. iii. 8–10.   [5] Gen. xxviii. 16.

the wilderness and the bush 'afire with God' and the command 'Put off thy shoes from off thy feet, for the place whereon thou standest is holy ground';[1] or Isaiah in the year of Uzziah's death, 'I saw the Lord. ... Then said I, Woe is me! for I am...a man of unclean lips'.[2]

It is important to stress the dual effect of this encounter, because too often these two, the moment of vision and rapture and the moment of self-consciousness and shame, are regarded as antithetical. It has, indeed, been a truism among students of early Christianity that the element of illumination with its stress upon man's capacity to live immortally belongs to the Hellenic, and the element of penitence and judgment and deliverance from evil to the Jewish presentation of the gospel. This dichotomy is then followed by a castigation of the Greek as shallow, optimistic and Pelagian and by insistence upon the profundity and realism of the Hebrew, and by an identification of Christ's religion with the darker utterances of St Paul as interpreted by Luther and Calvin. It need hardly be stated that such an attitude is psychologically false, since the two elements belong together, historically exaggerated, since Jew and Greek had been fused for three hundred years before Christ, and theologically distorted, since Paulinism as expounded by the Reformers is a parody of the Apostle's full teaching.[3] Yet in any mature religious experience, as in the primitive encounter with the unknown,[4] the two are one and indivisible. The sense of isolation and individuality is correlated with and arises alongside of the sense of awe and rapture, just as the consciousness of God and of creaturehood, exaltation and penitence, humility and joy are intimately and immediately linked. We cannot discover 'the self' save by simultaneous discovery of 'the other'. The mutuality of the I-thou relationship is fundamental.[5]

In these days, when the results of the scientific analysis of our

[1] Exod. iii. 2–5.   [2] Isaiah. vi. 1–5 (R.V.).

[3] For fuller treatment cf. Vol. I of this book, pp. 33–8.

[4] Cf., for exposition of this, R. R. Marett's insistence that the primary religious experience is a compound of *mana*, the source of exaltation, and *tabu*, the source of humility; *The Threshold of Religion*, pp. xviii, 183–91, etc.

[5] For full treatment cf. Dr J. Baillie, *Our Knowledge of God*, especially pp. 41–3, 219–27.

environment are so obviously far-reaching, it is hardly necessary to add that in thus calling attention to the danger of the method of alternatives we are not condemning the process by which the unity of infinite being is split up into the multiformity of the existential world. Plainly in our space-time existence we live in 'a dome of many-coloured glass' and can only in rare moments of integration see the varied hues combined so that they reveal for us 'the white radiance of eternity'.[1] If we are to grow into fully developed men and women, we must exercise and train these sense-perceptions of ours through which we can appreciate and understand the refracted bits of being which make up our earthly environment. To choose naïve enjoyment rather than the sensitive and intelligent valuation of our experience is to refuse the discipline and miss the opportunities of life: it is to endorse the modern craze for the barbaric as superior to the civilized, the craze which professes to prefer the art of the Baga tribe to that of Pheidias and of the jazz-band to the Bach Mass; it is to endorse the heresy which denies the possibility of progress, the cowardice which dare not face the adventure of going forward.

The danger that, as a result of three centuries of intensified analysis and of concentration upon its results, mankind may have forgotten the whole in the over-specialized study of the parts, and, since these parts belong to the ephemeral, become secularized and superficial, is a feature of our time to which attention cannot too often be drawn.[2] Plainly, if analysis degenerates into disintegration and existence becomes fragmented into a rubbish-heap of 'shreds and patches', coherence, significance and growth become impossible; the compass-bearings are lost; civilization founders; and mankind sinks to a level lower than that of the brutes. There are abundant signs in contemporary life and thought, particularly

[1] Cf. the familiar lines in Shelley's *Adonais* LII.

[2] In this respect Dr Emil Brunner's Gifford Lectures, *Christianity and Civilization*, are a notable contribution. Disagreeing as I do with his exaggerated transcendentalism which seems to leave no room for the conclusions which he seeks to draw from it, it is the more incumbent upon me to acknowledge gratefully my entire agreement with his intention as expounded in *Religion in Life*, XX, 3, pp. 323–8 (New York, 1951). But for the weakness of his general position, cf. the searching criticism by Prof. H. D. Lewis, *Morals and Revelation* (London, 1951), pp. 28–46.

perhaps in the West, that this is a real danger. When the young look only for a 'good time' and find it in a whirl of amusements and excitements;[1] when religion loses its joy and can only proclaim that existence is corrupt and behaviour a choice of evils; when the finest products of human science and effort are prostituted to purposes of mass-destruction, and fear, despair and hate seem to be supplanting faith, hope and love; there must needs be searching of conscience. But even so the return to the primitive is as futile as the flight to the desert.[2]

If disintegration involves the loss of all awareness of the eternal and can only be checked by its recovery, the converse is also true—that this awareness is attained if and when the personality attains integration. It has long been recognized that religious experience is not to be assigned to any particular instinct or faculty, that though psychic mechanisms may suggest and control its interpretation they do not originate it, and that it is a property of the whole self. The evidence of the great mystics supported by that of a mass of more ordinary folks, artists, poets, scholars and men of action, goes to show that ecstasy or its lesser equivalents are experienced when the personality has reached a measure of spiritual, psychic and physical integration, been freed from distraction, unified and harmonized in its interests, and then been enraptured by some unexpected and often hardly recognized event, seldom in itself of any great importance, which so to say fuses into a single cord of intense sensitivity every fibre of the self.[3]

The various techniques which can be used for promoting such integration fall into two main classes, negative and positive.[4] Those

---

[1] For a brief comment on this, cf. Note II on the idea of freedom, below p. 206.

[2] Cf. A. N. Whitehead, *Science and the Modern World* (Cambridge, 1936), p. 294: 'Nothing does more harm in unnerving men for their duties in the present than the attention devoted to the points of excellence in the past as compared with the average failures of the present day.'

[3] *Mysticism*, by Evelyn Underhill (London, 1910), is still valuable as a full and sympathetic survey of the subject; for my difference from it cf. Note III below, p. 206.

[4] I owe this distinction to E. Murisier, *Maladies du Sentiment Religieux*; cf. my *Jesus and the Gospel of Love*, pp. 82–9. It has much in common with the distinction between 'mystical' and 'prophetic' as drawn, for example, by F. Heiler, *Prayer* (Eng. trans., London, 1932), or even with that between 'exclusive' and 'comprehensive' mysticism in A. Caldecott, *The Philosophy of Religion in England and America*.

of the former type aim at unity by subtraction, the diminution and concentration of the field of interest. They range from the adoption of a posture and the recital of a monotonous formula with discipline of the breathing and inhibition of conscious thought, or the more elaborate preparation by fasting and penance and the ordered dismissal of all earthly interests and attachments, to the simple apparatus of the hypnotist or clairvoyant, or the dose of hashish or cocaine, or even the cigar and the mixed drink. The latter proceed by the opposite route directed not to the narrowing but to the enlarging of interest, to producing a high and intense vitality by the influence of a master motive and the removal of internal wastage and friction, and the sublimation of the whole self so that it can function as a single and fully co-ordinated entity. Each such method if successful produces a consciousness of the oneness and worth of existence and at its best an exaltation that thrills and satisfies; but some of them, as will be obvious, produce their effect merely by chemical action upon the frontal cortex, and most of those which we have classified as negative must be regarded with suspicion: they can produce a sense of peace out of pain, of escape into the infinite, of security and comfort which may indeed have a profound and haunting influence; they cannot directly energize or inspire or qualify for effective service, and usually only increase the sense of contrast between the world of claims and counterclaims and the world of changelessness and peace, and so result in an after-effect of dissociation and the familiar conflict between religion and everyday life. Even the ecstasy which some have regarded as the consummation of religious experience is not commended very highly by the most judicious students of the subject.[1] If we may follow up a familiar metaphor already used, positive awareness has the effect of combining all the colours of our refracted existence into the white light; the *via negativa* blacks out a number of them and gives a defective colour-compound as the result.

Students of mysticism will protest that the classification thus

[1] Cf. F. von Hügel, *The Mystical Element in Religion*, II, pp. 44–9; H. Delacroix, *La Religion et la Foi*, pp. 268–71; J. B. Pratt, *The Religious Consciousness*, pp. 467–9, etc.

proposed identifies 'positive mysticism' with inspiration and depreciates the significance and value of many of the greatest adepts. This criticism of the discipline and abstraction of the way of negation would condemn methods commended not only by Plotinus but by the whole tradition of the Pseudo-Dionysius and his followers. Moreover, although to suggest that their practices have something in common with the practice of Yoga may be permissible, the extension of this suggestion to include self-hypnotism, anaesthetics and stimulants is unjust and even cruel. This treatment, indeed, will seem to be a rejection of the mystic claim to be 'in communion with the infinite' and to 'live eternally'.

We have in fact insisted that such communion, whether men recognize it or not, is the hall-mark of the human species, and have suggested that each of us becomes conscious of it as he achieves integration. We do not deny but affirm that this experience is real and primary, and that only as men live eternally and fashion their conduct on the pattern thus disclosed can they develop individually and collectively their true potentialities. The ecstasy that comes to the broken-hearted when in their agony and exhaustion suddenly the world of the senses is splintered and they find themselves in a relationship that abides changeless and sustaining; the exhilaration that is wrung from pain when the tortured nerves can endure no more and the whole being is thrilled with a sense of victory; the release that sets free from its prison-house the mind obsessed by fears and perplexities and presents it with a clear solution of its problems; these moments are among the supreme experiences of men. If results of a similar kind can be obtained more artificially by the lulling of the fretful and distracted self, they are not on that account to be dismissed as illusory or mischievous. Here as elsewhere the test of fruits is the only safe criterion. That which produces finer sensibilities, profounder insight and stronger affection may be tentatively accepted: that which fosters escapism and divides the natural from the supernatural, even if it does so in the name of religion, is rightly suspect. It is hardly disputable that disciplines which strengthen the contemplative life and detachment from ambitions and fears are a witness to man's essential nature which in these days of secularism and strife is of high value. If they are interpreted in terms which reduce physical existence to the level of illusion, lay chief stress upon the salvation of the individual soul and identify salvation not with service but with escape from the wheel of things, their value will be less highly regarded. Lower in the scale are practices which minister solely to the obtaining of moments of expansiveness and uplift, the satisfaction of spiritual aspirations and relief from frustration and guilt. Practices of this kind, even if unaccompanied by consciously hypnotic or narcotic influences and pursued with a religious motive, are exposed to devastating criticism by the psychologist and should be ruthlessly scrutinized and tested. Many of the methods of popular evangelism and many of the manuals of private devotion advocate practices and produce effects which if recognized would surprise and horrify their advocates.[1]

We have classified the religious experience as negative and positive according as the method of its attainment is by subtraction or sublimation. But from what has been said of the former it is plain that the distinction cannot be sharply drawn. The preparation by which Plotinus sought to fit himself for ecstasy could almost as well be described as an integration of his whole personality. Plainly, to sublimate is to discipline; and if the process is rather one of ardent aspiration than of abstraction and of active than of passive service, this does not mean that it can be less exacting or continuous. Probably the difference lies rather in the attitude towards this world: the negative road sees it as a place of darkness and illusion from which a definite withdrawal is demanded; the positive regards it rather as a field of service and training, its dark places as the shadows cast by the light of reality, dark enough yet capable of illumination rather than compelling flight. The distinction is one that goes deep; indeed, the great religions of the world can be readily classified by means of it: the

---

[1] Sinclair Lewis's exposure of them in *Elmer Gantry* was too savage to be fully effective. Few tasks are more urgently needed for religion than a drastic examination and purge of its methods of propaganda and discipline.

three chief categories, world-acceptance and world-rejection and the more profound concept of world-redemption, reproduce themselves in the religious experience of the individual.

For on the positive side also there is a wide range of experience. On the higher levels are those for whom after long periods of effort in pursuit of an objective beyond their grasp and when all the powers of imagination and thought and will are dedicated to it there comes an inrush of illumination and power, a creative energy which inspires and constrains and impels. The familiar imagery of light and flame, whirlwind and convulsion is alone adequate to describe the effect of such rapture, and those who have known it not only display a dynamic influence beyond all expectation but depict it in terms of possession.[1] With them are those who draw an oft-repeated inspiration from nature or music, from their fellows and their religion, and without any great moments of achievement maintain a steady activity of devoted and unselfish service, the 'Saints of common life', who live in the world but not wholly of the world, and who by their patience and cheerfulness and self-giving sweeten and encourage all with whom they come in contact. At a lower level are those amiable and optimistic folk who succeed in shutting out the stress and sin of human life, who have no sense of tragedy and are apt to run away from pain, and who talk easily of God's care and goodness in a way that commends the comfort of religion and encourages the belief that all is for the best in the best of all possible worlds.

Beyond the world-rejection and world-acceptance which these types of experience respectively express lies a relationship to the two spheres, absolute and relative, being and existence, which holds them in a closer and more realistic unity, which recognizes both the value and the estrangement of the phenomenal, and while discovering in it the eternal, yet accepts and suffers with its disintegration. This rejects as oversimplified the easy verdict 'good' or 'bad' and insists that if the purpose of creation and of the

---

[1] Lest Christian sources be suspect, appeal can be made to F. Nietzsche, *Ecce Homo* (Eng. trans.), p. 96.

spatio-temporal process be taken into account the response to it must be both 'good and bad and therefore redeemable.' For if there be any meaning in the refraction of the infinite into the multiform, of unity into diversity, it must surely be that those who have experienced the whole with naïve apprehension may learn, by the process of experiencing, understanding and co-ordinating its parts and through the effort and agony which this involves, to recover the wholeness of life with an added conscious-ness of its quality. The human pilgrimage proceeds just in so far as its members bring fresh ranges of the ephemeral into conformity with the pattern and being of the eternal.

In this task of bringing the phenomenal into conformity with the eternal, two obvious means are available, first the almost universal practice of prayer, and secondly, since prayer to the infinite is difficult if not impossible, the interpretation of the infinite by the appropriate symbol and instrument.

We have claimed, and with a strong balance of evidence, that the reality with which man is in contact, though ineffable, is yet rightly apprehended as personal or, if the term is preferred, super-personal. We have hitherto hesitated to use the word *God*, though the majority of mystics of all schools and the experts of most religions insist upon doing so. Certainly prayer assumes not only that there is one to whom prayer can be addressed but that relation-ship with him of a kind analogous to that which links person to person is possible and existent. For prayer necessarily begins with an act of acknowledgment and of worship such as implies a God active and accessible; continues with confession of our own worthlessness—thus repeating the universal rhythm of religious experience; and culminates in the business of intercession, that is the effort to lift up into the light of God ourselves and our neigh-bours, and the needs and concerns of men, a business whose inten-tion is not only that we may see them all *sub specie eternitatis* but, much more, that the love and power of God may flow out to them as we hold Him and them together in our consciousness.[1]

[1] The problem of intercessory prayer is a familiar difficulty; cf. the suggestions in Note IV below, p. 207.

Prayer makes urgent what the whole experience demands: that we find a description for the ineffable, a definition for the infinite, an effective symbol for absolute being, an image of the invisible God. Logically, no doubt, the position can be so stated as to make such discovery impossible: if God is the ground of all existence, the subject but never the object, then He is plainly, in the general as well as the theological sense of the word, 'incomprehensible', and every image will be an idol. But in fact the paradox with which logic and neo-orthodoxy confront us is resolved in experience as well as by Christendom. Absolute Being enters into communion with us: we respond to His presence and by that response know that in some sense He has 'visited and redeemed His people'. Nor is our union with Him solely 'a visitation from on high'. However lowly our state, however earthbound our love, yet we can and do 'lift up our hearts' and our love recognizes and meets and is at one with His.[1] Moreover, if God is, as Dr Barth and his followers insist, the 'wholly other' standing to us as the vertical to the horizontal[2] and only cutting our plane at the sole point of Christ, then incarnation in any except a Gnostic or Arian sense would seem to be impossible, and any such relationship of religion with civilization, as Dr Brunner advocates in the second series of his Gifford Lectures, can have no theological basis.

The fact seems to be that if in our thought of God we begin from the details of our partial and specialized lives and proceed by a process of generalization to eliminate all that is concrete, and so from abstract ideas produce a concept of infinity formulated in negations, we shall conclude that God is not only beyond all description but can only be regarded with a complete and ultimately sceptical agnosticism. He may or may not be the ground of all being; but if so, we cannot state that He exists or assign any solid reasons for believing in Him.

---

[1] The contrast between ἔρως and ἀγάπη is seriously overstated by Dr A. T. S. Nygren, *Agape and Eros*. It is encouraging that Dr P. Tillich, that austere transcendentalist, can write 'If eros and agape cannot be united, agape towards God is impossible', *Systematic Theology*, I, p. 281.

[2] This favourite but very difficult analogy is accepted by Dr Brunner (cf. *Christianity and Civilisation*, II, p. 22), and by a host of lesser men.

If, on the contrary, we start from the experience of wonder and the assumption that the universe thus manifests a reality, unity and life, from which all existence derives its character and by which it is permeated and sustained, then we shall be justified in claiming that this reality is capable of confronting us with a valid and authentic presentation of itself. For in our experience, in this mosaic of our transiency, we can trace the cartoon which depicts the lineaments of the eternal. Man has in fact always accepted the belief that he could express the likeness of the divine, and in the attempt to do so he has developed his art, his codes of conduct and his folk-lore. From the crudest fetishes, lightning-stricken tree or twisted rock, or the artifacts of his earliest instruments, to the Parthenon and Chartres and the frescoes of the Sistine Chapel; from primitive taboos and food-laws and marriage rules to Moses and Solon, Augustine and Justinian; from tales of the egg and the tortoise, of dragons and heroes, of deluge and deliverance to prophecy and speculation, science and theology, Plato and Aristotle, Origen and Aquinas: so it has moved. And always, behind these symbols of the aesthetic, moral and intellectual values, there is constant evidence that only in terms of personalities embodying and transcending such values can we find full satisfaction.

And in that case the goal of its movement may be forecast. The ineffable which we encounter can be *shown* (as L. Wittgenstein[1] has put it) but not *said*—shown by a fully integrated person in his way of life, rather than said in any symbolism, Hebrew or Greek, music or mathematics. We, being human and conditioned in our whole quest by the limitations of our status, must surely look for the showing-forth of the ineffable in terms of the perfect Son of Man. Nothing less will serve; for, as Guye has put it,[2] 'Il n'y a pas un homme *moral*, un homme *intellectuel*, un homme *physiologique*, un homme *physico-chimique*. Ces distinctions résultent de nos classifications arbitraires. Il y a L'Homme tout court. Le réel est un.'

---

[1] Cf. *Tractatus logico-philosophicus*, §6. 522 (Eng. trans., p. 187) and Margaret Masterman in *Theology*, LIV, pp. 53–8.
[2] Ch. Eug. Guye, *L'Evolution physico-chimique*, p. 149.

III

RELIGIOUS EXPERIENCE:
ITS INTERPRETATION

WE have argued that religious experience is fundamentally an awareness of Absolute Being, of a reality, itself infinite, of which the finitudes of space-time are in differing degrees the symbols and instruments, and that this awareness is a universal characteristic of mankind. If so, then the precise modes of its interpretation and expression are plainly, as the religions have always declared, matters of primary importance: the symbols and instruments chosen to reveal it must be the best available.

That the experience itself in its simplest form is essentially similar, whatever interpretation be put upon it, seems probable from the evidence. Obviously, since such evidence consists mainly of recorded experiences and the records are inevitably coloured by the knowledge and beliefs of their authors, it is difficult to disentangle the original event from the meaning put upon it in the telling. But anyone who analyzes carefully the data supplied by the Yogis and the Sufis, Plotinus and St Teresa and Eckhart will find that when allowance has been made for the presuppositions of their respective metaphysical and theological beliefs the basic encounter of the self with the ineffable seems in each case to show the same characteristic quality. This result is confirmed by the work of those students who have striven to show that the ecstasy of non-Christians or even of non-Catholics is a state of unconsciousness, whereas the true supernatural mysticism has its culmination in communion; it is not unfair to say that in so doing they have misinterpreted the evidence in regard to the non-Christians and have read into the Christian records elements

44

which belong rather to the interpretation than to the experience itself.[1]

An instance will make this clear. Father Maréchal, the Jesuit authority on mysticism, asserts that he is bound to regard Plotinus' experience, the culmination of his concentration, as a passing into 'absolute unconsciousness', and its unitive ecstasy as an illusion due to the sudden snapping of the interior tension.[2] There is nothing in Plotinus' own account to justify this charge: his language, though it lacks the warmth and passion of some Christian mystics, describes an event no more and no less exposed to the charge of illusion than theirs, an experience of liberation and life, and a flight of the alone to the Alone.[3] Far from being illusory it is, as Dean Inge points out, 'unusual but in no sense abnormal'; 'it closely resembles the records of the Christian mystics, indeed of all mystics whatever their creed, date or nationality: the witness of the mystics is wonderfully unanimous.'[4] The parallels which he quotes from Philo[5] and Dante,[6] Mozart[7] and Wordsworth[8] could be multiplied indefinitely; and most normal people will at some time in their lives have known something not very dissimilar. The experience seems, as we have urged, to be universal.

Just on this account it is probable that if they could give a completely independent description of it no two individuals would do so in precisely the same form and imagery. Their record would vary first owing to the circumstances preparatory to and accompanying the experience: where, as with Plotinus or 'The Cloud of Unknowing', the approach is by the *via negativa*, it will be in terms of abstraction and release; where it is by sublimation and

---

[1] Cf., for example, J. Maréchal, *Studies in the Psychology of the Mystics*, pp. 222–3 and 285–339.

[2] *Ibid.* pp. 222–337. F. von Hügel, *Eternal Life*, pp. 87 ff., does not challenge the reality of his experience, though he criticizes the consistency of his experience and his ethics.

[3] For a translation of the chief descriptive passages cf. W. R. Inge, *The Philosophy of Plotinus*, II, pp. 133–43.

[4] *Ibid.* pp. 143–4.

[5] *De Migratione Abrahami*, 7 (Cohn and Wendland, *Philonis Opera*, II, p. 275).

[6] *Paradiso* XXXIII.

[7] The origin of the passage quoted seems obscure.   [8] *Excursion* I.

inspiration, fulfilment and creative rapture will be its dominant notes. It must be conditioned also by the history and interests, temperament and convictions of the experient; these will not only supply the language and metaphors but will colour the whole substance of the record.[1] So, too, we must take account of the psychic elements to which Leuba and so many hostile critics have drawn attention: these elements do not fully explain, still less explain away, religious experience, but they manifestly influence subtly and powerfully its interpretation and the inferences drawn from it. Finally, and principally, we must consider the intellectual problem and ask how far the mechanism of the mind can give a valid account of what appears to be in itself indescribable. It will be well to begin with this last problem: for all interpretation, being undertaken in order to impart to ourselves and others a communicable account of what has happened, assumes that the mind can translate an experience by the whole self into categories appropriate to the self as the subject of fragmentary and partial episodes, an experience of the absolute into adequate spatio-temporal symbols.

Such an assumption is of course the necessary basis for any intellectual effort, be it scientific or religious. We are bound to assume that space-time existence is congruous with our intimations and apprehensions of the eternal experienced in it, that the functioning of the 'self of contemplation' bears a real relation to the activities of the 'self of enjoyment', or (to state it on a lower level) that the paradoxes which Eddington made familiar to us in describing our entrance into a room do not in fact imply a radical derangement in our reaction to our environment; that in fact the logos in us, the 'depth of reason', as Tillich calls it, has contact and affinity with the divine logos or ground of reason. We all, in our everyday behaviour and in the postulates of our thinking, accept the belief that existence is coherent and intelligible, although such a belief must involve the corollary that relativism cannot be

[1] An example is supplied by Dean Sperry, *Jesus Then and Now*, p. 207, who states a belief, which I have also held, that Dr K. Barth's condemnation of nature and the natural man would have been much modified if he had spent the First World War in the trenches instead of in neutral Switzerland.

universal, but that there are principles of absolute validity even if, like the Platonic ideas, they remain in the heavens. Even if Dr Jaspers be right in insisting that we cannot bridge the gulf between existence and being, yet he does not and could not say that there is no contact between them. It may be true that we do not know how to translate eternity into time; yet 'both time and eternity are involved in every act of our moral and rational life'.[1]

It is noteworthy that in the many recent attempts by scientists to find a basis for ethics in the evolutionary process[2] there has been a deal of ingenuity and of psychological jargon, and some protests that the apparent evidence of standards of absolute value is 'not valid'. There has also been much confusion of thought and self-contradiction. Even in Dr Simpson's chapter on 'The Ethics of Knowledge and Responsibility' it is clear, as Dr W. H. Thorpe has pointed out,[3] that his conclusions depend upon assumptions which are neither contained in nor consistent with his premises; and this is demonstrably true of the work of the biologists upon whom he relies. That evolution can be so interpreted as to present a case for the validity of ethical standards is a conviction which we shall strongly affirm; that these standards are themselves a product of the evolutionary process is a belief which T. H. Huxley was more successful in attacking than his grandson has been in defending.

In considering this basic disparity between experience and interpretation it is permissible to return to a point already noted that in this respect the religions and the personal encounter have in common this same quality. As soon as we treat a human being not as a thing but as a person we discover in him elements that we can apprehend but not describe. It is only on the surface that we can define one another; even when, as we say, we know our friends through and through, share their impulses and react to their every mood, yet such knowledge when we try to express it remains ultimately mysterious: 'I know but cannot tell.'

[1] W. R. Inge, *The Philosophy of Plotinus*, II, p. 101.
[2] As, for example, J. Huxley, *Evolution and Ethics* (London, 1947); C. H. Waddington, in the symposium *Science and Ethics*; G. G. Simpson, *The Meaning of Evolution* (Yale, 1949).
[3] *Evolution and Christian Belief*, p. 12.

A. N. Whitehead's words are significant here: 'It is characteristic of the learned mind to exalt words. Yet mothers can ponder many things which their lips cannot express. These many things which are thus known constitute the ultimate religious evidence beyond which there is no appeal.'[1]

Man, as we have seen, turned naturally to an anthropomorphic symbol for his gods; and though this is due in the first instance to his dependence upon mother and father, to family and tribal loyalties, and to projection and personification, it has also a deeper and more mature significance. Only by the analogy of our human contacts, only from the ecstasies and the agonies of our human intimacies can we expect to draw any adequate interpretation of the adoration and abasement which the religious encounter evokes. Man who in his infancy makes his god after his own image discovers, when he has ransacked every other field for more appropriate imagery, that only on the level of the personal can any satisfying analogies be found. We can note this at the moment and return to it more fully later.

If we examine the character and effects of this personal encounter with the ineffable, it may be tentatively argued that the first stage in the transition from the experience to its interpretation consists in an awareness of certain constraints and intuitions, a repulsion and attraction deeply felt but not as yet rationalized, and that these convey and constitute an appreciation of value.[2] We discover a simple scale of aesthetic, cognitive and conative discrimination in regard to our environment; there are objects which evoke in us a sense of joy and humility similar to that of the religious experience itself; and we begin to assimilate them to beauty as contrasted with ugliness, truth with disorder and the good with the bad. The absolute passes over into the relative; for although here and there we encounter something like perfection and bow the head before it, our contacts are for the most part on a lower level where there is little to suggest or recall the absolute.

---

[1] *Religion in the Making*, p. 67.

[2] Is this what Dr Tillich calls the ecstatic reason—'Ecstatic reason is reason grasped by an ultimate concern' (*Systematic Theology*, I, p. 53)?

In this business of carrying over the unitary experience into its spatio-temporal expression as soon as we pass from the naïve personalism of our infancy, although the whole self continues to function, its emotional and artistic reaction is more immediate than any other. We respond to the aesthetic appeal before we begin to categorize and cross-question. We are musicians, painters and sculptors before we begin to be scientists or philosophers, though to say so suggests a segregation of our faculties which is false to the facts. We are artists; but art is never, even in its most naïve forms, divorced from curiosity and the desire to understand; and as it becomes appreciative it develops the desire to categorize and compare. So the musician begins to develop a sense of number and its properties; and the painter a perception of the relation of form to function. Questions arise and demand an answer; and from the problems of his environment man is led on to the problems of his own origin and nature and of those haunting moments in which he was aware and afraid. All knowledge has, indeed, followed this path from awareness to explanation; and at each stage of the journey the scope of our experience is narrowed, attention is restricted and concentrated, and what begins as an activity of the whole self in relation to its whole environment becomes, when analysis is complete, a minute and abstract interpretation of one aspect of one particular unit selected from the whole.[1]

That such a process of selection and examination enables us to understand, explain and control our environment and is essential, not only to education, but to life at the human level, is sufficiently evident. The naïve enjoyment and creative imagination of the child must be submitted to the discipline of criticism, to analysis, classification and comparison, if mature appreciation and use are to be attained. This is as true of our personal and religious experiences as of any other. But there is manifestly danger that the products of analysis may be taken as the sole reality and that we may be misled into the common error of supposing that we can explain the whole in terms of an arbitrary selection of its part.

[1] For an illustration, cf. J. Oman, *The Natural and the Supernatural*, pp. 120–1.

Science and psychology have been conspicuously at fault in this respect. They have perpetually sought for a magic formula, a philosopher's stone which being effective in its special field should be proclaimed as the universal solvent of all our problems; and man's integrative experience is explained away in terms of the Oedipus complex! This procedure falls, of course, into both the familiar fallacies, the denial that the whole merely by being a whole is greater than the sum of its parts and the assumption that, the parts being original and the whole merely the product of their combination, to explain them is to describe and account for it.[1] Both fallacies ignore the fact that the wood has a life of its own which is not described by an explanation of the trees that compose it.

This limitation of the analytical intellect which, as von Hügel has said, 'seems habitually to labour at depersonalizing all it touches',[2] serves to illustrate the character of the mental activity and the relation of its products to the full human experience. When Professor Norbert Wiener demonstrates how closely the automata of cybernetics resemble in their functioning the nervous system and mental processes of mankind, he is not entitled to conclude from this similarity that a thorough-going materialism is in any way more arguable.[3] That the human brain is an instrument closely analogous to the computing machine and other servo-mechanisms is a discovery of high importance—the more so if it enables a vast field of human effort to be transferred from mankind to his robots. But that this makes it in any way more plausible that a human being is, as De la Mettrie supposed, himself nothing but a machine, is a wholly unjustifiable inference. As Wiener insists,[4] the machine, however perfect its functioning, does not replace the mathematician who sets up its problem and

[1] For an exposure of these fallacies, cf. J. C. Smuts, *Holism and Evolution*, pp. 19–20.

[2] *The Mystical Element in Religion*, 1, p. 76. The recent revolt against reason is partly a protest against the exploitation of this tendency in the name of science.

[3] Cf. *Cybernetics* (New York, 1948). It is not always easy to see in his book how much the machine can already accomplish and how much he thinks it may some day achieve. Similarly his own philosophical position is by no means clear. These two objections apply also to Dr J. Z. Young, *Doubt and Certainty in Science*.

[4] *Cybernetics*, p. 154.

50

gives the necessary instructions upon which it operates. The machine can analyse and compute and control: it cannot experience or apprehend or initiate. In other words it is not alive, and the whole realm of personal contacts is outside its range. The robot remains a robot.[1]

Nevertheless, as we have been constantly suggesting, Wiener is right in saying that 'the whole mechanist-vitalist controversy has been relegated to the limbo of badly posed questions'.[2] Anyone who will reflect upon the curious fact that for the past half-century scientists have assumed that mechanism and teleology are contradictory notions, that a machine can exist without any purposive function, and that purpose is inconsistent with the existence of machines to give it expression, will realize that this absurdity has arisen because of the controversy in question. We can see that the two words had come to symbolize two rival methods of interpreting the universe; that teleology seemed to ascribe everything to the arbitrary will of an omnipotent deity whose recorded actions though not always miraculous or magical were yet such as often to conflict with the observed facts, while mechanism implied a purely materialist outlook and accepted in spite of its difficulty the belief in self-impelling, self-constructing, self-repairing, self-reproducing automata, in a design without a designer.

It is easy to say that each of these assumptions is ridiculous, but much less easy to surrender the basic antitheses from which they are derived. Mind and matter, spirit and body, the world and God, not to say science and religion, have been for so long accepted as statements of a common-sense dualism too obvious to need examination that they form not only the axioms of our normal outlook but the presuppositions of our religious formularies. Acceptance of them as the terms of peace after the Darwinian controversy[3] fixed them upon the outlook of the present

---

[1] For electronic brains, cf. D. M. Mackay in *British Journal for the Phil. of Science*, II, no. 6, pp. 105–21; and for their analogy with us cf. Prof. J. Z. Young, *Doubt and Certainty in Science*. [2] *Cybernetics*, p. 56.
[3] Cf. Vol. I of this book, pp. 187–9, for the gentleman's agreement after the Huxley-Wilberforce affair.

older generation; and the replacement of the Platonic division of phenomenal and eternal by the contrary classification of fact and fancy, endorsed by Logical Positivism, perpetuated the same dichotomy. When mankind found philosophers insisting that all the experiences that really matter were unknowable and that all statements about them were nonsense, they naturally protested that, although they were used to this sort of proclamation from scientific materialists, it was for philosophy an act of suicide—reason had betrayed itself, and them; a revolt against it was inevitable. The wave of anti-rationalism which swept over theology was hardly so swift or so intense as that which flooded the world of painting and poetry, of literature and art. It is time that we looked at this reaction more closely.

It is unnecessary, and would be out of place, to examine in detail the revolt against reason which has been so characteristic of recent orthodoxy. To ascribe it solely to the reaction against the identification of reason with scientific and quantitative studies would be to ignore two other elements which contribute to its support, the continuance of fundamentalist beliefs in the infallibility of Scripture and the revival of transcendentalist insistence upon the unknowable 'otherness' of God.[1] Each of these characteristics found their prophet in Sören Kierkegaard, the Danish man of letters of a century ago;[2] and the immense influence of his works during the past twenty years has been at once the sign and the instrument of irrationalism. They satisfied the longing for authority and pandered to the general despondency both by their denunciation of human thought and effort and by their insistence that the Word of God can only be accepted with creaturely and unquestioning

---

[1] The confusion arising in relation to Natural Theology illustrates the plight of orthodoxy. Out of many examples two may be mentioned. E. Brunner, *The Christian Doctrine of God*, insists (pp. 65–6) that the witness of the Bible must be formulated in terms consistent with science; then he admits (p. 132) that there is a revelation in nature; and again insists that there is no such thing as natural theology and that no effort of philosophy or of the non-Christian 'can possibly be combined with the Christian idea of God' (p. 136). P. Tillich, *Systematic Theology*, I, pp. 44–6, has almost similar inconsistencies in his treatment of experience.

[2] Cf. particularly *Concluding Unscientific Postscript* for his insistence that any attempt to interpret God or the Bible objectively is unchristian.

obedience. They cut the sinews of faith by declaring that there could be no coming of God's Kingdom within history, and provided excuse for acquiescence in sin by proclaiming that fallen man could only face a choice of evils. To argue against them was impossible and wicked, since reason was the enemy of faith and the proof of self-will.[1]

Influential as this revolt has been, its error is evidenced not only by its character but by its effects. Reason may be, and is, a defective instrument: in its present obsession with the mathematical and quantitative it is obviously ill-fitted to deal with personal experience and the encounter of man with God. But although it is at best interpretative rather than creative, its function being to explain and so to enable communication, yet it is still our only means to this end, our sole instrument for the understanding and the debating of religion. Theology is only a handmaid of faith; but her service is indispensable. We can have, if we are worthy, good theology, if unworthy bad theology: an irrational theology would be a contradiction in terms; and a religion without theology would be a dumb and mutilated torso.

Moreover, the revolt has not in fact made for a more vital and personal commitment to religion nor for a more imaginative and practical faith. Anyone who compares the present concern of Christians with that of a generation ago will find it hard not to confess that in evangelism, in social service, in moral and intellectual effort, in scholarship and educational activities and in Church membership there is evidence rather of decline than of advance. In the special subject with which we are occupied, the relation of religious to scientific effort, there has been, as we have seen,[2] in consequence of the revolt a very evident set-back. The fact is that, just at the time when sound and adventurous thought was most needed and most practicable, theology like philosophy disavowed its responsibility. The result has been bewilderment, a tyranny of catch-phrases, and many 'struggles in the dark'.

[1] For an examination and refutation of Kierkegaard and his followers cf. L. H. De Wolf, *The Religious Revolt against Reason* (New York, 1949); H. J. Paton, *In Defence of Reason* (London, 1951), pp. 213–28.
[2] Cf. Vol. I of this book, pp. 200–3.

It has been necessary to note thus briefly the contemporary difficulty that has arisen in relation to the attainment of a reasonable faith, in order to insist that whatever the obstacles such effort is essential. If, as is plainly the case, our encounter with the ineffable quickens in us apprehensions and intuitions which seek expression in emotional, cognitive and conative activity, and if the resultant achievements are to be prevented from becoming merely chaotic and anarchic eccentricities, the original experience must be represented, at each level of its translation, in terms of daily happenings. This would seem to involve the development of a graded system by which the primary quality of religion should be transmitted, through the broad principles which constitute the good life, into the details of social and individual living—by which, in fact, the ephemeral should be fashioned after the pattern of the eternal and human affairs ordered 'according to the vision revealed in the mount'. Plainly all the religions of mankind have, to some extent at least, set themselves to fulfil this ideal, producing a cultus or form of corporate and private worship, a creed or similar statement of its beliefs, and a code of conduct or moral theology prescribing the ethics appropriate to the expression of cultus and creed in secular affairs. Any study of the evolution of religions or any analytical comparison between them will show how the general character of these systems is determined by the reaction of the particular faith to its physical environment.

We are not here so much concerned with the general characteristics of the various religions as with the means by which mankind in general has striven to find a true and satisfying representation of the ineffable. When the diffused and undifferentiated animism of primitive times gave way to the various pantheons of polytheism, these personified aspects of nature or of human excellence, of social life and its activities, of sky and sea, beauty and wisdom, home and state, sex and war. They tended to attach reverence to places of natural grandeur, Delphi or Tempe or the crest of Olympus, to symbols expressive of fertility and birth, of strength and speed, the tree and the pillar, the bull and the snake, the hero and the virgin, or to the ordered life, the ceremonies and duties of the community, the burial-place and the temple, the festivals and mysteries, the law and the prophets. The variety of these symbols is itself a proof of the universality of the religions: it is linked naturally with such elements of man's normal experience as impress his powers of appreciation and arouse or recall the wonder and awe, the joy and humility of the basic encounter. As Oman has so fully demonstrated,[1] these symbols can be grouped in accordance with the general valuation of the natural world: if it is accepted as, broadly speaking, it is in Hinduism, or rejected as in Buddhism, or regarded as a scene of conflict as in Zoroastrianism and to some extent in Islam, or of redemption as in prophetic Judaism and Christianity, this verdict has its influence in determining the main features of the cultus, the doctrine and the ethics which embody it, and is clearly related to the character and history of its followers. This correspondence between the religions and the character, the beliefs and the practices of mankind as expressed in the quality of their divinities gives rise to the theories of anthropologists and certain psychologists which accept the adage that men make their gods in their own image, and explain away religion in terms of projection or escapism, sexual complex or social behaviour-pattern. Such theories throw a valid light upon certain phases in the development of infantile personalism into its fully matured shape; for in that process as in the similar business of individual adolescence there is room for large variation, for perversion and a wide divergence. But as an interpretation of the fully developed product they are sufficiently refuted by their failure to explain how, if religion has no other source than such partial and diverse origins, it displays in its highest exponents so remarkable a similarity of experience. The testimony of the saints and mystics, reflected as it is by vast numbers of much less exceptional folk, should be the norm and criterion in the study of religion. Starting from that we can see how the stream of awareness is split up into main branches, divaricated through a multitude of channels, and finally

[1] Cf. J. Oman, *The Natural and the Supernatural*, the third part of which (pp. 358–471) is a most impressive exposition of the chief types of religion.

represented by such drops of the water of life as individuals like ourselves may receive.

In all this variety—and in religion as in sex the multitude of experiments has been almost countless—we can trace clear proof that it is in personal categories that the finest, truest and most effective interpretations are to be found. As we have indicated there have been individuals and phases, cults and even religions, in which the vagaries of perverted relationships reproduce themselves. So much Leuba and his colleagues have shown. But here as elsewhere in life *abusus non tollit usum*. If even in Christendom there has been eroticism and sentimentality, sadism and masochism, hypocrisy and self-seeking, there has also been the purest, noblest and most creative of human relationships, a transformation of the human individual into a personality that carries with it in emotion, thought and will, indeed in the whole range of its being, the quality of the Christ. As we survey the vast field of man's quest for God it is difficult to deny that, only when the divine is interpreted in terms of the Word made flesh, can awe and obedience and curiosity be quickened into love and so individuals and communities be integrated and energized for the fulfilment of His purpose.

Hitherto we have been considering man's encounter with the ineffable solely from the human side in terms of awareness and interpretation. But plainly what we meet supplies the standpoint from which the experience is to be more truly described. Discovery as it is in the one aspect, is also, obviously and primarily, revelation. We are caught up into a presence chamber, we become aware of a reality, we strive to interpret God. We do so in terms of His effect upon us; and the more we enter into the appreciation of what has happened, the more plain does it become that the initiative, the character and the influence of it are from Him not from us. He gives; we respond and receive. He is always giving; we can only seldom and partially reply.[1]

---

[1] Cf. W. Temple, *Nature, Man and God*, p. 306, 'We affirm, then, that unless all existence is a medium of Revelation, no particular Revelation is possible'; and p. 266, 'When we see nature truly, we see God self-manifested in and through it'; and A. N. Whitehead, *Religion in the Making*, pp. 155–6, 'Every event on its finer side introduces God into the world'.

It is important to recognize clearly this element of mutuality in His relationship with us. Some of those who have recently emphasized their belief in God as living and active have seemed to imply that revelation can be and must be wholly independent of human response; indeed, that divine action can only be known as such when it is miraculous—by which word they appear to mean contrary to the normal sequence of cause and effect. In addition, there is, of course, a mass of traditional evidence in most religions which ascribes to God arbitrary and spasmodic actions whose common quality is that they are unpredictable and inexplicable—'acts of God' in the lawyers' sense. Deliverances and calamities, inspiration and judgment regarded as due solely to God give the impression that He acts as an individual king or magistrate would do towards subjects and cases who have no right of reply.

Such insistence upon the supremacy of God, such refusal to admit any conditioning of His will, are the natural acknowledgment of our creaturely status. Obviously we are in no position to 'reckon on His ways or bargain for His love'. But we must not on that account impute to Him caprice or changeableness or a nature that operates by after-thoughts. He is essentially constant and self-consistent, fulfilling His own purpose without haste and without rest, and offering to His creatures the invitation to know and to share His way. And in our moments of awareness we do in fact find that we are caught up and inspired, sustained and encouraged by the power that floods in upon us and the peace that sets us free from fear and self-esteem. A life intense and joyous, an energy which convulses and impels us, a sensitiveness which quickens our insight and deepens our sympathy are the sequel to such moments; and though the revelation fades it does not leave any of us unchanged; none of us can altogether forget, and some are permanently transformed. Hearts and minds and wills are enriched and directed.

In their accounts of such experience there is wide difference between people of varying temperaments and traditions. By some it can only be described in terms of drama, 'I saw', 'I heard', 'He said', 'I replied'. No doubt some of us visualize more clearly and express more vividly an encounter which others would interpret in less sensational imagery. But when all allowance is made for the danger of applying the language of sense-perception to events not on that plane, it is evident that for many at least the only possible analogies are those of personal contact. The experience is emphatically not to be explained in lower than personal categories: it is not abstract or aesthetic; nor is its subject a fantasy or a theorem; whatever the inadequacy of such accounts of God's dealings with us, they are at least less mistaken and debasing[1] than the presentations which treat the divine as impersonal or subpersonal, as mechanism or the life-force. For, however much we may be on our guard against anthropomorphism, human personality cannot but be the most appropriate as well as the highest and worthiest category in our experience; and to accept a lesser *morphé*, be it mathematical formula or mechanical analogy, is not only to fall into idolatry but to declare that the whole is lower than its part. A universe which contains the personal must not be interpreted on a lower scale.

With temperamental differences there are also those that arise from tradition. A Plotinus will interpret his ecstasy in language and imagery somewhat unlike that of an Origen and widely divergent from that of (say) St John of the Cross; and the description as given by any of these and by a mystic trained in modern psychology would vary still more radically. Indeed, to determine how far if at all religious experience can properly be regarded as validating the interpretation put upon it demands a sensitive appreciation and an exegetical skill of the rarest kind. Manifestly the method which would accept the fact of experience as authentic and dismiss its interpretation as subjective is too simple: there are too many instances in which experience and interpretation 'belong together', too many in which what might be dismissed as mere description is on inspection seen to be in fact integral and even

---

[1] For justification of these epithets cf. Rom. i. 23–32, where St Paul shows that a distorted concept of God involves a degraded valuation of man and thus leads to sexual exploitation and so to the corruption of human relationships.

essential. There are cases in which closely similar accounts can be found from mystics of contrary traditions, for instance that of the martyred sufi of Bagdad, al-Hallâj, and Christians who proclaim as he did a true union through love with the divine;[1] and even when explanations differ in their choice of symbol and analogy, careful consideration discloses an underlying and evident identity. In face of the evidence it is not easy to escape Professor W. E. Hocking's conclusion that 'the love of God is the one natural instinct of man: worship is the one deed which answers as an echo all other deeds of history: all special desires are refracted desires for the Absolute Good'.[2]

Light, life, love: so the Fourth Evangelist defined the Godhead. If here as in every other field of human endeavour the expert has a right to be heard, that definition may be given high authority; it is in fact one to which the great religions of mankind would give assent and which might go far to provide a basis for discussion between the two chief of them, Christianity and Buddhism. To accept it would be for the Christian to reaffirm the general conviction that belief in a personal God does not mean that God is an individual, and for the Buddhist to assert that he does not regard the ultimate substratum of the world as subpersonal.[3] Certainly for the vast majority of mankind, even for those outside any religion, the belief in the ultimacy of materialistic categories seems to have been generally abandoned.[4] It is becoming clear that Buddhism in its higher forms does not mean, by Nirvana or by its doctrine of the Way, an escape into non-entity, nor could it find basis for its ethics in a non-personal reality. Light is for man the universal symbol. Life, unless it means merely individuality,

---

[1] Cf. L. Massignon, *La passion d' al Hosayn-ibn-Mansour al-Hallâj* (Paris, 1922); J. Maréchal, *Studies in the Psychology of the Mystics* (London, 1927), pp. 241–81; and A. J. Arberry, *Sufism*, pp. 59–60; and for his relation to the doctrine of the Perfect Man, R. A. Nicholson, *Studies in Islamic Mysticism*, pp. 77–89.

[2] *The Meaning of God in Human Experience*, p. 577.

[3] A. N. Whitehead, whose treatment of the subject in *Religion in the Making*, pp. 58–67, is marred by lack of definition of 'personal', declares that Eastern philosophy asserts that 'The substratum is impersonal'. Does this mean unindividual? It should mean subpersonal and if so is not (I believe) true. Both East and West could perhaps accept super-personal.

[4] The change in Communist doctrine in this respect has been very remarkable.

and love, if it is agapé and not eros, would be acceptable to the experts of all traditions.[1]

It is a short step from such a statement to the conclusion that the quest for an adequate symbol of the divine can only be satisfied by the acknowledgment of the perfect Son of Man as the 'express image' of God. It is plain that human personality, at the highest level of which men and women can conceive it, is for us humans the appropriate category in which to find God revealed; that if the ultimate reality is to be interpreted for us it can only be in the terms of our own highest knowable; that if there be a perfect man then he will represent God to us with a fulness that no other sacrament can approach. Moreover, the instinctive response of worship and abasement, of joy and humility, of love in fact, which we make to revealed deity is only satisfying if the object of our adoration is in some sense one of ourselves. As has repeatedly been demonstrated, mankind cannot adore or love the Absolute, or the Life-force, or the Laws of Nature, or Chance any more than he can adore the terebinth of Mamre or the bull of Bethel or the serpent called Nehushtan. Worship and abasement can be quickened into love only as the communion of person with person is established. And love is the sole alchemy by which we can not only adore but become one with what we love. The Ineffable may exalt and overwhelm me; the Lord of Nature may inspire and sustain; the Incarnate transforms and integrates. God thus giving Himself does indeed visit and redeem His people: for not only, as J. T. Merz put it, 'did humanity look up into the face of Christ and found itself',[2] but it learnt to say 'we live: yet not we: Christ lives in us'.

The reason for such a contention is explained if we press to its conclusion the argument that what is discovery on our side is revelation on God's, if, that is, we insist that our union with God and His incarnation in Christ are congruous with and vindicated by the indwelling of His Spirit in us. Our experience, be it at its

---

[1] On the relation between Buddhist and Christian ideas in this matter, cf. Note v, below, p. 209.

[2] So G. E. Newsom, in *Great Christians* (London, 1933), p. 382.

simplest level or in the rapture and inspiration of the saints, is not an achievement of our own: to claim it as due to our human merit or effort is to follow the heresy of Pelagius. It is itself God's gift, the evidence of His energizing presence, the proof that we are made in His image and are in some sort His children. In us as men, the divine Logos, the divine Spirit operates; in us the divine springs up to meet and welcome and adore its own source and sameness. Not of ourselves, but by virtue of His good gift to us and in us, we can be at one with God. It is the appropriate response to His gift, that, having by a long process of trial and error discovered that we can in some dim fashion reflect the nature of the divine, we should in the fulness of time be led to confess Jesus as the image of the invisible God, truly Son of Man and truly Son of God, God and Man one Christ.

IV

THE SIGNIFICANCE OF JESUS

IF we are right in claiming that in view of our experience, both of ourselves and of the universe, any presentation of reality in lower than personal terms is inadequate and in religious regard idolatrous, and if we are constrained by the evidence of His character and influence to endorse the apostolic confession that Jesus, the Christ, is the image of the unseen, the Son of the Father, the Word of God, then we are faced by the immediate problem that confronted the early Church, 'How is such a belief consistent with monotheism?' or 'What is the nature of the Christ? is He God or man?'

It is proof of the importance of the question that Jesus Himself raised it at the two critical turning-points of His mission, when at the end of His work in Galilee before beginning His last journey to Jerusalem He asked His disciples 'Who say ye that I am?', and when, in what was perhaps His last public utterance at the close of the great day in the temple before His arrest, He said to the Pharisees 'What think ye of the Christ? whose son is he?'—and when they said 'The son of David', asked again, 'How then doth David in the Spirit call him Lord?'[1] Plainly to men brought up in the intensified monotheism of contemporary Judaism such a problem was obvious and urgent. The tension is shown by a notable coincidence: at the very time when Saul of Tarsus was risking his life in becoming the servant and evangelist of Christ, his Jewish contemporary Philo of Alexandria was running a similar risk on an embassy to Caligula in order to plead that no Jew should be compelled to break the first commandment by offering incense to the emperor.[2]

[1] Cf. Matt. xvi. 15 and xxii. 41–6; Mark viii. 29 and xii. 35–7 (R.V.).

[2] Cf. his *Legatio ad Gaium* ap. Cohn and Wendland, *Phil. Op.* VI, pp. 155–223; and H. St J. Hart, *A Foreword to the Old Testament*, p. 12.

It is, indeed, one of the most remarkable proofs of the impression made by Jesus that the very people who were least of all likely to deify Him and who in fact had sent Him to death on the ground of His claim to be Messiah should have produced in the writings of the New Testament a varied literature, the common element in which is its agreement that in Jesus God had visited and redeemed His people. The several writers approach the proclamation of this belief by different roads: they express their conviction under different metaphors and describe the central fact in different terms.[1] But each of them is plainly attempting to find symbols adequate to an event which has brought to him a new and transforming experience and compelled him to rethink and to redescribe his concept of the nature of God and the relationships of men to God and to one another. We can see not only from such contrasted documents as the Epistle of St James and the Epistle to the Hebrews, but from the divergencies between the Synoptists and the varying elements, ethical or apocalyptic, conservative or revolutionary, in their portrait of Jesus, how hard they found it to discover a simple and consistent interpretation of their experience. There is no one type of theology in the New Testament; and even the Fourth Evangelist, who more than any other has arrived at a complete and coherent exposition of the meaning of the good news, is not always characteristically Johannine.

It is of course in the series of St Paul's letters that we can most plainly trace the sequence and quality of the process. Constrained by temperament and education to fasten upon the problem of suffering which had haunted Israel and so to reject Jesus as accursed by the evidence of His crucifixion,[2] he shows in the Epistle to the Galatians how his conversion involved an inevitable break with the Law. It was apparently not until his sojourn in Corinth that the full significance of the Cross became plain to him. In Thessalonica, by his own showing, he had preached the 'man from heaven' in terms of miracle and apocalyptic and the power of

[1] The present emphasis upon the uniformity of the kerygma must not blind us to this diversity.

[2] Gal. iii. 13; for the reasons for believing this to be an early, perhaps his earliest, letter, cf. my *Jesus and the Gospel of Love*, pp. 306–8.

God; in Athens, according to the Acts, he had played the philosopher, argued his case on the Areopagus and proclaimed the
wisdom of God. In both methods he had accomplished little
upheavals and derision were not a satisfying result; he had
adulterated the word.[1] Not the Jewish craving for miracle nor the
Greek concern for knowledge nor the concepts of deity as all-
powerful and all-wise could yield a satisfying interpretation of
reality. God had revealed Himself in Christ in terms of a man on
a Cross, a scandal to Jews and folly to Greeks, but to those who
respond to its meaning God's power and God's wisdom.[2]

That, so soon after his conversion and by concentrating his
attention upon the crucifixion, he should have realized the
revolutionary effect of that event upon the traditional ideas of
God's nature and upon the corporate, not less than the individual
life of man is proof not only of the depth of his experience and the
brilliance of his intellect but of the unique consistency and influence
of Jesus Himself. It is not merely that an orthodox Jew found himself compelled to confess the Crucified as Lord and Son of God
but that in doing so he saw that the traditional doctrine of God
and of man could no longer stand, that God must be Father not
Sultan, Love not Power, and that man must be not God's servant
but His child, not His instrument but His embodiment. He was
thus able to resolve, as none of the Old Testament writers who
had wrestled with it had succeeded in doing, the ancient problem
of the justice and mercy of God and of the unmerited suffering of
the innocent; and to express the new concepts of love and community without diminishing the sense of God's majesty or of
man's sin: indeed, as any student of the first eight chapters of
Romans will recognize, though his basic picture is new and unprecedented it is indeed the 'fulfilment',[3] as much as the super-
session, of the Law and the Prophets.

This radical change in religious values was accomplished in
terms of personal religious experience rather than by ethical or
metaphysical exposition. Doctrine in St Paul, as in the New

---

[1] Cf. II Cor. iv. 2.   [2] Cf. I Cor. i. 23-4.
[3] So Jesus had proclaimed, cf. Matt. v. 17.

Testament generally, is the expression of a way of life, not a code of conduct or a system of thought. Indeed, as we have indicated, the various writers do not share any exact or consistent vocabulary or ideology, and interpret their experience in forms which can easily be set in contrast. It required three centuries of analysis and debate to fashion out of the records and heritage of their experience an orthodoxy of morals and theology—and perhaps as much was lost as was gained in the process. But these earliest witnesses were united in their central testimony. They had found in Christ 'the way, the truth, and the life', and in that way all things were made new for them. The discovery was not only true and real but illuminative. It made sense both of their own lives and, so far as they could see, of the universe.

We have already[1] discussed the fresh and characteristic attitude of Jesus towards nature and the extent to which, contrary to tradition, this attitude was shared by St Paul. Its revolutionary character may most clearly be seen by the failure of Christendom in later ages to appreciate and accept it. But at the time it was plainly a chief cause of the impact which Jesus produced on His contemporaries. Unlike the rabbis[2] He taught not by precept or convention, but with authority and at first hand. When first they heard Him, a murmur ran round the synagogue, 'What is this? a new teaching! with authority he commandeth even the unclean spirits, and they obey him';[3] and He Himself fulfilled their expectation when He based His discourse upon the antithesis 'it was said to them of old time,...: but I say unto you,....'.[4] He 'spoke things' as a great interpreter of Christianity in our time has said of Him;[5] and men were stabbed into sensitiveness by His words. This is indeed the 'authority', the originality and efficacy, of His teaching, that He took the simplest and most universal experiences and activities of mankind, expressed them in aphorism or parable, and challenged His hearers to discover their significance. He tells the story of a sower or of a seed, of

---

[1] Cf. Vol. I of this book, Ch. II.   [2] Cf. Matt. vii. 29.
[3] Cf. Mark i. 27 (R.V.); the word ἐξουσία is nearer to creativity than to power.
[4] Matt. v. 21, 27, 33-4, etc. (R.V.).   [5] The phrase is characteristic of T. R. Glover.

something that we all know and take for granted, and asks 'Do you *see*? Is it, as Wordsworth would put it, "a yellow primrose and nothing more"? or do you glimpse "the many-splendoured thing"? Do you *really* see?' And some saw. But if not, then He will try again—neither forcing nor arguing—until at last the hearer sees and is tempted to exclaim 'Why didn't I see that before?'

If this sounds elementary, if (as is indeed the fact) it seems very unlike the Redeemer God, the wonder-worker and oracle of tradition, yet it is precisely thus that Jesus vindicates the claim, 'I am come that they might have life': it is exactly what He stated in His message,[1] 'Go your way and tell John the things which ye do hear and see: the blind receive their sight, and the lame walk, the lepers are cleansed, and the deaf hear, and the dead are raised up, and the poor have good tidings preached to them.' We may interpret those words physically if we will; but spiritually each clause describes precisely the effect of His teaching upon His contemporaries and upon all who through the ages have been to school with Him. Sensibility, which as the course of evolution demonstrates is the true equivalent of life, must always be the educator's objective; and no one has ever aroused it so fully and passionately as Jesus.

But, as we saw when we considered His attitude to nature,[2] His power to evoke wonder and heighten vitality is only one side of His influence: if He illuminates He also challenges and condemns, and with an austerity that often seems ruthless and even cruel. Indeed, the most familiar of the paradoxes ascribed to Him is that of a gentleness that is almost sentimental and of a severity that is almost savage; for He is described as having said, 'Whosoever shall say to his brother, ...Thou fool, shall be in danger of hell fire',[3] and also, 'ye compass sea and land to make one proselyte; and when he is become so, ye make him twofold more a son of hell than yourselves'.[4] How could so strong a contrast be displayed by One who nevertheless has always impressed students

---

[1] Matt. xi. 4, 5; Luke vii. 22 (R.V.).   [2] Cf. Vol. I of this book, pp. 30–3.
[3] Matt. v. 22 (A.V.).   [4] Matt. xxiii. 15 (R.V.).

as being singularly consistent and integrated, 'the same yesterday, and to day, and for ever?'[1]

This particular paradox is already familiar to us. We have seen that it belongs to the fundamental religious experience of mankind and is perhaps specifically characteristic of man's primary reaction to his environment. *Mysterium tremendum et fascinans*: in such terms might our remotest forbears have described the universe or its God: the self-same moment which terrifies also attracts; what exalts also abases; wonder effects penitence; adoration is the obverse of self-consciousness. If Jesus is in any sense divine, we should expect to trace in Him the same quality, the same rhythm, the same paradox as we trace in man's first religion and find repeated at every stage in his development. The experience of Adam in the garden,[2] of Moses at the bush,[3] of Isaiah in the year that King Uzziah died[4] is inevitably repeated when Simon Peter, convinced in his boat of the miracle of Jesus, can only cry 'Depart from me',[5] and when Saul seeing the Lord in the way learns through a life-time of service the self-emptying which he describes as the supreme act of Christ.[6] Indeed, we can go further; for the two complementary elements in the teaching of Jesus, His power to illuminate and sensitize, and His power to test and to reject, belong together, and His training of His disciples, as indeed His whole mission, involves them both. Life, the life abundant which He imparted, can ultimately only be attained through failure. 'He that loveth his life loseth it.'

If this double experience is, as we have claimed, the basis of man's nature and status, then Jesus, whose whole teaching and influence repeats and emphasizes it, is thereby linked at once with the essentials of religion. In fashioning His ministry on this rhythm He is vindicating the title which He chose for Himself, 'Son of man', and fulfilling the conditions which accompany and enable the manifestation of God. As He initiates us into this experience He enables us to grow up into our own true nature and to gain our freedom from the pride and the conflicts which enslave

---

[1] Hebrews xiii. 8 (A.V.).   [2] Gen. iii. 10.   [3] Exod. iii. 4–6.
[4] Isai. vi. 5.   [5] Luke v. 8.   [6] Phil. ii. 5–7.

5 2

our will and dissipate our energies. He illuminates, condemns, and forgives; and we are exalted, broken, restored and united. If individuation and its completion in community is the significance of the evolutionary process, then by His character, achievement and permanent value Jesus is demonstrably linked with that process as its symbol and instrument. Its meaning is illuminated and its fulfilment guaranteed by Him; and the early confessions which hailed Him as the embodiment of the divine Word,[1] the image of the unseen God,[2] the hall-mark of deity,[3] the Alpha and Omega of the creation[4], can be endorsed by modern man.

If life abundant is both the goal of evolution and the purpose of Jesus, it is important that the content of this description should not be narrowed. Plainly it is the whole sphere of our being that is to be made alive; the self in its threefold aspect 'spirit and soul and body', as St Paul calls it,[5] that needs renewal and redemption; the person in all its relationships, temporal and eternal, secular and religious, individual and corporate, that is to live here and now in the heavenlies. If this seems vague or pietistic or impossible of fulfilment (as, indeed, to most of us it certainly will do), we can look to Jesus, and in confirmation also to the saints, to see what is involved. What we must not do—though it has only too often been done—is to scale down the extent and wholeness of the adventure so as to make it fit our competence or serve our appetites and interests. When religion becomes the vested prerogative of a class or clique, then 'life' is fashioned according to their design; and its integrity is impaired if not perverted. The full-grown man whom the writer to the Ephesians proclaimed can be measured by 'the stature of the fulness of Christ'[6] but by no smaller standard. It would be good if all who speak in the name of Christianity and the Churches would on occasion take stock of their procedures and equipment and see how far each of them is adequate to the wholeness of their obligation.

Jesus Himself, as the New Testament shows Him, had plainly

---

[1] John i. 14. [2] Col. i. 15.
[3] χαρακτήρ; Heb. i. 3. [4] Rev. i. 8; xxii. 13; and cf. Col. i. 16.
[5] I Thess. v. 23. [6] Eph. iv. 13.

a many-sided and indeed universal sensitiveness. The range of His teaching; the variety of His technique; the power to take any simple thing and make it transparent and luminous; the particularity of His response to each individual according to his or her special need; whatever allowance we make for the conditions under which the books came to be written or for the personal equations of the several authors, the freedom with which He strikes the appropriate note in the scale of man's highest experience must always excite our wonder. It is all so fresh and spontaneous, so vital and so relevant, that we begin to exclaim for ourselves 'Never man spake like this man'[1] or, as we realize the quality of the experience to which He initiates us, 'Thou hast the words of eternal life'.[2]

The New Testament evidence is reinforced and enlarged by the verdict of subsequent ages. It has been a frequent taunt that each age and each people fashions Christ after its own image; and whether we look at the artists or at the preachers of a period the charge is plainly not unfair. After the first joyous centuries when Christ was not only the shepherd but the Orpheus of the Catacombs, interest becomes increasingly focused upon the Babe in His mother's arms and the Redeemer on His cross—though the Judge dividing the saved from the damned and delivering each to his apportioned doom played an even larger part in influencing opinion. It is one of the proofs of the rigidity of orthodoxy in the medieval period that it confined knowledge of the Scriptures and the content of popular religion to so small a selection of texts and stories; as with nature so with grace, the symbols are few and strictly standardized. But when with the Renaissance and Reformation a greater freedom is manifest, the Churches which did not follow the Second Commandment into iconoclasm show in their pictures something of the range of possible interpretations and of the movement of contemporary feeling. From the avenging Christ modelled upon Jupiter with his thunderbolts to

---

[1] John vii. 46 (A.V.).
[2] John vi. 68; here, as in the other sayings that we have quoted, the Fourth Evangelist sums up exactly the impression produced in detail by the Synoptists.

the Light of the World thorn-crowned and patient or the Gentle Jesus praying in the garden, it would be possible to find examples of each mood of theology and of devotion:[1] and of most of them, particularly the sentimentalities of Protestant piety and the Sacred Heart of Roman Catholicism, it is difficult to speak with reverence. Freedom of imagination and variety of significance are restricted by the almost universal dominance of the traditional Christ—the long-haired, smooth-bearded, flowing-robed figure which as far back as the sixth century had become the accepted portrait:[2] it is difficult to bring fulness of life into anything so formal and statuesque. But those who in recent years have broken away from it have, so far as I can judge, found the task too much for them. Indeed, it may well be that the Puritans were right after all and that in the media of the artist and the sculptor Christ must remain the 'great unknown'.

In literature the case is different. Though for the experienced Christian to write a life of Christ will seem almost as impossible as to describe the character of God, yet it is plainly the function of an 'image' to be capable of description; and the New Testament is an ample precedent. It is significant of the extent to which interest in the manhood of Jesus had been lost that no attempt was made to study His life till late in the eighteenth century.[3] But since the days of Strauss and Renan when the taboo had been broken by the critics, it has been natural that those who were facing the question which Jesus Himself invited should answer it in terms of a biography. On the whole, and with the exception of one or two writers whose work has been merely pretentious and of a few others who meant to scoff, the results have been significant and valuable. Inevitably they have been limited by the author's personality and experience; he has told, and told at his best, what

[1] Cf. Mrs K. L. Jenner, *Christ in Art* (London, 1906) and J. Burns, *The Christ Face in Art* (London, 1907), the latter an admirable study of the myriad variations upon a traditional theme.

[2] This is described in the spurious letter of Publius Lentulus, and became usual in the fourth century. It was adopted by the mosaic-workers of Byzantium and is finely shown in St Appollinare Nuova at Ravenna.

[3] The earliest seems to have been that by Reimarus in 1778; this was published anonymously and as fragments.

1e was able to see and to understand. When this has been done by
1 person of wide sympathies and spiritual insight a portrait which
has disclosed a new aspect of Christ has often been given to us.
Those who sneer at such books by describing them as essays in
self-idealization are misjudging their author's motives by interpreting his limitations as his intentions. Others, professedly more
objective, have been in the main less satisfactory; a 'harmony' of
the Gospels or a speculative interpretation of the drama which
they indicate is only valuable if it combines first-rate scholarship
with the sort of intimate appreciation which is hard to reconcile
with objectivity. Yet here too it is not fair to dismiss such work
as if it merely tabulated the tradition or speculated upon its
improvement. Where there is sincerity—and the subject draws
out the best in us—the result has been akin to that achieved by the
sculptors of Greece when they set themselves to model the perfect
athlete. Each aspirant gives of his best; each reveals his own
predilections; but each gives us a work of art which illuminates
and interprets its theme.

The immense variety of such studies of Jesus illustrates most
strikingly the many-sidedness of His appeal. A quarter of a century
ago when T. R. Glover's world-famous book *The Jesus of History*
had been followed by a spate of similar volumes, it was easy to
collect a number of books written recently and in English[1] in
which Jesus was depicted as a pacifist[2] or a 'die-hard',[3] a dreamer,[4]
a rotarian,[5] a social reformer,[6] a mystic[7] or an apocalyptist;[8] since
then a number of others could be added, most of them characteristic of the reaction against liberalism and emphasizing the
healer, the miracle-worker, the Virgin-born[9] and the traditionally

---

[1] This list was printed in my book *The Creator Spirit*, pp. 234–6, where comments upon
some of them may be found. A somewhat similar list and commentary is in A. M. Hunter,
Interpreting the New Testament, 1900–1950 (London, 1951), pp. 49–60.

[2] C. J. Cadoux, *The Early Church and the World*.

[3] A. W. Gough, *The Fight for Man*.

[4] Foakes Jackson and Kirsopp Lake, *The Beginnings of Christianity*, I, pp. 267–99.

[5] Bruce Barton, *The Man Nobody Knows*.

[6] L. Dougall and C. W. Emmet, *The Lord of Thought*.

[7] J. Middleton Murry, *Jesus, Man of Genius*.

[8] S. A. Mellor, *Jesus of Nazareth*.

[9] D. A. Edwards, *Jesus, The Gospel Portrait*.

71

divine,[1] but one or two representing Jesus as a communist[2] and His Church as a world-revolutionary movement. Not the least valuable have been those written by Jewish scholars, among them the important study *Jesus of Nazareth* by J. Klausner.

It is worth remembering in this connexion that Western orthodoxy has, since the fifth century until lately, insisted that Jesus though man was not a man—that His manhood was representative not individual. This doctrine is closely akin to that which asserts that His manhood was impersonal, and, indeed, is often only a less negative statement of its conviction that He was in the centre of His being not human but divine. If this is indeed its meaning, then it implies a Christology indistinguishable from the Apollinarian heresy. Christ is the divine Son of God who takes to Himself the totality of human attributes and in them, as in an actor's role, plays out the drama of His sojourn on the earth. Apart from the difficulty of conceiving of human nature as separate from human personality (a distinction irreconcilable with the view which regards personality as the essential element in human nature), such a doctrine reduces the incarnation to a theophany and Christ to the status of a divine intruder. But while impersonal humanity seems meaningless and heretical,[3] it may yet be urged that Christ's manhood in its universality and completeness though fully personal was not in our sense of the word individual; and this would be in keeping with the view that individuality, the characteristic of the solitary self in each one of us, that which makes Peter and John separate entities, is transcended as each approximates to fulness of personal life and finds himself more and more completely at one with his fellows. If Christ as man is thus the consummation of our humanity, representative and therefore perfect, the Pauline teaching as to His body and as to our life in Him becomes plain. In us the broken arcs; in the Christ the perfect round. Before we can accept such an idea we

---

[1] For example E. C. Hoskyns and N. Davey, *The Riddle of the New Testament*.

[2] Conrad Noel, *The Life of Jesus*; the communist background had been suggested by A. Kalthoff, *Die Entstehung des Christentums* (Leipzig, 1904).

[3] Thus, for example, Dr D. M. Baillie, *God was in Christ*, pp. 11–20, describes 'the end of Docetism' as the first factor in the distinctive situation today.

must ask how it can be reconciled with the evidence of the New Testament writings and especially with the element of paradox and even contradiction which we have already noted.

It might be argued—indeed, at one time the argument was very familiar—that what we have in the several books is a series of interpretations reflecting the temper and outlook of their several authors but in their main lines increasingly supernatural. Even if recently and by a number of important books[1] the disparity of the writings in this respect has been denied, there is sufficient evidence to support it; and the matter is important. Familiar examples will suffice. If we compare the first three Gospels and the modification of St Mark by the two later evangelists, it is obvious that St Matthew gives the evidence an ecclesiastical and controversial colour, whereas St Luke is by comparison universalist and humanitarian: in the First Gospel the eschatological element is emphasized by a cruder type of apocalyptic language and the teaching by much violent denunciation of the Pharisees; in the Third not only is the Marcan material given a more cosmopolitan colouring but the Lucan sections, the great parables and the passion narrative, emphasize the compassion of Jesus and show a special concern for women and for the poor. In the period of intensive study of the parallel texts there was no doubt a tendency to exaggerate such differences; but the reaction which has done good service by its stress upon oral tradition and the importance of the catechetical and evangelistic motive[2] has too often tended to neglect previous conclusions; and by its depreciation of the human element and reversion to a fundamentalist outlook has obscured the historical value of the evidence.

It can hardly be questioned that there is a real difference of Christological language and idea between such different strata as the speeches of St Peter in the early chapters of Acts, the Epistle of St James, the Epistles of St Paul (and these though in the main similar show from first to last considerable development in thought

---

[1] Prominent is Hoskyns and Davey, *op. cit.*, where it is argued that the whole literature testifies to a similar Christology 'Son of Man and Son of God'.

[2] For a brief comment upon Form-criticism see Note VI, below, p. 210.

and expression), the Epistle to the Hebrews, and the Johannine writings. Similar differences can plainly be traced even in the Gospels. We can see it in the matter of miracles where St Mark ascribes to Jesus the use of contemporary methods with gradual effects, whereas the later evangelists eliminate such signs of humanity and concentrate upon the 'word of power';[1] and of prophecy where the exact fulfilment of scripture, even to misinterpretation of the text and evidence, is progressively emphasized, as, for example, in such familiar instances as the sign of Jonah[2] and the triumphal entry into Jerusalem.[3] It may well be argued that changes of the same kind are responsible for the disappearance in St Matthew and St Luke of the clear indications of development and of a sequence of events in the Marcan record.[4]

But this evidence of diversity of standpoint and interpretation and of a tendency to heighten the supernatural, to idealize the disciples and to substitute hagiology for history does not give sanction to the freely expressed suggestions that the New Testament, like the stories of Mithra or Apollonius of Tyana, deals with myth;[5] or that it testifies to the deification of a peasant-prophet; or that the records belong to a time so uncritical and so unlike our own as to be for us of little value or relevance.[6] Each of these three points deserves attention, though any adequate answer would involve the citation of a mass of detail and a lengthy examination of it. The dating and authorship of the particular books—now so

---

[1] Cf. the use of saliva and the hand in the miracles in Mark vii. 31–7 and viii. 22–6 and a formula of exorcism in i. 25 and iv. 39, and the treatment of this subject in Hoskyns and Davey, *op. cit.* pp. 163–77.

[2] Luke xi. 38 elaborated into Matt. xii. 39, 40.

[3] Matt. xxi. 2–7 (the ass and the colt).

[4] B. S. Easton, R. H. Lightfoot and the scholars who accept the 'Form-criticism' in its entirety are prevented by their theory from recognizing the evidence for a sequence of events in St Mark's record dictated not by his ingenuity (since in many cases he is plainly unconscious of it) but by history. This evidence collected by many earlier scholars is best summarized by F. C. Burkitt, *The Gospel History and its Transmission*, pp. 65–105; its validity is accepted and defended by Dr T. W. Manson, *The Beginning of the Gospel* (Oxford, 1950).

[5] For a sufficient refutation of the Christ-myth theories, cf. C. Guignebert, *Jesus* (Eng. trans.), pp. 63–75.

[6] For the general question of the relation of Christianity to history cf. the lecture by A. E. Taylor, *The Faith of a Moralist*, II, pp. 109–49.

often dismissed as insoluble and unimportant—cannot but be matters of high significance for the historian; the present insistence, that as we believe them to be inspired any human details of time and place, of language and character are subsidiary if not trivial, seems inconsistent both with the literature itself and with an incarnational philosophy. But even without entering upon such problems [1] certain comments can be made.

In the development of Christianity during the first four centuries the mystery religions and especially Mithraism were its most serious rivals. That a certain amount of assimilation took place, and that this was not always in one direction, can hardly be disputed. Just as the development of the Church owed much to Greek philosophy and to Roman law, so in its ritual it was influenced by the ceremonies and discipline of the Mysteries. But the parallelism reveals beyond doubt the radical differences of origin. There is neither in Mithraism nor in any other of the cults anything like the New Testament or any grounding in history, or any such theological debates as its Jewish ancestry and factual origin made inevitable for the Church. Alike in the earliest Kerygma of the Gospel and in all its doctrine the manhood of Jesus constitutes the basis both of the message and of the problem. [2] We know from the Apocryphal Gospels and Acts what Christian literature would have been like if it had been mythical in origin, and not the record of one who lived a human life at a particular time and place.

That this historical origin does not consist in the transformation of the prophet of Nazareth into the Son of God is perhaps less easy to demonstrate. We have seen that in the New Testament there is evidence of a heightening of the supposedly divine element in the

[1] It is perhaps not improper to say that though I should alter details and revise the whole of my treatment of these questions in my Alexander Robertson lectures of 1931, *Jesus and the Gospel of Love*, pp. 129–228, this still represents my opinions on these matters. The alternatives in nearly every case seem to me to be open to insuperable objections. For a summary of recent scholarship, with which I am in general agreement, see A. M. Hunter, *Interpreting the New Testament, 1900–1950*; it is a pity that his last chapter is so complacent over the present and so unfair to the past.

[2] The centrality of Jesus is well brought out by Dr John Baillie, *The Place of Jesus Christ in Modern Christianity*, and Dr Donald Baillie, *God Was in Christ*.

account of Jesus; it is on the face of it easy to argue that this proces
has been solely responsible for turning the preacher in the synagogue of Capernaum of whom they said 'This man speaks with
authority' into the expected Messiah, and so into an incarnation o
the deity, and so into God the Word. We have already pointec
out one fatal objection—the engrained and fundamental monotheism, at this time almost deistic in its isolation of God from the
world, which characterized contemporary Judaism. Nothing bu
overwhelming conviction could have constrained orthodox Jew
to violate the First Commandment and commit the mortal sin o
blasphemy. But general considerations, however strong, are no
enough. The New Testament itself is proof that such a theory i
untenable.[1] During the past century and a half it has been sifted anc
twisted by the most acute critics in order to make it yield evidence
of a deification. Such evidence, if in places it indicates a tendency
to mythical accretions, does not lessen the unique quality of the
historic figure. On the contrary, what we have is the picture o
one whom His contemporaries at first took to be a Nazarene anc
therefore of no account, whom they discovered to be of unique
stature and divine quality, and for whom finally they ransackec
the vocabulary of religion in order to find an adequate description
Prophet, Messiah, Son of Man, Son of God—in none of them, no
indeed in any of the descriptions in which they are found, is there
any suggestion of the sort of process which deification involves
Indeed, even the contrasts of the portrait—those seeming paradoxe
of gentleness and austerity—when we see them in their proper
setting have an obvious congruity. In Christ, as in the Universe
there is this simultaneity of the adorable and the overwhelming
the mystery which fascinates and terrifies, the reality which we
cannot categorize or comprehend but which satisfies even though
it transcends.

The remaining point for our consideration is at once more vague
but perhaps more influential, especially among the scientifically
trained. It arises out of the recognition of the profound differences
in outlook—in knowledge of the character and scale of the

[1] For a clear examination of this cf. J. S. Stewart, *A Man in Christ* especially pp. 273–98

universe, of the normal laws of cause and effect, and of the nature and experience of mankind—which separate modern man from his forbears. Great as were the achievements of Hebrew and Greek genius, their cosmology and demonology,[1] physiology and psychology were so totally unlike ours as to render their descriptions not only of the supernatural but even of the natural and historical deeply suspect. Any field-naturalist who listens to the descriptions of bird and insect behaviour from his untrained friends will know how easy it is to see what you expect to see even if the occurrence is demonstrably impossible. Can we honestly accept as factual the record of events which presuppose and if accepted would demonstrate the reality of magic and diabolism? And if not, how can records written by those who accepted such occurrences as a familiar part of their general outlook be treated as historically valuable?

Anyone who studies books like T. R. Glover, *The Conflict of Religions in the Roman Empire*, or W. L. Knox, *St Paul and the Church of the Gentiles*, or the writings of Dr A. D. Nock will see how vast is the gulf that separates the *Weltanschauung* of the Graeco-Roman or even the Jewish intelligentsia of the first century from our own. He will discover that the familiar language of the Authorized Version, which he can usually assimilate and accept, covers a strange world of astrology and demons, amulets and exorcisms, the speculations of the Gnostics and the spells of the *Mathematici*; and that doctrines originating in the Epistles to the Colossians and Ephesians refer primarily to a realm of 'principalities and powers' with which he is wholly unfamiliar. Events, especially those of supernatural or religious significance, if described by anyone whose background is of this sort, must inevitably be interpreted and indeed apprehended in terms of esotericism and thaumaturgy. Those who believe that demons can enter into swine or that food can be miraculously multiplied will be liable to affirm that they have seen such marvels and will

---

[1] For this cf. E. Langton, *Essentials of Demonology*. He concludes that Jesus accepted the contemporary outlook, but adds 'Such an acceptance does not prove that these popular beliefs correspond with reality', p. 224.

sincerely believe the truth of their affirmation. But it is notable that in several of the most difficult of the New Testament miracles there are details in the narrative which suggest that, though the authors manifestly believed the story as they told it, a modern observer might perhaps have described it in somewhat different terms.[1]

It is obvious that in records dealing with unique events and the person of Jesus it is presumptuous to suppose that miracles could not happen: indeed, there are today few who would seriously doubt His works of healing and His power to meet human need. But for those who believe that the evidence for an orderly world, the cosmos of modern science rather than the chaos of magic and demonology, is one of the best gifts of God, it is surely proper to insist that each case must be examined and that in some the difficulty of literal acceptance is much greater than in others. But our point at the moment is not whether particular details are accurately described, but that, even if in these respects the authors being men of their time were mistaken, this does not impugn their evidence in general or imply that in other matters they are unreliable.[2]

Two other and somewhat similar points must be added. It is clear to anyone who compares the treatment of 'speaking with tongues'[3] in the second chapter of the Acts and the first letter to the Corinthians that there is not only a difficulty in distinguishing between the psychic and the spiritual but that in this case at least widely different estimates of the religious value of the phenomenon are manifest. Modern psychology and psychotherapy have made it impossible for us to accept emotional excitement or even the healing of disease as in themselves evidence of high moral and religious attainment. The cures at Nancy by Coué or at the grotto

---

[1] For example, in the raising of Jairus's daughter Mark v. 39, where the word for sleep is καθεύδειν not as in John xi. 11 κοιμᾶσθαι; in the feeding of the five thousand, Mark vi. 40, John vi. 10, and the eucharistic language 11, 12; in the walking on the water, John vi. 21, and the repeated use of ἐπί.

[2] For further detail see Note VII below, p. 212.

[3] The fullest study is still H. Weinel, *Die Wirkungen des Geistes und der Geister*, pp. 71–101; and cf. J. B. Pratt, *The Religious Consciousness*, pp. 183–7.

at Lourdes, like those by a Zulu witch-doctor or a Christian exorcist, are sufficiently authenticated and sufficiently similar in spite of the contrasts in technique to make us hesitate about accepting the event as proof of miracle or of the sanctity of the healer.[1]

More important still is the change in the attitude towards miracles if and when they occur. It was and still too often is an important element in traditional apologetics to insist that God who made the laws of nature proved His presence by breaking them and that miraculous events being breaches of the laws demonstrated the divine power of the miracle-worker.[2] In ages when the activity of God was associated only with the abnormal, and for folks who cannot realize that the whole realm of our experience, indeed all that is, exists by reason of God's sustaining energy and reveals Him to those who have eyes to see, such an argument was simple and effective. It is, surely, impossible for most of us; for as commonly presented it comes near to reducing the deity to the level of a chess-player who when threatened with defeat is entitled to alter the rules of the game. Such a concept is unworthy of the teaching and example of Christ, of this world as we have come to know it, and of a universe measurable in light-years.

These three points about miracle are of high importance, although even today they are largely ignored by students both of the Old and of the New Testaments. Yet this does not of course mean that miracles do not happen or that when unique personalities and conditions are in question events wholly beyond normal experience will not occur. Christ, as we believe, reveals the truth about nature and the universe in a way that no other has done; yet it is at least arguable that He does so not by thaumaturgy or psychic influence so much as by the way in which He discloses the beauty and meaning of common things, the eternal significance of common people, the mind and method of God in dealing with the world's sin and the world's woe. God, as the Fourth

[1] Jesus Himself regarded it as primarily due to the faith of the recipient or of his friends.
[2] The 'unfortunate consequences of so doing' and the subject as a whole are wisely treated by H. H. Farmer, *The World and God*, pp. 107-27 and 145-79.

Evangelist would teach us, is best described as light and life and love; then it surely follows that it is Christ's unique illumination of our darkness, His power to awaken and quicken our sensitiveness, the wonder and wisdom of His love that proclaim Him to be the 'image of the invisible'. All else, the works of power, the fulfilment of prophecies, the Virgin-birth, the physical resurrection, are no doubt appropriate but surely secondary; and if the evidence for them does not convince us, we need not therefore feel that we are outcast from Christendom. It is, to many of us, a cause for thankfulness that today men find the miraculous rather in the unique quality and abiding presence of Jesus Christ than in the mode of His conception or the emptiness of His tomb; and that we associate miracles rather with the love of God than with His power, rather with His encounter with us and response to our need than with such events as we cannot otherwise explain. Whatever may have been the case in the past, it is not the case today that the supernatural is equivalent to the thaumaturgic or that the evidence which a Christian would use to commend his Master would be such as a scientist would be bound to reject.

The fact is that after a century of the most intense and critical analysis and when every allowance is made for discrepancies in the records, for errors of observation and interpretation, and for the influence of theological and traditional presuppositions, the impression of Christ that results from them is one not only of universality but of uniqueness, not only of His many-sidedness but of His consistency, not only of His human perfection but of His deity. We start where every student must start with the assumption that He is one of ourselves, the Son of Man. Only so can we hope to understand Him or to learn of Him. We test Him as best we can by the standards of value that we recognize, in the categories of character and achievement. We scrutinize the evidence, ancient and modern, as to His impact and influence. And having studied, we experience that which happens to men when they confront perfection, we 'consider and bow the head'.

And if, as will certainly be the case, we are asked 'Why all this effort? The Church has always known that Jesus is the Son of God.

What need, what right have you to verify its conviction? You must begin with an act *not* of enquiry but of faith', we shall reply that, only as we discover and approve for ourselves the grounds and validity of the confession, can we avoid the twin mistakes of reading into Him our own preconceived ideas of the Godhead, and of isolating Him from our species and ignoring or denying the inclusive and representative character of His holiness. Only if we have made an honest and strenuous effort to answer His question, 'What think ye of the Christ?' shall we escape the condemnation on those who say 'Lord, Lord' without changing either their outlook or their actions.[1] Recent theology is full of instances of those who magnify the 'cosmic Christ' but ignore or even disavow the sayings of the historic Jesus.[2]

Nevertheless, though we seem to have reached the same conclusion as traditional orthodoxy we have to consider how far the language of its definition has meaning for today. We still have to formulate a Christology.

[1] Cf. Luke vi. 46.
[2] For a powerful demonstration of the weakness of neo-orthodoxy in this respect cf. Dean W. L. Sperry, *Jesus Then and Now*, particularly pp. 190–211.

V

THE DOCTRINE OF THE PERSON OF CHRIST

I T is a commonplace that the confession of Christ as Lord and God inevitably produced a dilemma which it took the Church three hundred years to resolve. For the Jew the First Commandment and for the Gentile the movement of all educated men towards a vague monotheism involved them both alike in the search for a description which should do full justice to the unique and divine quality of the Saviour and yet should not infringe the unity of God or move back towards polytheism. It is equally commonplace that almost at once Christian thinkers solved their problem by fastening upon the term Logos. This was familiar to the Jew as translating Memra, the Word of the Lord by which creation took place[1] and the prophets were inspired,[2] and as already the subject of much learned apologetic by Philo the scholar and spokesman of liberal Judaism. It was equally familiar to the Gentile in the popular philosophy, part Platonic, part Stoic, in which it was used to denote mind and reason—the mind which was the controlling element in the universe and in the individual, the reason which separated man from the unreasoning brute, linked him with the supreme reality by the quality and exercise of his intelligence, and was thus both the symbol and the instrument of his status; and in the prologue of the Fourth Gospel it was already used of the divinity of Jesus Christ. As we see most plainly in Justin Martyr's three writings, the combination of the two meanings, the transcendent Word and the indwelling Reason, not only won acceptance from both parties but produced a simple, coherent and sufficient Christology. By it Christ could be defined

[1] Ps. xxxiii, etc.   [2] Ezek. iii. 16, etc.

both as God's final and perfect expression of Himself to His people and as the embodiment of the rational principle which gave the world its meaning and direction, and was the particular prerogative, the divine element, in humanity, and when perfect the true self, the archetype and consummation of all mankind. When Justin's work was taken up by Clement of Alexandria, he purged the term Logos of its intellectualism by his stress upon love as always the motive of the whole creative process, by his robust concern for moral righteousness in practical life, and by his common sense, his cheerfulness and his wide range of learning. It only needed the theological genius of his successor Origen to provide Christians with a full library of scholarship and a complete system of doctrine—though Origen replaced the term Logos by the more scriptural term, the Son, and did not in fact work out the proper distribution of the prerogatives attaching to it.

By this Logos-Christology, Christ was presented as not only unique but representative: He was akin to us organically because Himself the perfection of that which each of us possesses as our birthright; He consummated for us the whole story of creation and history in which He is the supreme agent. Both Clement and Origen set the Christian revelation against a universal background and as the culminating event in an age-old evolutionary and educational process; and this in itself makes their theology far more appropriate to modern man[1] than that which took its place two centuries later. When we add, as we surely may, that they were not only the most learned and brilliant of all early Christian scholars[2] but were also men of the widest sympathy and interests, free from the organizing efficiency and intellectual mediocrity of the Roman Churches and from the pessimism that accompanied the Gothic invasions and twisted the genius of Augustine, their

[1] The criticism of the Logos-theology as a secularizing and intellectualizing of the Gospel by Greek thought advanced by A. von Harnack in his *History of Dogma* is rightly rejected by Dr P. Tillich, *Systematic Theology*, I, pp. 157–9; Tillich's sympathetic understanding of the Greek Logos-theology is in striking contrast with the hostility to it in Dr Reinhold Niebuhr, *The Nature and Destiny of Man*, II, pp. 129–33.

[2] It is disappointing that C. N. Cochrane, *Christianity and Classical Culture*, ignores Clement altogether and only mentions Origen three or four times and then to disparage him, cf., for instance, p. 234.

relevance to our own age with its cosmopolitanism and its despair is both positively and negatively invaluable. They understood, as no subsequent Christians until very recently could do, those esoteric elements in theology which the East has always emphasized—elements which the West expelled but never absorbed or answered when it dealt with Gnosticism by the argument of the *De Praescriptionibus* and which after constant returns during the centuries now again confront us in India. They realized, as few of their predecessors and no one after them until modern times have done, the immensity of space and time, and could see the Gospel not as a mere *Interims-ethik* but as disclosing the age-old purpose of a God for whom a thousand years were but as one day and who was neither to be defeated by Satan nor to be rushed by His creatures into impatient or spasmodic action. Indeed, Origen's great passages like that in which he expounds the struggle for existence, the relationship of man to the animals and the origin and progress of man's arts and knowledge[1] or that in the same book in which he answers the old objection, 'why if Christ is Saviour was His coming so delayed?' by insisting that we must first consider the distribution of the races of mankind, the religious pre-eminence of the Chosen People and the differing status and treatment of individuals,[2] have so modern a tone that it is difficult to realize that they were written sixteen hundred years before Darwin. It is not surprising that when Christians have taken science seriously they have returned to the Christian Platonists of the third century.

So large and coherent a view of the relationship of God to the universe did not long outlast the martyrdom of Origen and the period of mediocrity and decline that followed.[3] It is customary to criticize the Alexandrians on three grounds, first that they used allegory in interpreting Scripture and in consequence took a low view of the importance of history; secondly, that their doctrine was in fact Binitarian, and did not clearly distinguish between the Second and Third Persons of the Godhead; and thirdly, that their

[1] *Contra Celsum* IV, 75–90.   [2] *Ibid.* 7, 8.
[3] For which cf. Eusebius, *Hist. Eccles.* VIII, 1.

theology gave too much heed to education and evolution and not enough to redemption and revolution. The first of these is true; and in defence we can only reply that like other Christians they could neither live with the Old Testament nor live without it, that literary and historical criticism was not yet understood, and that in these days of typology we are ourselves falling into the same method of interpretation. The second is only valid if theology is a matter not of exegesis but of formulae; the Logos plainly included the functions of the Son and of the Holy Spirit, but the result of its use was to give real meaning to the immanence of the divine and to emphasize its connexion with other aspects of deity; when the orthodox Trinitarian formula replaced the Logos-theology a careful discrimination of the contents of the idea of Logos should have been made so as to secure that the concept of the Holy Spirit covered all that was previously believed; but nothing of the kind was done, and the doctrine of the Spirit has been impoverished ever since. The third criticism is only true if the elements of education and redemption are set in contrast and the experience of the twice-born regarded as the only road to salvation; but even so the glib charge that the Alexandrians have a defective sense of sin is hard to maintain against Clement, who devotes most of his space to warnings against occasions of falling, and Origen, who is also, and by others, accused of a streak of morbid asceticism.

Although the background of his theology was the Logos-doctrine, Origen had himself stated his position in the Trinitarian language of the New Testament. But he was not greatly interested in formularies; his doctrine of the Holy Spirit is notoriously hesitant; from his own utterances in different connexions he can be claimed as the forerunner both of the Arian and Nicene Christologies. After him the triune formula of the 'Grace',[1] already used in baptismal creeds, became almost universal, and the term Logos—and the ideas associated with it—disappear.[2]

[1] II Cor. xiii. 14, chronologically the earliest Trinitarian statement.
[2] Logos was used in the Creed proposed by Eusebius at Nicea (A.D. 325); it was removed in revision. It occurs for Holy Spirit in the epiclesis of the liturgy of Serapion of Thmuis (c. A.D. 350). John i. 1, 3 is quoted in the Second Creed of the Dedication (the Lucianic; A.D. 341).

But in spite of the Macedonianist Controversy and several large books upon the Holy Spirit, the problem of His divinity and of His personal distinctness was settled by analogy from the similar problem of the Son, and the content of the doctrine hardly went beyond the epithets and three short clauses that made their way during the fourth century into the Nicene Creed.[1] Very soon the fact of divine immanence was limited to the baptized and to members of the Catholic Church upon whom its clergy could bestow the gift of the Spirit.

The Trinitarian language though both more scriptural, more personal and therefore in the long run more profound, had one serious danger. Whereas God and His Word or Reason could not be regarded as essentially separate, the term Son suggested not only a distinct person but one derived and subordinate. Difficulties arose in both directions, the former tendency led to Tritheism, the latter to Arianism. The Western mind, with its passion for legal order and for precise definition, insisted upon a uniform and official formula which all Churchmen should accept; the Eastern, more deeply concerned with meaning than with formulation, but passionately argumentative and incurably given to factions, plunged into debate. Historians have divided and classified the several parties and groups, and given us a picture of friction increasingly embittered by political and personal ambition until at last the dispute involved the holders of the ancient sees of the Eastern Church, and the conflicts became almost suicidal. In the first phase it was the doctrine of the Trinity, the necessity to vindicate the essential unity of the Godhead as against tritheism, and the equality of the persons or modes of the Godhead as against a graded 'ladder' of deity. In the second it was Christology, the problem of the nature of Christ, the answer to His own question, 'Whose Son is He?'; and the parties to it reproduced the double significance of the Logos; for the Syrian Church and the great School of Antioch accepted the divine Word as an inspiration operating from without, and therefore posited a perfect union of this Word with the man Jesus, the two natures being welded together by

---

[1] In 325 the Council's Creed only contained 'We believe in the Holy Spirit'.

mutual love and by the goodwill of God given and received; and the Greeks, thinking of the indwelling wisdom, held to the archetypal relationship of the divine Reason to the human and therefore could not accept two separate natures, and either like Apollinarius denied a human spirit to Christ or like Cyril and the Monophysites treated the human as swallowed up by the divine. Their objection to a perfect manhood in Christ was later reinforced by their acceptance of the Augustinian doctrine of the universal corruption of human beings, and also by their lack of psychological and abstract language and the consequent habit of treating spiritual realities as if they were physical and chemical entities.[1]

Behind these controversies and rendering any solution of the Christological issue unattainable were the changes in the whole attitude towards nature discussed in the earlier series of these lectures, enhanced as they were by the calamities of the age. We have seen in the past twenty years how catastrophe produces a religion of despair, a stress upon the remoteness of God, separated as He is by a vast gulf from contact with the world and unapproachable by any human effort of mind or will, and consequently upon the helplessness and corruption of man whose state is that of the victims of Noah's flood, inescapable doom, unless they be taken up into the particular ark in which the prophet of disaster is afloat. The historian recognizes it as a repetition of the despair which blighted the first great phase of Christian history and has reappeared at times of crisis ever since. God and man are set in contrast; God ceasing to be the Father and becoming the Impassible and Unchanging, the Sultan and Judge; man ceasing to be His child or even, in any real sense, His creature, and becoming a thing of naught, a child of Satan, suffering deservedly in the present and damned to torment throughout eternity in the future. In face of such a paradox there can be no significance in the phrase 'God and man one Christ'; for we dare not, if this indeed be our state, insist that in fact and in our own experience the paradox cannot be ultimate, since even in ourselves forgiveness resolves it and proves that divine love and human sin are not mutually exclusive.

[1] Cf. Gregory Nazianzen, *Ad Cledonium* (Ep. CI).

The interpreters of Jesus, confronted with this antithesis, found themselves already committed to lay stress on the aspects of His work and character which proved Him to be in the conventional sense divine. Even in the Gospels this tendency was already present; signs of human weakness in Him and in His disciples are recorded in St Mark and eliminated in the later Synoptists; if He is hailed as the friend of publicans and sinners, whose mission is to the lost sheep of Israel, yet more and more He becomes the worker of miracles, the fulfiller of prophecies, the herald of judgment, with legions of angels to do His bidding and all power in heaven and earth at His disposal. The Son of Man tends to disappear; the Son of God begins to be arrayed in those splendours which contemporary piety thought proper to the divine; and by the end of the second century apologetic, in Western Christendom, at least, has fastened upon the *Testimonia* or Old Testament evidences to Him in the past,[1] and the miracles wrought by Him and by the Church[2] as the characteristic features of His ministry and the sufficient demonstration of His Godhead. By the fourth century Athanasius and his friends in their struggle against Arian error have eliminated almost every trace of human semblance from their picture of Him.[3] It is not surprising that the Eastern Church was so largely monophysite.

At Chalcedon the final formula did indeed preserve the two natures of Christ in their entirety and by the four adverbs, ' unconfusedly, changelessly, indistinguishably, inseparably,'[4] safeguarded their union in Him and so left the way open for subsequent research; but its result is plainly not a solution but a statement of the limits within which Christian convictions believe a solution to lie. When the Church after periods of further controversy proceeded to reaffirm it by deciding that there were two wills as well as two natures in Christ, it became hard to believe that the

---

[1] Cf. Pseudo-Cyprian, *Testimonia adv. Judaeos*; Justin, *Dial. c. Tryph.* etc.

[2] Cf. Irenaeus, *Adv. Haer.* II, 31, 2 and 32, 4 that miracles are the prerogative of the orthodox.

[3] Cf. for example, Athanasius, *De Inc.* XVIII, 1, 2; *Or. c. Arian.* III, 30, 31; 37 (denying Christ's ignorance); 40 (His weakness); 56 (His fear).

[4] Cf. A. Hahn, *Symbole*, p. 166.

unity of His person had not been in effect denied. By dividing the natures thus widely His removal from our species was almost as effectively accomplished as it was by the monophysites and their successors. In each case Christ is presented to us not only as uniquely divine but as divine in an exclusive, not as hitherto a representative, sense. In East and West alike and among Christians of all sorts, the manhood of Jesus was forgotten, and for those in need of His compassion or His example His mother and the Saints filled His place.[1]

The importance of this for future development and indeed down to our own time need not be stressed in detail. It is sufficient to recollect that, as recently as 1933 when controversy arose about the fact that a Unitarian, Dr L. P. Jacks, had preached in Liverpool Cathedral, the Bishop of Durham in order to condemn it appealed to the clause 'who for us men and for our salvation came down from heaven' as the criterion of orthodoxy. That any modern man, let alone one so clever and at one time so liberal as Henson, should have chosen a phrase so archaic in its cosmology and so open to criticism in its theology, is evidence of the extent to which the Nicene and Chalcedonian Christology proves itself inadequate and misleading. It is to lay stress upon a metaphysical and one-sided statement of His origin and 'nature' rather than upon His relationship with us, His quality, His influence and meaning. It is to accept the definition of deity as an essence, a quasi-physical 'stuff', and of God as a society of persons acting under conditions of space and time. Such language appropriate to the imagery and ideas of the fourth century can perhaps still be translated into the thought and speech of modern man and may then be found to be arguably correct; but our whole concept of deity, of heaven and of salvation has been so transformed as to make the credal formula unreal and to many of us a serious stumbling-block. To a scientifically trained generation it is difficult to justify the use of definitions of which it is constantly necessary to explain away the plain meaning. Anthropomorphism may be in the last resort inescapable;

[1] For the significance of The Assumption of the Virgin in this respect cf. H. Chadwick in *Journal of Theol. Studies* (N.S.), II, pp. 162–4.

and as we have seen the so-called 'higher anthropomorphism' is intelligible and valid; but a faith which at once defines God as 'without body, parts or passions' and then says that God's Son 'for us men came down from heaven' is unnecessarily bewildering.[1] If we are defending the divinity of Christ, we shall not today do so on quite these lines. We shall be concerned rather with experience than with abstractions; first, with what He has done and does and only then with what He is. We shall in fact be concerned rather with Atonement than with Incarnation; for it is only as we perceive the scale and significance of His atoning work that we shall be in a position to appreciate His divine nature.

In His own time, as we have seen, the influence of Jesus upon His disciples was such as to constrain them, being orthodox Jews, to proclaim Him Lord and God. Such influence has in fact been continuous ever since. We have seen how men and women of all types have found in Him the satisfaction of their ideals and described Him in the language of their own most intimate experience and aspiration. But it is not only in the range but in the intensity of His appeal that we shall best discover His secret. Still today as in the first century He can transform the stuff and substance of our characters by the alchemy which only love given and received can accomplish. Still today there are those who find themselves honestly compelled to say of Him that He is to them more certainly real and more vividly present than any object of sense-perception, and whose whole lives testify that like the Christians of the first century they have been with Him,[2] and that He lives in them.[3] These are people sensitive and unselfconscious, free alike from self-pity and from self-esteem, from fears and from ambitions, for whom to see is to act, full of humility and of humour, of sympathy and of joy; people who having themselves suffered cannot lightly inflict suffering, and having descended into hell have learnt that God is there also.[4] There is in them a serenity and detachment which contrary to popular expectation stimulate

[1] In his valuable chapter on symbolism in *Miracles*, pp. 83–97, Mr C. S. Lewis interprets these words as 'entered the universe', which is surely still more misleading.

[2] Cf. Acts iv. 13. [3] Cf. Gal. ii. 20.

[4] See prayer-book version of Ps. cxxxix. 8.

practical wisdom and enable a sense of perspective and proportion. They live here and now 'in the heavenlies', in the last things, the realm not of means but of ends,[1] in the Christ in whom God here and now gathers together all things into one.[2]

That this is not rhapsody but 'plain tale' will be recognized best by those who have met and known such rare folk. Rare they certainly are—and perhaps for obvious reasons[3] seldom to be found in high places or official positions. But having seen one such we can recognize the characteristic quality in a great multitude of others—so much so, indeed, as to change our whole estimate of humanity, not only as it might be, but as it is. For they are those who, being in Christ, have received His power both to illuminate and to redeem. We not only see from them what we ought to be and to do, but seeing we receive, if we can accept it, in some small measure at least, 'grace and power faithfully to fulfil the same'. They disclose to us the image of God in the common man—in those 'people of the land' whose fate so perplexes the sages and preachers,[4] who yet heard Jesus gladly,[5] and whose response to Him throughout the ages is perhaps the most interesting evidence of His divinity.

For, indeed, here we are struck by a fact which has received little attention and which deserves careful study. In the doctrine of the Incarnation the Church fought its way through to the great doctrinal and metaphysical structure of the so-called Athanasian Creed by process of argument and controversy. The arguments were not always sound, the controversy was violent and in its later phases wholly unscrupulous. The result was an undeservedly satisfactory paradox which, becoming sacrosanct, put an end to discussion. But in the doctrine of the Atonement there was no such struggle; no single authoritative formula was accepted, and each epoch produced a generally approved explanation. As we examine these successive theories we find not only that each one

[1] This is the significance of eschatology, see below Ch. x.
[2] Cf. Eph. i. 10.
[3] Best expressed in the Lucan version of the Beatitudes, Luke vi. 20–6.
[4] Cf. Ecclesiasticus, or Reinhold Niebuhr, *Moral Man and Immoral Society*.
[5] Mark xii. 37.

is representative of the Christian life of its period but that each is in fact expressed in terms of that period's deepest corporate need. It is as if men, striving to proclaim what the Lord had done for them, found nothing else adequate except the fulfilment of their own most intimate and profound desire; no lesser symbol would do justice to the good gift of Christ. There could hardly be more significant evidence of the fact that from age to age and for men of widely varying environments and social conditions Christ has been disclosed as unique, representative and divine.[1] If this be true, then plainly the apostolic confession 'my Lord and my God' has been validated not by formal acknowledgment but by testimony from the depth of experience. We must examine the claim in some detail.

In the earliest days when the new life in individual and community was in its first rapture the sheer joy and power of it expressed itself simply in a sense of victory. Christ had conquered sin and death and in Him the conquest was shared by His people. The joy which shines out from the records of the martyrs and the *graffiti* of the catacombs is plain evidence of 'the victory that overcometh the world'; it is also the cause of that victory's efficacy. Dr Aulen's claim that the first doctrine of Atonement is centred upon the two words 'Christus Victor' is amply demonstrable.

When men came to theologize the doctrine and to give it fuller interpretation they had recourse to the event which for most of them, being slaves or freedmen, was the most important in their lives, the manumission which accomplished their release. Ransom was a word already familiar from St Mark;[2] it was taken up and developed into the elaborate theories of redemption which posed such problems to the Fathers.[3] Who paid the price? Christ. To whom? Was it to God, or to the devil? The metaphor had its difficulties. But its significance is plain to all who know or can

---

[1] For an analysed list of examples of Christian thinkers illustrating this contention, cf. H. Richard Niebuhr, *Christ and Culture* (New York, 1950).

[2] Mark x. 45; Matt. xx. 28.

[3] For this cf. the catena of passages from Origen in H. Rashdall, *The Idea of Atonement*, pp. 282–7, and the evidence that his successors tended to materialize and literalize thoughts which in him were spiritually, philosophically, and ethically intended (*ibid.* pp. 288–312).

magine the condition of the Roman *ergastula*.[1] Slavery in Israel had been mitigated by the Law. In Greece it had not been in-human. But after Spartacus,[2] Roman society had a phobia on the subject; and the blood-lust fed by the orgies in the arena found an outlet in the slave-quarters of their palaces. Those who knew in their own bodies what it was to be the chattel of a Lucullus and who proclaimed Christ as the Redeemer gave to Him thereby the name that for them was above every name.

The ransom theory dominated theology through the dark ages, often in the crudest forms, until the absurdity of the claim that the devil had just rights against man which God could only annul by the payment to him of the sinless Christ was exposed by Anselm and Abelard. The latter is one of the only theologians to appeal in this matter to the realities of experience, and therefore replace the legal and commercial metaphors of contemporary metaphysics by a simple and realistic exposition of what actually happens when men become 'at one' with God.[3] The former in his famous treatise *Cur Deus Homo* developed an alternative doctrine based upon the analogy not of slavery but of the tenant's obligation to his feudal overlord. Anselm trained as a lawyer at Pavia and coming to his life's work in the England of William Rufus found himself principally concerned with the business of creating a system of stable justice in a land ravaged by civil war and the chaotic feuds and pillaging of predatory barons. His theology reflected the passionate desire of the Church and of average men and women for security from rapine and for a recognized status in an ordered society. The honour of the overlord obliging him to protect and respect his people; the service due from them in return; and the satisfaction that must be offered for the failure to meet honour's demands; these supply the imagery and language for the feudal

---

[1] Private prisons for ironed slaves were not abolished till a law of Hadrian.
[2] In 73–71 B.C. he led the revolt of gladiators and slaves; there had been two previous slave wars 134–131 B.C. and 103–100 B.C.
[3] The story of Abelard (for our present purpose 'another story') is a striking example of the extent to which sophistication blinds men to reality; and the usual comment on him, 'he reduces the Atonement to a manifestation of God's love', proves how persistent is such blindness.

doctrine of Atonement. Man's sin violates God's honour, set man outside protection, and exposes him to vengeance. Christ offers full satisfaction for his fault; man is restored to his overlord.

In these two theories, ransom and satisfaction, Christ's work is regarded as universal and corporate. The next great analogy, that which has for its theme the idea of substitution, treats it as appropriate to the individual. At that time the old order in society and in the Church, the old tradition in knowledge and belief was being challenged by a multitude of pioneers, each one of whom whatever his special interest, felt constrained to break away from the herd and adventure into the wilderness. Whether he were hesitant or aggressive no one could attack the venerated structure of medievalism without a sense both of rebellion and of loneliness. To reject the obligations of feudalism or the fables of the bestiaries or the indulgences of the papal Church involved not only a high courage but to some degree at least a feeling of shame and almost of remorse: the very violence of their diatribes against the whore of Babylon is proof of their subconscious guilt. For such pioneers standing alone with Christ it was natural to say, 'I am a sinner but my sins are laid on Him' and 'He did this for *me*'. The doctrines of imputation and of assurance, the two new articles in the Reformation theology,[1] meet the guilt and the loneliness of the Reformer. 'He did this for me; He is my substitute.' 'I believe it and can therefore go forward no longer guilty and no longer alone.' At its best such an interpretation of atonement teaches that strength is made perfect in weakness, that Christ lives in me and I can do all things in Him.

It is hardly disputable that the independence and fortitude which this doctrine enabled not only made possible a rebirth of Christianity but recovered for Christendom something of the dynamic vitality of the earliest Church. In it the Reformers turned the world upside down; in it Puritanism 'made all things new'. If it fell short of the fulness of the faith by reason of its lack of any adequate experience of the community of the Holy Spirit, it at least cleared away the formal legalisms and encrusted trivialities

[1] So Rashdall, *op. cit.* pp. 404, 409.

94

which for the mass of traditional believers had made Christ of none effect and produced the superstitions and profligacy of papal religion. It restored Christ to His place as Saviour, even if faith, the *sola fides* of Lutheranism, did not always involve either love or goodness.[1] It interpreted His work in language and a setting that sprang not only out of the Epistles but out of the deepest need and aspirations of the time.

Victory, ransom, satisfaction, substitution—if our own age has not yet found a single term to express its particular approach to Christ, we may yet conclude this brief survey of a vast subject by noting that the same correspondence between the characteristic need of the age and the contemporary exposition of the Atonement can still be traced. The quickening of the social conscience, the swing from individualism to collectivism, and the consequent fear that the ordinary person will be crushed by a soulless and mechanical system have all had their effect upon the theology of Atonement. On the negative side there has been widespread recognition of the unworthy and indeed immoral character ascribed to God by each of the three doctrines: ransom, with its suggestion of a fraudulent settlement of the devil's legitimate claims; satisfaction, as if to a feudal baron jealous for his honour; substitution, when the blood-lust of a vengeful deity was appeased by the sacrifice of the innocent. Such ideas might claim sanction in parts of the Old Testament; but the same development which rejected them as no longer decent even in a human sovereign recognized that, like much else in the Scriptures, they belonged to a primitive and sub-Christian era. On the positive side the reaction against individualism led to a stress upon the representative and universal element in Christ's person and work, such as was stressed by appeal to experience in F. D. Maurice's sermons on the doctrine of sacrifice[2] and to orthodox theology in R. C. Moberly's *Atonement and Personality*. In general, the significant note in most of the best work on the subject is that struck first by Abelard—a presentation

[1] It is not sufficiently recognized that both Luther and Calvin explicitly deny that love or good works are necessary to 'saving faith'.
[2] Cf. Note VIII below, p. 213.

of the work of Christ in terms of the primary attribute of God. The declaration that in the climax of His life of love Christ dis closed the essential nature of the Godhead, proved its triumphan efficacy against evil, accomplished as man's representative the perfect response of obedience and sacrifice, and so initiated for u as we live in Him a new world of relationships towards God and one another, came as peculiarly appropriate to a generation fo which the universe seemed mechanical and empty, God a primitiv anthropomorphism and the individual a helpless victim of vast and ruthless evils which men were powerless to escape or to restrain

At the same time the growing sense of solidarity which ex pressed itself in the spread of socialism and the great missionary activity of the century emphasized the limitations of the variou theories of the Atonement and suggested that to isolate the death of Christ from His ministry and indeed from the divine revelation in creation and in the work of the Holy Spirit was a source o misunderstanding. The separation of faith from love and goodnes and the contrast between faith and works were manifestly due or their theological side to the antithesis between God the Father and God the Son inherent in most doctrines of Atonement and to the poverty and neglect of the Church's thought and experience o the Holy Spirit. Atonement had been detached from Incarnation that is, from the loving purpose of God in relation to His world and from the indwelling of His Spirit by whom the efficacy o being at one with God was made fruitful. The answer to those who feared that a doctrine of Atonement in terms of love was a diminu tion of the fulness of Christ's sacrifice was to demonstrate it as the culmination and consummation of the whole creative-redemptive process.[2] The answer to those who argued that any confusion o

[1] It is a striking proof of the extent of our failure to Christianize the idea of God tha writers as orthodox as Moberly speak of a revelation of love as if it were a poorer thing than a vindication of justice or less effective than a metaphysical transaction.

[2] So in effect Dr V. Taylor *Jesus and His Sacrifice* (London, 1937). Though he declare the Abelardian view inadequate, he in fact expands and vindicates it by ruling out from his concept of sacrifice all that is inconsistent with it (e.g. p. 304). His effort to go beyon it is marred by inconsistency: arguing in each case from the silence of Jesus he rejects th belief that His death embodies the love of God (p. 302), and then accepts that it is 'a sacri ficial work for men' (p. 306).

he *sola fides* with change of character or the doing of works was subtle Pelagianism was an insistence that faith had its fulfilment n the life-giving energy of the Spirit who unites the believer with he community and works in him both the will and the power to erve.

The fact that in each age it has been appropriate to describe the vork of Christ in terms of the prevalent human need is perhaps he plainest possible proof of the reality and the universality of His divine status; at least it corroborates very powerfully and lown to our own day the verdict which pronounced Him the mage of the invisible God and the Saviour of the world. Having hus reaffirmed orthodoxy we can proceed to suggest that this is precisely what the doctrine of the person of Christ was intended o maintain whether we take it in the form 'God and man one Christ', or as 'truly Son of man and truly Son of God'. But before accepting the conclusion and drawing the corollaries that St Paul vas so quick to draw, we must ask whether, in view of our present knowledge of the creative process and of human nature (that is, of volution and history), even if Christ has the value which we once learnt to associate with God, we can any longer affirm it s appropriate to deity. We must, in fact, face the question put to us in the statement that modern man is prepared to accept esus but could not identify Him with the power responsible for he universe and for mankind. Must we not accept T. H. Huxley's hesis that the high adventure of humanity and therefore of the Son of Man is to challenge in the name of morality and strive to everse the amoral and immoral movement of the natural order? Or, if such presuppositions are unwarranted and absurd, is not he honest course to respond as best we can to the demands of Christian living but while acknowledging Christ's example as our ideal to reject the metaphysical assertion of His divinity and o maintain a reverent agnosticism as to the ultimate character of he universe?

It is, of course, evident that this particular problem did in a lightly different form underlie the long debate which gave the Church the Nicene Creed and the formulated doctrine of the

Trinity. In the discussion the orthodox insistence on the super
essential nature of the Godhead and the consequent rejection c
patripassianism as a heresy opened the way for the Arian belie
that the Father, being transcendent and indefinable, differed i
essence from the Son who was capable of becoming incarnate an
thereby of experiencing suffering and death. As was proved b
the success and vitality of Arianism, the simple belief in an un
knowable deity represented by a cosmic and subordinate repre
sentative would have been readily accepted by most of the paga
world. Yet the Church, recognizing not only that it was a ste
back into polytheism but that it failed to explain the nature an
influence of Christ, rejected and condemned it; and subsequen
events demonstrated that it was right to do so. The unity of th
Godhead could not be surrendered; yet it must be so interprete
as to emphasize the fact that the divinity acknowledged in Chris
and experienced in the indwelling of His Holy Spirit was identica
with that manifested in the creation and maintenance of th
universe. The Nicene Council's chief purpose was not to defin
the equal status of the three persons, but to insist that thougl
distinct the three were in fact permanent aspects of the single an
unique Godhead. In spite of previous decisions and of the anti
thesis between God and man the Council made it plain that any
attempt to separate Christ's revelation from the processes o
creation and sanctification was destructive of the basic faith o
Christendom; and though, as seems certain, the 'New Nicenes
in the middle of the subsequent controversy shifted the emphasi
from the unity to the trinity,[1] it was still evident that no sucl
distinction between the God of the Gospel and the God of th
universe would have been tolerated for a moment. Even in th

---

[1] The 'Old Nicenes' like Athanasius and Apollinarius thought in terms of one divine
being existent under three eternal modes; their favourite analogy was the sun, its light
its rays: cf. G. L. Prestige, *God in Patristic Thought*, p. 214 and the note in C. R. B. Shap
land, *Letters of Athanasius on the Holy Spirit*, pp. 108–9. The 'New', like Basil of Neo
Caesarea and the Gregorys, thought of three eternal persons united in a single divine
substance; they employed the analogy of three men, Paul, Silas and Timothy; cf. the
famous letter of Basil to his brother Gregory, *Ep.* xxxviii, 2. J. F. Bethune-Baker is righ
in arguing that this is not a concession to Arianism (cf. *Texts and Studies*, vii, 1); its motive
was against the supposed Sabellianism of Ancyra. But it did in fact encourage Tritheism

fifth century when secular calamity had hamstrung all hope for this world and produced monasticism in ethics and transcendentalism in doctrine, though Leo's *Tome* divided up the actions of the Christ between His two contrasted natures and Cyril of Alexandria had advocated an almost Apollinarian Monophysitism, the Council of Chalcedon insisted that Godhead and manhood were verily united in the one Christ 'without confusion, without change, without distinction, without separation'. If no attempt was made to resolve the paradox, at least it had been vindicated and affirmed. It was not, of course, a solution of the problem; a paradox is never anything more than an acknowledgment of a logical impasse, a challenge to further and fuller intellectual effort, a notification of the dilemma and a definition of its constituent elements. But though as propounded it went far to destroying the real unity of the one Christ and thus the essential significance of the Incarnation, it left the way open, as Monophysitism or Humanism would not have done, for development along the line of the primary Christian experience.

That the controversies did not prove more fruitful was due not only to the trends in Christian thought and life which divorced the natural from the supernatural,[1] but to a more fundamental cause. In the New Testament we have the record not of a speculation but of an encounter, not of an abstract and metaphysical enquiry into the nature of God but of an immediate and personal experience of relationship with Him. In the business of giving theological interpretation to this experience, its reality was treated objectively and almost in a physical-chemical fashion,[2] Godhead and manhood being regarded as stuffs or substances and their union in Christ as analogous to the fusion of gold and silver to make electrum[3] or the mixture of wine and water which can be poured into the same vessel and yet remain in some sense distinct.[4]

---

[1] For these cf. Vol. I of this book, pp. 48–50, and *The Gospel and The Church*, pp. 59–90.

[2] How rapidly this took place is shown by Professor T. F. Torrance, *The Doctrine of Grace in the Apostolic Fathers*. The classical treatment of the subject is J. Oman, *Grace and Personality*.

[3] So, for example, Tertullian, *Adv. Praxean* xxvii; he repudiates the idea of mixture.

[4] So, for example, Apollinarius, *C. Diodorum*, ap. H. Lietzmann, *Frag.* 127.

Consequently the segregation and definition of the two substances became inevitable; their contrasts, immortal and mortal, eternal and ephemeral, supplied the requisite characterizations; and the proven unity of the two in Christ was rendered logically impossible. Study of the language used in the New Testament to describe the disciple's new life in Christ shows that words like faith and grace speedily lost their essentially personal significance and were interpreted, the one in terms of intellectual assent, the other in a form appropriate to medicine or magic. Sacraments, effective symbols like the handshake of friends or the kiss of lovers, became ritual acts whose validity was conditioned not by the spiritual quality of the participants but by the status of the celebrant and the correctness of the formularies. System and regularity were no doubt desirable, if not actually necessary, to unify and consolidate Christendom in the dark ages; but personal relationships, as St Paul had insisted, cannot be standardized by law nor established by definition. A Church which could declare Origen damned and Cyril of Alexandria canonized had gone far towards making the word of God of none effect.

This replacement of the personal by the legal and metaphysical produced, as we have seen, a particular problem for Christology and a similar problem in relation to the whole field of religion. If Christ were divine and if therefore, as the example of Athanasius shows, we must explain away all evidence of His human weakness, then all that is truly religious must be given the divine attribute of absolute perfection. Either the Church is inerrant or it cannot be the divine community. Either the Scriptures are infallible or they are worthless. Either the elect are assured of salvation or the promises of God are not trustworthy. So the arguments have run. They have produced the belief that if we can say only that Christ is the image of God, or is God for us, then we are in effect saying that He is not really God at all. And this is a matter of vital importance if we are to be honest in our thinking.

For it is precisely this claim to an absolute finality whether in the Church or the Scriptures or in Jesus Christ or in anything else, this claim that revelation belongs to a totally different order of reality from discovery or that a creed is something more than a working hypothesis, that perplexes and affronts those of us who have a proper sense of our own human limitations. We can be utterly convinced as we encounter Christ that He expresses for us in terms of human life the quality of God, that He fulfils and surpasses all that we know or can conceive of God, that abstractions like the Absolute, or the Life force, or the Soul of the World are inadequate and idolatrous beside Him, that we can and must offer to Him adoration and penitence, that He is for us 'of one substance with the Father'. We can therefore make the venture of faith and stake our lives on the truth of His revelation. But we cannot, if we are to be truthful, say more than that He is God for us; for this is the most that in our finite and human state we can say of any such conviction; God for us, God in the sense in which alone we can understand and use the term, God in so far as His being and nature can be reflected in the perfect Son of Man. Like Origen we may affirm a ὑπερουσιότης in the Godhead or like Dr Paul Tillich may define Godhead as pure being, beyond essence and existence; but such acknowledgment of our creatureliness does not absolve us from the necessity to respond as best we can to the mystery of that being, and to draw from the encounter with it in Christ and in the universe as clear an interpretation as our condition allows of its quality and character. In so doing we must accept our human status without arrogance and without despair; and formulate 'in Christ', as St Paul would say, the interpretation of His person. The result may not even then be expressible in the thought forms of Nicea and Chalcedon. If it verifies Christ's picture of the Father, and enables our fellowship in the Spirit, it will vindicate our faith.

What then is our Christology? To answer such a question at all may well be outside the scope specified by Lord Gifford for his lecturers: to answer it in detail would require a course of lectures to itself. But we have at least defined certain limits within which our interpretation must fall. Christ by the witness of the Church to His atoning work throughout the centuries has established a claim to meet the deepest needs of man, to be in a unique sense their Saviour, and thereby to be the image, the representative, the embodiment of God. At the same time we as human creatures limited by our status cannot speak with knowledge of what transcends our experience: we may lay down certain propositions about the nature of the Godhead, we may support them by inference and analogy, but it is sinful pride, and great foolishness, to talk as if we could define the infinite or formulate absolute truth. We must beware of claiming for our words an ultimate wisdom, an inerrant authority.

Recognition of these limits may help us to indicate the lines of a Christology. Its background will plainly be the view of nature and history and the creative process which three hundred years of scientific study and of the attempts, from Cudworth to Whitehead, to give an organic interpretation of that process have provided for us. Like Dr L. S. Thornton, whose book, *The Incarnate Lord*, is probably the most important modern attempt in this field,[1] we shall use the record of the successive stages of evolution—the schema of emergence—to describe the 'setting of the stage', the preliminary activity of God as creator and sustainer of the world; for this schema not only allows both for continuity of process and for the appearance of real novelty, but is compatible with belief in God as Love, since it is the right fellowship[2] of the constituents that accompanies and conditions the manifestation of the new. Dr Thornton's own doctrine was rendered inconsistent by his insistence that although the creative process disclosed a series of emergents, life, mind, spirit, and thereby foreshadowed the culmination of the series in the coming of Christ, yet that event differed radically from all its predecessors and signalized not the consummation of the process but the intrusion into it of a Being wholly distinct and independent.[3] It was of course evident that the motive

---

[1] Published London, 1928; and welcomed in these terms e.g. by Prof. L. Hodgson.

[2] C. Lloyd Morgan does not hesitate to apply this word to all such relatedness as enables the emergence of novelty, cf. *Mind at the Crossways* (London, 1929), p. 6.

[3] Cf. *The Incarnate Lord*, pp. 232–9, 260. I may refer to my criticism of this in *Jesus and the Gospel of Love*, pp. 430–1. It is this statement by Thornton rather than the characteristics of emergence (as Dr D. M. Baillie, *God was in Christ*, pp. 91–3) that denies Christ's true manhood.

f this discrepancy, which as Professor Dorothy Emmet has ointed out[1] vitiated his argument, was the desire to insist upon nd to safeguard a finality of revelation.[2] It was analogous to the ssertions of those who repudiate all connexion between inspiration and incarnation; and come near thereby both to a tritheistic oncept of the divine operation and to a refusal to interpret the ature of Jesus or a denial of any meaning to His manhood. lainly Dr Thornton in over-emphasizing one of our limits has efused to observe the other.

It was perhaps natural that Dr Thornton should wish to protect imself against seeming to accept too fully the position which Whitehead had taken about the personality of God. He had been ollowing Whitehead's exposition very closely, and may well ave shared the conviction expressed by Archbishop Temple[3] hat this exposition lays such stress upon process as to leave no oom for any sense of finality or of the otherness and transcendence of God. If so, he might feel that to represent Christ as vithin the emergent series was to deny to Him any but a transient uthority. He would be merely the next stage of development.

Yet, even so, it may well be argued that the schema proposed y Whitehead does not necessarily involve his peculiar insistence pon the distinction between organic and personal or the conlusion which Temple ascribes to it.[4] Christ by it is represented s bringing the series to its culmination. He is the new man,[5] the ew creation,[6] the Man from heaven[7] who not only transcends ur individualities and imperfection but sums up in Himself the vhole process of the creative, redemptive and sanctifying work

---

[1] Cf. *Whitehead's Philosophy of Organism* (London, 1932) pp. 254–5 n.

[2] Thornton, *op. cit.*, pp. 256–62, gives three reasons for refusing to follow his own chema to its logical conclusion. The first argues that to do so would be Adoptianism, ince Christ would then be 'an individual human organism'. But this surely contradicts he principle of emergent levels of novelty. The second and third both insist that Christ nust be the final and absolute revelation and therefore cannot be within the organic eries.

[3] *Nature, Man and God*, p. 259; I confess that I can attach no clear meaning to the note n which he comments upon Dr Thornton's use of Whitehead.

[4] Cf. D. M. Emmet in F. A. Iremonger's *Life of William Temple*, pp. 528–9.

[5] Cf. Col. iii. 10; Eph. iv. 24.   [6] Gal. vi. 15.

[7] I Cor. xv. 47.

of God. He is at once the new species of humanity and also the embodiment in its fulness of the Godhead[1] towards which the whole process has aspired. 'One and the same, truly Son of God truly Son of Man',[2] as the ancient formula of the Faith maintained 'He became what we are that He might make us to be what He is' said Irenaeus.[3] 'God and Man one Christ' says the Church from the author of the Athanasian Creed to Bishop Frank Weston. That the two are indeed one in Him would seem to be in keeping not only with the testimony of the Saints but with the aspiration and to some degree the experience of mankind. Is it not then, as Dr Tillich maintains, the Final Revelation?[4] Can it not as such find confirmation in the character of the creative process of which man is on earth the present culmination?

[1] Col. ii. 9.

[2] Leo, *Ep. dogmatica* (The Tome of Leo), iv.

[3] *Adv. Haereses* v, pref. 'Jesus Christus factus est quod sumus nos, uti nos perficeret esse quod est ipse'; this Harnack, *History of Dogma*, II, p. 286, declares to be his prevailing conception of Christ.

[4] Cf. P. Tillich, *Systematic Theology*, I, p. 136, 'the final revelation, namely as the Messiah, the Christ, the Man-from-above, the Son of God, the Spirit, the Logos-who-became-flesh, the New Being. All these are symbolic variations of the theme "Thou art the Christ"'.

VI

CHRIST AND THE UNIVERSE

FOR mankind there are two unique sacraments which disclose the meaning and convey the experience of reality: they are the created Universe and the person of Jesus Christ. Such was the contention of one of the most brilliant and orthodox of English theologians of my generation, Oliver Chase Quick,[1] whose premature death so soon after his appointment as Regius Professor at Oxford was a loss to Christendom and a bereavement to his friends. It is our business, having looked at the revelation in the person of Christ, to look similarly at the Universe so as to test the truth of the claim that what we see in the intimate and intelligible sphere can be apprehended and perhaps even confirmed in the elements of the vast and less accessible medium. When St Paul spoke of Christ as God's Mystery[2] he surely meant this, that, as in the initiatory drama of Cybele or Isis the myth enacted for the postulant disclosed the secret meaning of existence, so for His disciples the person and work of Jesus was a true revelation of the eternal. Can we today see in Christ the solution of what in the vastness of the creation is otherwise beyond our ken?

To ask that question may be to suggest one more attempt to pick out from the natural world such examples of its beauty and order and worth as will produce the required effect of similarity or correlation. It has been done a hundred times since John Ray wrote *The Wisdom of God in the Works of Creation*; and, indeed, to some extent every poet and every philosopher thus studies and selects and generalizes. It is from this world of our sense-perceptions that we draw the symbols for our speech, indeed, for the

---

[1] Cf. O. C. Quick, *The Christian Sacraments*, pp. 84, 85.   [2] Col. ii. 2.

whole many-sided intricacies of our explanations and communications. We could not 'grasp this sorry Scheme of Things entire', even if our apprehension of it were as restricted and distorted as Omar's or Fitzgerald's. Nevertheless, our inability must not be made an easy excuse for deliberate refusal. To treat Nature as if it were a picture-gallery or a chamber of horrors is to confess our own triviality and pride. The typhoon as well as the sunrise, the tiger not less than the gazelle, must come into our experience before we dare attempt an interpretation. It is in this preliminary enlarging of our range that we begin to suspect that the casual encounters that bring us into an awareness of God are reproducing bits of a pattern with which we are familiar elsewhere.

It is normally as we have seen[1] in terms of its aesthetic and emotional appeal that the universe first reveals itself to us. We are artists—of a sort—before we are thinkers or moralists; and before we have begun to speculate or to manipulate we have been thrilled by the beauty that surrounds us. Where all is 'many-splendoured' each one of us will find his own special object of delight—*cuique suum sacramentum*—and for the sensitive it will be almost a religious exercise to find out new sources of pity and fear, of wonder and joy. But soon the mind is aroused: questions are asked and explored, differences noted and compared, analogies discovered and investigated; and we plunge into the correlation of form and function, the disclosure of causes and effects, and the evidence for continuity of process combined with the emergence of novelty: the universe which had at first looked like a work of art seems now to be a school of life. As we discover that it is a place where action is necessary and choices have to be made, where behaviour carries with it far-reaching consequences and survival belongs only to the fittest, questions of ethics, individual and social, begin to obtrude themselves: this place of enjoyment and of education now suggests the possibility that it is a home.

To recapitulate these naïve impressions is to prepare for the more difficult issues with which our environment confronts us. For no one, and least of all a Christian, can accumulate such impressions

[1] Cf. above p. 49.

without searchings of heart and perplexity of mind. If he is to live in the world he must come to terms with it, must form some opinion of its significance for him and of his place in it; he must, as a child of the twentieth century, face the problems that have made his traditional religion so often appear an anachronism; the scale and character of a universe measured in terms of astronomical space and geological time; the worth of a world in which struggle and suffering have played so large a part; the purpose of existence when progress is so precarious, sin so manifest and devilry at times so triumphant. The two latter, the problem of life and the problem of freedom, raise difficulties of profound intellectual significance. The first is on a different level of importance: but in recent years has become urgently oppressive.

So far as it has arisen in consequence of the changes in our concept of the size and age of the world, it is primarily emotional in its impact and produces for many of us a devastating sense of futility. We realize that in the days of the New Testament when the earth was pictured as a flat and relatively tiny ring of land around the Mediterranean, covered at no very great distance by the vaulted heavens, it was easy to feel a direct and intimate relationship between God and the human individual: everything was small and cosy, a realm not much larger than the Roman empire. In such a world the Babe of Bethlehem, His birth heralded by star and angels, was a lovely proof of the Father's nearness and care. Throughout the Middle Ages and even when Copernicus and his successors had displaced the earth from its central position, the Manger and the Cross stood out with dramatic fitness as the twin reminders of the divine condescension. Only when the antiquity of the earth, the scale of the solar system, and more recently the possibility of a myriad other inhabited worlds and the unimaginable[1] size of the universe became familiar, did the

---

[1] For most of us a book like Olaf Stapledon, *Last and First Men*, is an aid to the realization of the new concepts of space and time; and Mr F. Hoyle, *The Nature of the Universe* (Oxford, 1950), has made them widely familiar. Of this book it is sufficient to say that its theory of continuous creation may be provisionally adopted, its conclusions as to other inhabited worlds are highly speculative, and that the naïve religion of its last chapter hardly deserves the attention that it has received.

incongruity of the contrast between the span of a human life and
the immensity of the creation become overwhelming. For us
realizing it, to go out under the stars and to say 'The Father sent
the Son to be the Saviour of the world' is something of an ordeal.
Rightly used it may give us back the humility of the early
scientists or even the shuddering dread with which earlier
generations faced the unknown terrors of mountain and ocean.
We should at least have little temptation

> to take possession of the world
> And make of God a tame confederate
> Purveyor to our appetites.

This problem is, as we have said, emotional. Facing it we do
well to remember that at the other end of the scale the very small,
the potato virus or the elements involved in nuclear fission, are as
fantastically remote from us in scale as the starry heavens. Whatever our relative stature we have capacities and experiences wholly
independent of measurement; and such as must not be crushed into
contempt and self-negation by the tyranny of numbers. To accept
our human status and to live at our best within it remains our plain
obligation; that status enables us to contemplate ourselves and the
universe and to encounter within both of them a reality which
seems to be personal or super-personal, with which we can be in
communion and from which we can draw penitence and inspiration, humility and joy. The validity of this characteristic experience
is not conditional upon or determined by considerations of the
size and age of the world. If in face of our new knowledge we
echo the words of the Psalmist ('But for me, I am a worm, and
no man'),[1] such confession is only harmful when we begin to act
accordingly. There is a phrase in the Catechism of the Book of
Common Prayer which some of us dislike in its social application
but which may help us here: I will 'do my duty in that state of
life, unto which it shall please God to call me'.

Such an answer is perhaps sufficient when the problem is put in

---

[1] Cf. Ps. xxii. 6.

more intellectual form and in terms of the second law of hermodynamics. In its popular presentation the belief that by his law the universe like a watch running down was doomed inevitably to total inertia received brilliant expression in Bertrand Russell's *tour de force*, *A Free Man's Religion*. The eloquent exordium in which we were warned that the only foundation for a reasonable religion was an uncompromising despair found its way into anthologies and on to all the platforms of secularism and revolt. If the physical world had only a few billion years more of energy, then human life was indeed 'a striving and a striving and an ending in nothing'. 'Let us eat and drink; for tomorrow we die', or as Russell prefers to put it 'Let's be as happy as we can while we can'.

There was nothing new about it; for, as Archbishop Temple and others pointed out, the Christian and indeed every religion of any importance has refused to make belief in the eternity of matter an article of faith—indeed, has too often been attacked for regarding this world as transient and ephemeral. Moreover, in any case what may happen a billion years hence has little relevance for humanity. But many of us questioned whether entropy was the last word and suggested that if the watch had once been wound up it could be wound up again, or more seriously argued that creation was a process still going on. Recent developments in physics encourage us to believe that we were right.[1]

Before we pass on, there is one element in our relationship to our environment that must be briefly noted. If we are to look fairly at the universe we must recognize not only its scale and order but within that order the incidence of natural disasters, floods, hurricanes, eruptions and earthquakes. The unpredictable suddenness of these disasters and their tragic effects made them in earlier days peculiarly significant as 'acts of God'; and the Old Testament gave abundant authority for associating them with the divine chastisement of evil-doers. To many Christians they still

[1] Cf. Prof. C. A. Coulson in *The Frontier*, I, p. 428, endorsing statements by Sir E. Whittaker, F. Hoyle, etc.

present a difficulty; how can the indiscriminate havoc, the terrible death-roll at Lisbon in 1755 or San Francisco in 1906 or in Japan in 1923 or recently in Jamaica be reconciled with God's care for His children?

Such a question does not differ in essentials from that which used also to be asked about disease. In the Middle Ages consumption or ague were as much an act of God or the devil as tornado or lightning-flash. With the work of Pasteur and of Ross the history of the tubercle bacillus and the life cycle of the malaria parasite became familiar, and the mystery was explained. We are beginning to understand the conditions that determine the weather and will no doubt eventually learn the precise incidence and course of volcanic and seismic disturbances. Meanwhile it is evident that we are slow to use such knowledge as we already possess. To build cities on sites notably liable to earthquake and then to treat the consequent disaster as a proof of the non-existence or indifference of God is hardly a reasonable attitude.

On the broader issue it is clear that the earth is not a padded cell in which its inmates are sheltered from the consequences of ignorance or rebellion. It does not encourage comfort or carelessness: else growth and development would be inhibited. Human history and the previous course of evolution suggest that to live dangerously is a necessary condition of advance; and those who have maintained that here we have no abiding city can appeal for confirmation to the order of nature as endorsing the word of Scripture. What seems plain is that the whole universe is 'all of a piece'; that the very qualities in it which on occasion manifest themselves in calamity are those which condition its climate and fertility, its ability to bring life into being and to sustain it, its fitness as the school and home of humanity. Books like William Whewell's Bridgewater Treatise [1] or more recently Lawrence Henderson's *The Fitness of the Environment* deserve to be constantly remembered. They make it abundantly clear that we are not in a position to suggest casual improvements in the scheme of things

[1] *Astronomy and General Physics considered with Reference to Natural Theology* (London, 1838).

or to indict the order of nature because of particular details which we have not yet learnt to understand.[1]

Following this line of thought we can answer those who say 'Your view of the worth of nature is perhaps appropriate to an Englishman: you have a garden-land with a varied and favourable climate, a garden without a snake. If you lived in the tropics where the scale and fecundity of nature terrifies and oppresses with jungle and desert, pestilence and famine, you would find your talk about a loving Father intolerably unctuous'. Anyone brought up in Britain and transplanted to 'green hell', to the Antarctic or Central Africa will certainly find his complacencies challenged. But unless he has been wholly enervated by the ease of life, he will speedily discover the zest of uttermost endurance and verify the fact that those for whom life is hardest are not those who despair of the world or desire to renounce it. He may even wonder whether the natives of Africa are not in fact already proving themselves better equipped for life than those of older and traditionally more favoured cultures.

Before we leave this aspect of our approach to nature it should be noted that along with the new awareness of the scale and ruthlessness of the universe has gone a widespread and deepened appreciation of its beauty. With the opening up of the world the terror of the sea began in the fifteenth century to give place to enjoyment. The grandeur of mountains which Gesner in the sixteenth century was the first to proclaim was hardly recognized until Wordsworth's day and is still a recent discovery. The fascination of the stars is even today not wholly freed from astrological and horoscopic absurdities or given its full power to purge and exalt. But if neither the very great nor the very small has as yet a universal appeal, the sense of harmony in variety, that found expression in Albrecht Dürer's picture of grasses or in John Ray's response to the wonderland of plant and bird or in Richard Jefferies's *Pageant of Summer*, has become a general and important element in our human heritage. The way of an eagle in the air, of

[1] The problem is of course raised by the familiar cases in Luke xiii. 1–5.
[2] Cf. Vol. I of this book, p. 88.

a serpent upon the rock, of a ship in the sea, and of a man with a maid, the 'three things..., yea, four' that stirred the wonder of the sage of Israel[1] symbolize for us what Robert Bridges has called *The Testament of Beauty*; and a great multitude finds in such beauty a profoundly religious inspiration.

It is true that in the past decades fear of the camera and other less simple motives have produced reactions of all sorts against naturalism in painting and sculpture; and it is difficult to speak about any aesthetic subject without becoming involved in a maze of controversy. A full discussion of the modernistic movements in art or of the relation of art to nature would inevitably be long and very controversial and require qualifications and an outlook to which I can make no claim. But it is perhaps possible to find an overwhelming beauty in the pattern and colour and texture of plant and insect and bird without necessarily comparing them with the creations of Picasso or Mr Henry Moore or being entangled in the theories and dogmas of the art critics. In the present chaos of ideas about beauty the only alternative to a discussion of the nature of art is a personal statement.

For some years in the past, and even now at intervals, I have spent many hours upon the contemplation of certain species of British Lepidoptera, not as matter of science but simply from delight in the pattern and colouring of their wings. My chief subject was a long series of the very variable geometrid moth *Boarmia repandata*, chosen from many hundreds, grouped according to localities because each area produced a characteristic type, ranging from the golden brown of south Devon to the cool grey of Exmoor, from the almost white of Enniskillen to the almost black of Penistone, from the dull brown and bold bands of Surrey to the indeterminate smoky speckling of Galashiels. Every specimen differed from the rest, in detail from those of its own group, in total effect from those of others.[2] Each was in itself a perfect design, satisfying in whole and parts, inviting one to concentrate

[1] Cf. Prov. xxx. 18, 19.

[2] This diversity, 'inexplicable as completely adaptive', is illustrated on a larger scale in the widely varying horns of Antelopes by G. G. Simpson, *The Meaning of Evolution*, pp. 165–8.

ne's whole attention upon it.[1] To move from one to another, to ense the difference of impact, to work out the quality of this lifference in the detailed modifications of the general pattern, this vas a profoundly moving experience. Here is beauty—whatever he philosophers and art critics who have never looked at a moth nay say—beauty that rejoices and humbles, beauty remote from ll that is meant by words like random or purposeless, utilitarian or materialistic, beauty in its impact and effects akin to the authentic encounter with God.[2] So far as I can judge this represents for me he same aesthetic response as for others is evoked by pictures or music;[3] and it supplies me with a criterion by which to appreciate other forms of art. In any case such beauty is inherent in and not merely imputed to the insects: we discover it; we do not invent it: and it satisfies[4]—even though as artists or poets we can no more fix and express its quality than as thinkers we can fully interpret its meaning.

The other two problems, of suffering and sin or life and freedom, are for our present purpose far more important: each has always been and perhaps will always be too difficult for final solution; each has recently become specially challenging to all thinking people; in each there is a particular tension for the Christian; each for the student of natural religion deserves a series of lectures to itself.

To describe the problem of suffering[5] as the dominant element in the theology of the Old Testament is to do no more than justice to the succession of psalmists, sages and prophets who agonized

---

[1] A striking instance of this co-ordination of change in design is to be found in the sympathetic colour-changes in feathers shortly before the moult: cf. J. G. Millais, *The Natural History of British surface-feeding Ducks* (London, 1902).

[2] Cf. W. R. Matthews, *The Purpose of God*, pp. 122–6, 'Beauty in nature is expression which finds an echo in our own spirits—"Spirit greeting spirit"'.

[3] So too R. G. Collingwood, *The Principles of Art*, p. 39.

[4] A similar experience has constantly accompanied the production of life-sized water-colour drawings of the British flora, of which I have done some thousands in the past twenty years.

[5] Confusion will arise unless suffering is defined. I use it for the self-giving of love, the sharing of experience (not necessarily painful), the sympathy which 'gets alongside' another. Thus it is distinct from pain, though in a sinful world it usually involves pain. For further discussion of Christ's attitude to it see Note IX below, p. 214.

over it. For anyone who is concerned with the restatement or the exposition of Christianity it is of supreme importance to realize how inevitable was the tension and how heart-searching indeed how heart-breaking, were the efforts to resolve it. In no other field is the contrast between Old and New so obvious; in no other has traditional Christianity been more handicapped by its insistence upon scriptural infallibility.

The God of the Old Testament was to His people their King and Law-giver: for Israel was a theocracy rather than a family. His power, originally confined to the hills and to the land holy to him, was extended by the great prophets until it embraced the whole earth. But it did not change its character, or rather as its range increased so did its omnipotence. He was their God, He was Almighty; yet they suffered hunger and disease, conquest and captivity. It was valiant in their singers to declare that the righteous were never forsaken and would inherit and possess the earth: but when Sennacherib or Nebuchadnezzar was devastating the land and encompassing Sion it was hard to accept encouragement—so hard indeed that excuses had somehow to be found for the delays and displeasure of Yahweh. No doubt the law had been broken, and His people been negligent and rebellious: let them repent and offer sacrifices and He would surely respond and rescue them. No doubt the adversary was powerful and might even succeed for a little: he stood on slippery ground and his overthrow would come suddenly. No doubt God wished to prove them, whether their loyalty was strong enough to stand up against temptation; let them be patient and all would ultimately be well. We can trace such reasonings until they culminate in the superb decision of Job 'though he slay me, yet will I trust in him', and in the dawning of a conviction that suffering is not only, nor always, the punishment for iniquity, whether individual or corporate; that it may fall upon and be accepted by the innocent; and that as such it has a redemptive purpose. Yet even in the Second Isaiah there is no clear sign that the concept of God as unconditioned power has been abandoned; and this is hardly surprising in view of the plain fact that the same is still too often the case in Christendom.

Our brief survey of the metaphors of Atonement has shown that suffering both in Christ and in ourselves has been usually interpreted as the penalty of sin, as retributive rather than reformatory, and as in itself and always calamitous. That it could be the symbol and instrument of fuller life, the incentive to and occasion of sympathy, the primary means for overcoming evil, these are convictions of which Christendom has too seldom shown any serious comprehension.[1] In spite of Christ's plain example and repeated precepts the belief that life can only be attained as life is laid down, that the Cross is not only the sign and means of Christ's victory but the universal symbol and instrument for deliverance from sin and indeed the appropriate emblem of the whole creative process, has seldom if ever been fully accepted by the Church.[2] Here in the central event of His ministry, as in so much else, we regard His achievement as exceptional not representative.

Consequently when Darwin's doctrine of the survival of the fittest was interpreted in terms of the struggle for existence, and it might have seemed that the whole march of evolution was a *Via Crucis*, Christians were and have been almost more unwilling than pagans to acknowledge that such a method could be compatible with a divine creator. Even so sensitive and profound a theologian as Bishop Charles Gore put it on record that he felt the sufferings of animals to be the most serious objection to belief in God as our Father;[3] and it is probable that no other single difficulty was so generally regarded as insuperable. A Creator who accepted the intolerable pain of His creatures as a necessary element in the fulfilment of His purpose was surely fit to preside rather over an *auto da fé* than over a father's home. Anyone who has reflected upon the destruction that ranges from the nuptials of

---

[1] It is notable that most of the books on spiritual healing treat suffering as an evil and come dangerously near regarding religion as, in A. N. Whitehead's great phrase (*Science in the Modern World*, p. 275), 'a research after comfort'. Yet physical health is not an end in itself. Cf., for example, L. D. Weatherhead, *Psychology, Religion and Healing*, pp. 194, 461–2, etc.

[2] It is perhaps permissible to say that the accounts of suffering that have helped me most are a lecture on Creative Suffering by Julia de Beausobre (Lady Namier) and her book *The Woman who could not Die.*

[3] Cf. *The Reconstruction of Belief* (London, 1926), pp. 160–3.

the Praying Mantis to the mass-suicide of the migrant Lemmings or upon the parasitism of liver-fluke and tapeworm or of the nestling Cuckoo, or watched the agony of sufferers from tuberculosis or cancer will know how futile it can seem under such circumstances to believe in a God of love.

It has been already shown in treating of Darwinism that it owed much of its influence to its appeal to two of the strongest qualities of the Victorian age, its utilitarianism and its sentimentality. The belief that the world of nature was a charnel-house and its presiding goddess 'red in tooth and claw with ravine' was almost as congenial as the belief that every detail of structure from the corolla of the gentian to the face of the hippopotamus was dictated by its commercial value for the business of survival. In days when insect and animal behaviour was interpreted in the simplest anthropomorphic terms, it was useless to argue that there was little corresponding to pain as we know it until the appearance of the mammalian brain and nervous system—and hardly more before the arrival of the frontal cortex—and that in any case the absence of imagination and recorded experience involved freedom from anxiety and anticipatory fears. Such arguments, although used, then as now, to justify the killing of animals in sport and for fun, were nevertheless universally regarded as special pleading if employed to rebut the cruelty of nature. With the passing of the Victorian age and the spread of observation of birds and beasts a more realistic attitude has prevailed. It is generally agreed in accordance with the experience of field-naturalists that at the lowest levels of life there is a rudimentary pleasure-pain reaction accompanying the exercise of instinctive urges; that this develops in close correlation with the general increase of responsibility and becomes acute in relation to particular satisfactions and needs; that there is a remarkable extension of the range and depth of suffering in birds and mammals and perhaps some evidence of fellow-feeling for the sufferer; but that pain does not take a major part in the experience of any organism below the human level; and that the life of wild creatures far from being spent in constant fear is active, rhythmic and, if such a word be allowed, joyous.

Whatever be the case about suffering in the animal world, there can be no easy disposal of it at the human level. Even if we admit that sensitiveness is the synonym of life, and that power to suffer is the true gauge of sensitiveness, there are moments in the experience of us all when the sheer mass of physical pain in the world makes us sick at heart and rebellious in spirit. Not until we have known it ourselves in one of its fiercest forms, not until we have discovered the power to triumph over it, ought we to dare to say anything about it. For ignorance, on this matter at least, is almost always either glib or morbid or both. Perhaps there is nothing harder than to escape distortion when we are compelled to look on at the pain of others without having experienced it in our own bodies. It was not the martyrs who invented hell but their friends who escaped the fire; and the combination of compassionate heart-break with impotence to bring relief makes such vindictiveness intelligible and even pardonable. It is plainly part of the value of pain that it should evoke sympathy and enlist our best instincts in the effort to prevent and alleviate. If it were absent, our life would lose its qualities of mercy and pity, of patience and protection, of sacrifice and forgiveness.[1] Karel Capek in *R.U.R.* has analysed and presented the problem to us with a simplicity which, if sentimental, is also profound. Love itself is perhaps inseparable from suffering.

Moreover, the development in us of the pleasure-pain reaction into anxiety is an aspect of our self-consciousness which has far-reaching importance. It is not necessary or, to some of us at least, accurate to attach to anxiety such fundamental significance as Kierkegaard has done when he makes it the source of all human creativity.[2] The Christian contention that love is the source, and fear or anxiety only the spur and occasion, is a truer analysis. Affection and tenderness, the expansion of maternal instinct to include the sense of fatherhood in the male parent, and the enlargement of family love to include the neighbours—these are

[1] 'Joy and suffering are two equally precious gifts which must both be savoured to the full,' S. Weil, *Waiting upon God*, p. 75; but she deals also with '*malheur*, affliction or dereliction, which is the experience of the Cross'.
[2] Cf. R. Niebuhr, *The Nature and Destiny of Man*, I, pp. 184–6.

the basic elements in the evolution of our human status. But, as we have already said, love and suffering are intimately connected, and anxiety is their natural outcome. The stimulus to invention and technical skills directly due to it have given mankind forms of protection that range from the Devil's Dyke to the amulet, and from the umbrella to the atom-bomb. At the present stage of human history we hardly need to be reminded that Jesus spent much of His teaching [1] in warnings against it and that He gave us a salutary lesson by so doing. For anxiety, like fear, is the perversion of a virtue; and creativity thus motived is liable to be misused.

Suffering, being in essence the self-giving which love inevitably involves, would seem, despite the condemnation of Patripassianism as a heresy, to be a proper attribute of deity: certainly if it is not so, the claim of Jesus to be the image of God would be hard to maintain. For Jesus not only suffered, but deliberately chose for Himself and for His followers the Cross, such suffering as involved extreme physical torment, and also condemnation, mockery and failure. At the crisis of His fate when He could have more easily chosen to fight or to flee, He accepted all that His enemies could do to Him; and by so doing accomplished His purpose, disclosing both the monstrous character of evil and the only effective means for its overthrow. That thus He opened up new resources of life, revealed the true and hitherto unrecognized character of God, and made possible a new and organic fellowship for those who by His act were purged of their pride and inspired for service, is the evidence of the efficacy of His self-sacrifice. It is a tragic comment upon the unique splendour of His work that Christians, though accepting the Cross as their emblem and love as the first definition of deity, have not yet realized that other methods of overcoming sin and uplifting mankind are sub-Christian and superficial. But to regard suffering not as a tragedy but as a triumph and sufferers not as the wastage of the world but as its redeemers is a transvaluation which few of us are as yet prepared to make. We are still a long way from appreciating the significance of our emblem

[1] 'Do not worry' ('Take no thought' as the A.V. unhappily renders it) occurs some ten times in the Synoptic Gospels.

nd seeing in suffering the basic quality of the creative, redemptive
nd sanctifying process,

> That only black Gethsemane can prove
> The pain, the triumph and the peace of love.[1]

That love involves sympathy, and to that extent suffering, seems
obvious. It need not on that account necessarily involve pain. In
a world freed from evil, if selfishness and its accompaniments of
ambition and fear were transcended, there would still be love and
the sympathy that is suffering; there would, as it seems, be no
occasion for pain. In heaven, despite those who have argued that
its bliss is enhanced by contemplating the torments of the damned,
there can be no room for hell: if hell is eternal, it is difficult to
believe that Christ will remain on His throne, for He surely cannot
lay aside His unique prerogative or cease to seek and to save that
which is being lost.[2] That all sin works itself out in pain and can
only be redeemed by suffering is a plain lesson of the Christian
gospel. It can be confirmed from the evidence of nature and
history. But to discuss it raises first the question of human
solidarity, the relation of the individual to society and his environment, and then our second problem, that of evil. For suffering,
by compelling us to realize our membership one with another,
also provides the one adequate motive for persistence in what
Robert Louis Stevenson so finely called 'the lost fight of virtue'.
If our attitude to evil was dictated only by selfish motives[3] or
ignored the obvious fact that when I sin the folks that I love best
are the first to suffer, the fight would be lost indeed.

It is plain that we cannot see deeply into the nature of suffering
without realizing the defects of our normally individualistic outlook. So long as we are concerned with particular people as if
they were self-contained and isolated units (and this is the usual
attitude of Western man), the oft-repeated cry 'Why should *I* be
the one to suffer?' expresses an unanswerable resentment—

---

[1] Margaret Lloyd, *Late Harvest*, p. 46.
[2] For the eschatological question thus raised cf. below Ch. x.
[3] The prudential ethics of Catholicism and the individualistic piety of Protestantism
have too often been responsible for inculcating these motives.

manifestly the naïve notion that pain is the penalty of wrong-doing is only true if we take the widest possible view of our corporate relationships. The young man who says 'I know I've been selfish and broken most of the commandments; I know I shall have to pay for what I've done; but I'll take my punishment without whining' is boasting as if we could each and alone bear the consequences of our errors—whereas the simplest lesson of the Cross is that the innocent suffer for the ignorance and vice of others, that, at every point and in all that we do and are, each one of us affects or infects his neighbours, that we are members one of another in a community as wide as the world. We shall have to examine this whole matter more fully in a later connexion. Meanwhile it is sufficient to note that in Hebrew as in Christian thought there is full recognition of our mutual responsibility, an insistence that if one member suffer all suffer with him, and a vision becoming clearer of a world-wide and organic society in which 'There is neither Jew nor Greek, there is neither bond nor free, there is neither male nor female'.[1] The fellowship of suffering which St Paul learned to proclaim as the goal of discipleship[2] is perhaps the strongest link that binds us together.

It is significant that as a result of two world wars Christians in the present phase of opinion are apt to regard the 'bond of iniquity' as a more obvious characteristic than the fellowship of suffering. It has become a cliché to say that 'the Christian doctrine of man is that he is fallen', though this is plainly a half-truth and as such more misleading than a lie.[3] The Christian doctrine is of course that man is both sinful and redeemable, that he is born with a heritage of dim ancestral lusts and aspirations, and has to achieve self-hood by way of temptation, sin and forgiveness; that he is capable of 'pulses of nobleness and aches of shame', of bestial and devilish wickedness and of inspiration by, and response to, the

---

[1] Gal. iii. 28 (A.V.).

[2] 'That I may know him, and the power of his resurrection, and the fellowship of his sufferings', Phil. iii. 10; the order of the clauses marks a change from the days when he had regarded the Cross as he did in Gal. iii or even in I Cor. i.

[3] For a shattering criticism of this attitude to sin, especially as expounded by Dr E. Brunner, cf. J. B. Pratt, *Can We Keep the Faith?*, pp. 105–13, 191.

Spirit of the Living God. To state one side of the fact without the other is to produce a parody and to be committed either to the falsehood that man has only a choice of two evils or to the equal falsehood that all is for the best in the best of all possible worlds. But of this anon. We are concerned at present with a more fundamental issue—can we regard a world in which evil is so evident as in any sense compatible with belief in God?

If God be regarded in terms of power as primarily the Almighty, the King of Kings, the Lord of the Earth, Whose will is the unquestioned and arbitrary fiat of a Sultan, then Cudworth's dilemma becomes inescapable. Either God is neither able nor willing to eliminate evil; or He is able but not willing; or He is not able though willing; or He is both able and willing—of which only the last seems worthy of deity—and the last does not happen.[1] We have already noted the speed and completeness with which St Paul realized that Christ if accepted as Lord had made impossible such a concept of the nature of Godhead and saw that the new analogy of Fatherhood opened up a resolution of the dilemma. The Fourth Evangelist with his triple definition of God as Light and Life and Love made explicit what his colleague had affirmed. If God is thus defined then power is always conditioned by love, and creation instead of being visualized in terms of the architect and his mansion or the watchmaker and the watch will have to be thought out in terms of parenthood and education, a parenthood free from possessiveness and favouritism, an education for self-hood, self-sacrifice and freedom. It is permissible to take this hypothesis as it is outlined in the eighth chapter of the Epistle to the Romans and test it out by reference to our present knowledge of the creative process. In this way we shall see in a new perspective the problem that has occasioned such debate in Christendom. Before doing so we must look at the traditional setting and solution.

Creation both in the Hebrew and the Christian cosmology had been regarded as an event to which an accurate date, the year, the time of year, and even by some commentators the day and hour,

---

[1] Cf. Vol. I of this book, p. 114, and R. Cudworth, *Intellectual System*, I, p. 129.

could be attached. John Milton in *Paradise Lost* expressed the story as it was accepted by practically the whole of Western culture three hundred years ago. Linnaeus, a century later, endorsed it by defining the species of plants and animals as those forms which proceeded at the beginning from the hand of God. The orthodox in all the Churches maintained the same conviction until the middle of the nineteenth century. The Creator made the world and completed His work by the making of Adam and Eve, and it was all very good; He rested. How then came evil?

In the Genesis story it was the serpent who successfully tempted the woman; and this might easily be interpreted as the influence of our sub-human ancestry.[1] But after the exile when the rigid dualism of the Persians and their own calamities sharpened the vague Hebrew idea of Satan into the definite picture of a supernatural adversary, the enemy of God, the Power of Darkness, the Fall became a catastrophic and deadly defeat for the Creator which involved His whole work in disaster. Christendom, which, like the New Testament, in its early days was too sure of God and too conscious of the presence of His Spirit to have much interest in the Devil, at first accepted the demonology of contemporary culture and then gradually elaborated a dualistic schema which represented the present world as the scene of a still undecided conflict and, in moments of calamity, went near to surrendering it to the sovereignty of the Evil One. Milton's picture of Satan as Pride incarnate is at once more profound and more impressive than the popular figure with horns and hoofs and forked tail, but both represent the ever-active enemy for whom the conquest of God's new and rebellious province is only an incident in an age-old campaign.

That such a dualism can become a fine fighting faith is plain from all its variants, Zoroastrianism and Mithraism, Islam in its several shapes, and the Christendom of the Crusades and of the Reformers. That it is in the last resort irreconcilable with Christ's concept of God and man and the world is more obvious to us, as

---

[1] Cf. A. J. Heschel, *Man is Not Alone*, p. 210, 'Man is always faced with the choice of listening either to God or to the snake'.

t was to Origen, than it could have been in the centuries when
he natural and the supernatural, the secular and the sacred, were
et in rigid antithesis. It is open to one of two fatal objections:
ither it represents God and Satan as engaged in warfare on such
qual terms as to make the result precarious—in which case God
s no longer God, but has lost control of His creation and cannot
properly be called Almighty—or Satan exists on sufferance
drawing his power from his Adversary and no more able to defy
Him effectively than Ajax to defy the lightning. In either case it
s important to remind ourselves of our own status: we can surely
ee the life-and-death urgency of our own struggle against sin
without reverting to the pathetic fallacy and picturing the stars
n their courses as involved in the battle.

In this connexion a word may be said about the theory of a pre-
mundane Fall which some theologians[1] have devised in order to
account for the elements of imperfection and struggle in the world
of nature. Mythology of this sort is no doubt as legitimate as any
other speculation upon matters for which mankind can have no
clear evidence. But if we confine ourselves to the data that are
within our reach and examine them as closely as we can, there
eems sufficient available material to supply a working hypothesis.
To remove the problem to a pre-mundane realm of which we
can in fact have no knowledge is merely to open the way to guess-
work.[2] That there may be demonic or satanic powers, disem-
bodied spirits good and bad, angels and archangels and a myriad
of other worlds is a possibility which few of us would wish to
deny. That for these beings there is at present little or no evidence
uch as can be scientifically investigated, and that to maintain a
reverent agnosticism about them is not incompatible with
Christian theism seems plain. If we are to strive for a reasonable
faith it is important to maintain a sense of proportion and to
realize that many pious opinions are both unproven and

[1] Cf., for example, Canon Peter Green, *The Problem of Evil*; N. P. Williams, *The Ideas
f the Fall and Original Sin*.
[2] It is scarcely necessary to add that the theory of a prehistoric period of human perfec-
on in a golden, or neolithic, age is still harder to reconcile with science or history or
heology.

improbable. We would do well in this matter to return to the teaching of Jesus for whom sin was not a cosmic power but 'the totality of actual concrete sins'.[1]

If we accept the fact that Creation, even though it may have had a beginning, is for us a process as yet incomplete and in that sense, as St Paul insists, imperfect or 'subject to frustration'[2] by God's deliberate will, and if we see that process as involving the whole story of the origin and evolution of life, we get a vastly different outlook at once. Further, if we provisionally agree with the Apostle's hypothesis that this process is analogous to the agony of a parturition, the birth-pangs of the family of God, then we can regard it as preparatory to the emergence of creatures who will lovingly, intelligently and voluntarily respond to their Creator and co-operate among themselves. We shall therefore expect the process to show signs that it can bring into being not slaves but sons, not robots nor chessmen but creatures who can speak the truth in love and find their freedom and fulfilment in 'the blessed necessity of not doing evil'.[3] Obviously if this is to be its goal it must make possible a disciplined choice of love rather than hate, of truth rather than lies, of the better rather than the worse. A world in this sense 'a vale of soul-making', a creative process which makes possible such a result, must be one in which ugliness and illusion and devilry have their place. We need no display of proof other than recent events in our own history to convince us not only of the monstrous results of our own wrong choices but of the age-old inheritance of lust and ignorance and cruelty with which each one of us is born:[4] that man is fallen is plain fact whatever we think of the story in Genesis. We are saved from denying

---

[1] Cf. F. C. Grant, *An Introduction to New Testament Thought*, p. 172.

[2] This seems the true meaning of Rom. viii. 20 (A.V.), 'made subject to vanity'; the words that follow 'not willingly but by reason of him who hath subjected the same in hope' assert that such frustration is not due to the devil or to man but to God—this in spite of some of the commentators!

[3] Cf. Augustine, *De Civ. Dei* XXII, 30, 'Beata necessitas non peccandi'.

[4] In his writings on sin, F. R. Tennant, who has the threefold qualification of scientist, philosopher and theologian, has clearly drawn this distinction between hereditary predisposition and personal guilt. They deserve more attention than they have received. Cf. especially *The Origin and Propagation of Sin*.

hat, being what it is, our race can ever produce freedom and love by the fact of Jesus Christ and its corroboration in the saints.

The basis of this element of choice or autonomy, like the sensitiveness to rudimentary pleasure and pain of which we have already spoken, would seem to be found in the capacity to respond to stimuli characteristic of certain molecular substances essential to the functioning of living organisms.[1] If so, it may not be wholly accurate to define such autonomy and sensitiveness as characteristic of the animate as contrasted with the inanimate. But even if a choice of alternatives is correlated with such chemical tissues, the actual decision—for example, to move in one direction rather than another—would seem to constitute a real difference between the blob of colloid and the living amoeba. The mechanism may in each case be identical: in the one it is put into operation solely by external stimuli; in the other it is controlled to some degree at least from within by the organism itself. The choices thus made, small in scope and effect as they may be, help to determine the organism's future. As organic life evolves, a wider and wider range of decision has to be made. At about the level of the starfish such decisions appear to become conscious and even purposively adapted to the desired end. With the higher insects methods of communication, of learning by trial and error, and of consciously co-ordinated effort are apparent. With the vertebrates individual variation of the behaviour-pattern becomes noticeable; habits though largely fixed show evidence of modification; there are indications of the beginnings of an appreciation of value and a purposive plan. No two birds, as every bird-photographer knows, will react to his presence in precisely the same fashion: in spite of Descartes and the behaviourists, reactions even when stereotyped are not automatic; and with the mammals the range of unpredictable responses becomes wider and more characteristic. It is plain that at this level the conscious choices of the particular creature contribute largely to its survival and play a big part in its life. The way is being prepared for selfhood and self-consciousness.

How far such evidence of an increasing scope in the exercise of

[1] The problem of design thus raised is considered below; cf. pp. 135-44.

the will throws light on the problem of evil may at this stage of the process be open to question. That from the human standpoint there is ruthless greed and cruelty, ghoulish parasitisms and wanton desecrations is obvious to any reader of the *Souvenirs entomologiques* and though Fabre himself came to see in it what he called submission to a law of sacrifice, yet the evidence is hard to reconcile with the moralizings and sermons of Aesop and his medieval successors. We may legitimately urge that it is under the stress of such strife that life is sifted and the fit are selected. We may go further and argue that in its higher stages it is obvious that survival-value belongs rather to the social than to the solitary, rather to the sensitive that live dangerously than to the predatory or to the immune, that man does not derive descent directly from the tiger or the elephant. But it is difficult not to believe that the sheer fecundity of nature, the widening range both of physical form and of behaviour-pattern, the infinite variety of living organisms are somehow integral to the evolution of man. *Tantae molis erat Romanam condere gentem*: Vergil's aphorism in the *Aeneid* needs only a change of adjective to make it appropriate to evolution and mankind.

There is one factor in the process which has hardly received from moralists or theologians the attention that it deserves. Progress is apparently both individual and collective, the enlargement and improvement of each particular unit and the complexity and co-ordination of the society to which it belongs. In the course of evolution there is what looks like a spiral movement—at one time development takes place in the specialization of solitary species, at another the individuals lose their significance except as constituent parts in the community. In the Hymenoptera, for example, we have both the predatory genera, like *Ammophila* or *Sphex* where each individual female after pairing works out the life cycle in solitude, and the social like the Honey Bee which has since Vergil's time supplied a pattern for a commonwealth, or the Ants which combine differentiation of form and function with conformity to a corporate plan almost as if each was a cell in a single body. Among the vertebrates, and most notably in human history, similar alternations of individual and collective can be readily traced; and if the goal be a family in which each member finds its fullest satisfaction in the service of the whole and the whole is healthy when each and all are co-operating at their best, this would be in accordance with the premonitory symptoms that we have noted.

But if so then it is important that the individual should reach his own fullest possible development; and this necessarily involves the attainment of conscious and responsible self-hood. It would seem obvious that for such self-hood the loneliness and self-reliance, the self-knowledge and the self-discipline of adolescence are an indispensable preparation. Each one of us, if he is to become a mature person, must come to terms with himself and gain the mastery of his own soul. Every experienced parent or teacher knows the difficulty and necessity of the process, and realizes its dangers—that to evade it arrests development at the child level, to obstruct it invites distortion, to assist it requires a rare degree of wisdom and insight. Yet this phase of growth demands isolation of the self from the herd, the fostering of egoism, and in some measure at least the temptation to the primal sin of pride. How indeed otherwise can the individual be fitted for self-sacrifice and self-surrender except by having acquired a self?

Here is a moral dilemma. Catholic Christianity has on the whole insisted upon innocence and obedience, the maintenance of childishness, the cult of the Little Flower. Protestants, like Milton,[1] have usually taken the opposite course, have stood for the twice-born rather than the once-born, and would today endorse Alexander Whyte's great saying 'Penitence is better than innocence'.[2] Both would agree as to the sinfulness of sin; both would refuse to countenance the doing of evil that good may come. Yet perhaps both would assent to the dangerous doctrine that God who can bring good out of evil has so ordered the world that by

---

[1] Cf. *Areopagitica*, 'Assuredly we bring not innocence into the world, we bring impurity much rather; that which purifies us is trial, and trial by what is contrary'.

[2] Cf. W. Temple, *Nature, Man and God*, p. 511, 'I should not hesitate to say that a sinful world redeemed by such a sacrifice as the Crucifixion of Christ is better than a world that had never sinned'. This is the teaching of Augustine, *De Civ. Dei* XIV, 11 and of Milton in *Paradise Lost* XII, l. 470; cf. C. S. Lewis, *A Preface to Paradise Lost*, pp. 65–7.

permitting freedom to His creatures and accepting their misuse of it He can thus bring about results not attainable in any other way. It begins to look as if the possibility of disobedience was the price of liberty, just as liberty is the condition of self-hood and self-hood the preliminary to fellowship.

If it be argued that this is to make God responsible for evil[1] and that this involves a denial of God's essential goodness, we can only reply that here again the objection suggests a pre-Christian concept of God. If He is love, and creation an act of parenthood, then He cannot without being false to His own nature treat His creatures as slaves or chessmen. The production of persons must involve what Incarnation also and more obviously involves, a 'Kenosis' or 'self-emptying',[2] that is, it must condition God's exercise of power. If, as is apparent, He has given His creatures the freedom to choose and with it to accept or to reject His will for them, He is plainly responsible for this gift to them, but not in any real sense for their use of it. If, as Jesus manifestly shows, He does not intervene to remove the righteous from the consequences of human wickedness, but on the contrary has so ordered His world that only by such suffering can this wickedness be overcome, we get at least a glimpse of a solution to the problem. 'The divine Atonement cannot be confined within any one moment of time, but, so far as it can be described in temporal terms at all, is as old and as endless as the sin with which it deals'.[3] The attainment of the blessed community in which full-grown individuals find their perfect freedom is an adventure; progress towards it is neither automatic nor at any moment inevitable; but since God is Himself involved not as spectator or judge but as partner and guide, we can speak with a clearer conviction than Socrates 'The message of immortal hope',[4] καλὸν τὸ ἆθλον καὶ ἡ ἐλπὶς μεγάλη,[5] 'the adventure is noble and our hope is high'.

[1] I agree with Bishop E. W. Barnes, *Scientific Theory and Religion*, p. 522, 'In the end all attempts to take from God responsibility for the nature of His creatures must fail', but not with his estimate of the evolutionary process as non-moral.

[2] Such a contention is familiar to Russian Orthodox thought; cf. Dr D. M. Baillie *God Was in Christ*, p. 98.

[3] Dr D. M. Baillie, *op. cit.* p. 197.

[4] So A. E. Taylor, *Varia Socratica*, Epilogue.   [5] Plato, *Phaedo* 114 C.

VII

NATURE AND GOD

FOR any Christian interpretation of the Universe it is not sufficient to show that the familiar objections which we have been considering are not fatal. We must look at what St Paul did not hesitate to call the witness of creation,[1] and see how far the new concepts supplied by the sciences are compatible with traditional beliefs. The contrast between new and old is manifest.

Three hundred years ago in Western Europe every educated man from Thomas Hobbes to Robert Boyle and from John Milton to Isaac Newton would have agreed that creation was an event taking place at a fixed and calculable date some 4000 years before Christ; that at that date and, as most supposed, in the autumn of the year the earth gave birth to its plants and trees, its fishes and birds, its reptiles and mammals, each as we still know it,[2] and that when all was complete man was made and supplied with a mate. As we have seen, this picture persisted well on into the nineteenth century—though by then knowledge of the story of the rocks and the age of the earth was well established. Until the Darwinian controversy it is probably true that public opinion generally still regarded creation as an act and the appearance of new species as in some sense a renewal of it. Evolution was in the air; the evidence for it was available and obvious; but its acceptance was only effected by the publication of the *Origin of Species*.[3]

---

[1] As evidence not of God's existence but of certain aspects of His nature; cf. J. Baillie, *Our Knowledge of God*, p. 126.

[2] One of the strongest arguments against the organic origin of fossils was the belief that God could not have allowed any one of his works to perish; cf., for instance, J. Ray, *Observations* (1673), pp. 113–31.

[3] So even Samuel Butler, Darwin's life-long critic; cf. *Life and Habit*, p. 277.

It is unnecessary here to repeat the story of the development of evolutionary theory—of the narrowing of Darwinism by Weismann and others so as to eliminate the Lamarckian elements which Darwin had inserted and strengthened, of the formulation of the Mendel-De Vries alternative to Natural Selection by stress upon genetics and the appearance of large-scale mutations, of the continuous production and abandonment of neo-Lamarckian evidence, and of the replacement of Huxley's 'gladiatorial' picture of the struggle for existence by concepts of survival as due to the whole life-effort, psychic as well as physical, social as much as individual. The rise and fall of hypotheses and the movement of opinion among scientists have been full of interest and deserve close attention. However, it is not only in Russia that a connexion between biological theory and political attachment can be demonstrated: we have noted that Malthus can be regarded as the ancestor through Darwin and Galton of the Nordic doctrines of Nazism and equally through Ricardo and Marx of the economic determinism of the Communists; Lysenko as an example of such connexion does not stand alone.

At the present time the position is by no means clear. Evolution as a demonstrable and omnipresent characteristic of life on the earth stands secure. Creation, as we can know it, is a process not an act, continuous not complete. God is not to be pictured as sculptor or watchmaker, nor as interfering in the realm of nature and history from outside it, nor to be fitted into the gaps left by natural events. He is at once universal Being, the one subject beyond all predicates or objectification, and also, if there is any validity in religious experience or any integrative connexion between the eternal and the phenomenal, He is the source and agent of all that is; and yet also, if space-time is to have any meaning or events in it to be more than illusory, random and kaleidoscopic, He is the inward *nisus* or urge whose significance it discloses and whose purpose it fulfils. To admit the impossibility of establishing any objective knowledge of the universal subject can only lead to agnosticism, or to an arbitrary and baseless acceptance of a revelation which leaves the whole secular realm meaningless and profane. Only a thoroughgoing belief that 'the things that are made'[1] do, in spite of the Fall and its consequences, manifest the true nature of their Maker can give any foundation for a reasonable faith. Seen at its most revelatory in the personality of the perfect Son of Man the natural order should supply us with a satisfying image of the invisible.[2] We have seen that the whole sequence of our experience as this ranges over the field of creation, redemption and sanctification seems coherent and congruous; that the world of nature and history can interpret and be interpreted by the person and work of Christ; that natural theology and the Christian religion are not necessarily incompatible. Does the study of the creative process from the standpoint of the scientist refute or validate such a hypothesis?

Evolution is demonstrable: its method, though less uncertain now than some few years ago, is by no means generally agreed. Few of us who once defended the common-sense belief, that to some degree at least acquired characteristics must be inheritable, can have found it easy to ignore the constant disappointments which have arisen from ill-observed or ill-interpreted observations and sometimes from less excusable sources. That the Weismannist objection based upon the total isolation of the germplasm can no longer be accepted as final,[3] and that a Lamarckian theory seems congruous with the general character of development, may be freely admitted: the influence of environment is obvious and may eventually be so restated as to find a place in a final interpretation.[4] But at present Lamarckianism is not proven nor in its traditional form probable. What is clear is that the interaction between the organism and its environment is very much closer and more subtle than biologists have until recently recognized; that mere study of physiology in a laboratory or of psychology

[1] Cf. Rom. i. 19, 20.

[2] It is notable that St Paul couples this phrase with the words 'firstborn of all creation' in his description of Christ, Col. i. 15.

[3] It has never been fully accepted by botanists, and now appears to be not universal in zoology; cf. E. S. Russell, *Interpretation of Development and Heredity*, pp. 291–3.

[4] The botanical evidence for the inheritance of modifications due to environment, e.g. prostrate growth in maritime ecotypes, is plainly demonstrated; cf. G. Turesson, *Hereditas*, III, pp. 211–350.

in cages or mazes is insufficient; and that if we are to interpret evolution we must obtain much fuller knowledge of the living creature in its natural setting and relationships. Too many of the data on which theories have been based have been derived from speculation upon museum-specimens rather than from observation of life in the field. With such observation we may well discover that, though acquired characteristics are not immediately inherited, they at least modify the way of life, promote the survival and thus influence the evolution of the species; and moreover, as expounded in the theory of organic selection,[1] may well have a direct influence within the organism itself.

The position of the mutationist hypothesis is more doubtful. Until recently, while it was assumed that each Mendelian factor was represented by a separate gene, it was easy to suppose that by gene-change, whether in a single factor or simultaneously in a large number, practically all hereditable variation could be explained; that sexual reproduction by recombining the genes gave continual opportunity for the appearance of fresh syntheses; and that the chief problem was the analysis and control of the causes of gene-change. Now this picture of a very large number of independent genes has been replaced by a recognition of the relatedness and mutual interaction of the whole gene-complex; but in spite of this it is maintained that large-scale changes by mutation are, if not impossible, at least exceedingly unusual—too rare to account for the amount of evolutionary change within the available time-span.[2] It is difficult for one who is not competent to estimate the value and completeness of the elaborate data upon which this conclusion is based to appreciate its strength, especially as there seems no evidence that variation and natural selection can in fact produce large differences any more easily or rapidly. But,

[1] For this cf. C. Lloyd Morgan, *Animal Behaviour* (London, 1900), p. 115, and J. M. Baldwin, *Development and Evolution* (New York, 1902).

[2] So, for example, T. Dobzhansky, *Genetics and the Origin of Species*, p. 223, rejects altogether the sudden appearance of new species by gene-mutation. This 'universal negative' is based upon two arguments in ch. III of his book, that mutation rates are known and always slow, and that whereas for a new species many gene-changes are requisite each such change is independent and random. Neither of these is demonstrated: instead he emphasizes the obscurity, variety and incompleteness of the evidence.

among zoologists at any rate, Darwinian rather than Mendelian views are at the moment fashionable. A botanist can only observe that in particular geographical areas there are genera, mainly apomictic in their reproduction, as in Britain *Hieracium*, *Rosa* and *Rubus* which display extreme variability; that they are obviously both adaptable and vigorous; and that neither the causes nor the significance of their variations, though theoretically explicable, seem as yet to be satisfactorily understood;[1] and that it is difficult not to believe that such instability must play a more important part in evolution than zoologists are ready to allow.[2] He will also wish to investigate the problems arising out of the remarkable fecundity and 'success' of allopolyploid hybrids like the familiar grass *Poa annua*,[3] the very recent invader of our mud-flats, *Spartina Townsendii*,[4] and the cornfield Labiate, *Galeopsis tetrahit*.[5]

It is perhaps permissible to conjecture that the gene-complex in the chromosome behaves in a manner similar to that of the atomic complex in the molecule. There, in the highly elaborate molecules which constitute the chemical compounds essential to the discharge of the vital processes of the organism, there is evidence of a correlation, control and sequence of change which may have to be explained in terms of organic design.[6] A similar correlation seems plainly manifest in the order and the simultaneity with which changes affecting the whole system and functioning of the organism take place. That genes are interconnected, so that a

[1] The fullest account in English seems to be G. L. Stebbins, *Variation and Evolution in Plants* (New York, 1950), and for details A. Gustafsson, *The Genesis of the European Black-berry Flora* (1943) and E. B. Babcock and G. L. Stebbins, *The American Species of 'Crepis'*, pp. 44–68. Though the main lines of the problem seem clearly traced, there are many points of detail and one or two larger issues on which the British evidence is not easily reconcilable. Nor does the disputable evidence on the *Rosa canina* group seem consistent with the interpretation of that on *Rubus*.

[2] See Note x below, p. 215.

[3] This is now thought to be a hybrid between *Poa infirma* and *P. supina*.

[4] A hybrid first appearing on Southampton Water between the native *S. stricta* and the American introduction *S. alterniflora*.

[5] Apparently a hybrid between *G. pubescens* and *G. speciosa*: so A. Müntzing in G. L. Stebbins, *op. cit.* p. 299.

[6] I borrow this term from a paper to the British Association, 9 August 1951, by Dr C. F. A. Pantin; cf. *The Advancement of Science*, no. xxx.

mutation in one of them has far-reaching consequences upon the whole complex, may involve not only that large-scale alterations are normally difficult to imagine, but that under particular conditions the interconnexion itself enables the co-ordination of changes as far-reaching as the appearance of new types. Any theory which leaves no room for such large-scale correlation has to face difficulties which the Neo-Darwinians dismiss far too lightly. It has always been enormously difficult to maintain, for example, that the primitive bird *Archaeopteryx* had been evolved at random and by the requisite astronomical number of variations, each by itself a hindrance, which gradually transformed arms into wings, provided a sternal keel and girdle, the aeration of bones and skin-sacs, the warm blood, the feathers, and all the essential modifications of reptilian structure.[1] It is not made easier by the absence of the myriad missing links of which geology should give evidence.

But if most zoologists minimize the effect of mutations and so agree that natural selection remains the most satisfactory hypothesis, they hasten to explain that they now put a different interpretation upon it. When first propounded, it was the struggle for existence that dominated the whole picture: the victim found itself in an environment to which it was imperfectly adapted and surrounded by its rivals and foes; its life was conditioned by conflict. Now we take into account the congruity of the organism to its world, the supple adjustment between them, the element of purpose unconscious or conscious in the adaptation of means to ends, and the development of perception, of behaviour patterns and social habits: the efficacy of such factors not only in sifting out the unfit but in promoting and developing fitness looms much larger than struggle in the story of selection. It is not true to say that the creature determines its own fate; but neither is it true to treat it as a helpless and predestined victim: its survival depends not only upon the accident of circumstances, but upon the quality

[1] For the adaptation of birds for flight, cf. D'Arcy Thompson, *Growth and Form*, pp. 961–71. For the difficulty of explaining its evolution, the speculations discussed by B. W. Tucker in his essay in *Evolution* (Oxford, 1938) are proof enough.

of its own responses to them; existence is less like a struggle than an adventure; the way to succeed is to live to the full. On the average, and as statistically tested, the course of evolution favours the sensitive, the swift-moving and swift-minded, the best equipped representatives of the species. The world is so ordered that life and life more abundant prevails in it.

So far most biologists were prepared to go when the exaggeration of the gladiatorial concept of nature was abandoned. The coming of an increasing recognition of the element of design both in organism and in environment has inevitably raised the question whether we can be content to formulate our conclusion 'the world is so formed' merely in terms of a consecutive clause: is not the evidence such as to encourage, indeed to compel, us to replace 'so that' by 'in order that'? Has not the time come to remind ourselves that whereas most writers suppose that Darwin overthrew teleology, the ablest of his contemporaries insisted that he had vindicated it?[1] Whatever we decide about that question, it is at least important that the mass of research which lies behind it, some of it very recent and very striking, should be fully considered.

Take first the problem of design in the organism itself. Ever since D'Arcy Thompson published his *Growth and Form* there has been available a vast collection of examples of the correlation of size and shape to use and function, much of it so intricate and exquisite as to defy any reasonable possibility that it is the result of random variations sifted by natural selection. Dr C. F. A. Pantin has described one such, the siliceous skeleton of the Sponge, *Euplectella aspergillum*. It lives in the Pacific and at a depth so great as to necessitate a structure at once rigid and light and designed to withstand not only direct pressure but the powerful twisting of oceanic currents; and its cylindrical framework braced by hoops and strengthened by a spiral network of lighter ties 'recalls the geodetic construction familiar to aeroplane designers'.[2] A somewhat different type of case, in which the structure of a Tunicate

---

[1] Cf. T. H. Huxley in *Life of C. Darwin*, II, p. 201, and Asa Gray, *ibid.* III, p. 189.
[2] Cf. C. F. A. Pantin, 'Organic Design', in *The Advancement of Science*, no. XXX, p. 2.

was modified by adaptation to its environment, has been reported to me and is highly significant.[1]

A similar instance of a somewhat different order can be studied by anyone, namely the design and construction of its web by the common Diadem Spider (*Epeira diademata*).[2] Some years ago my friend Dr G. T. Bennett, the stereometrician and inventor whose help as a mathematical expert and a first-rate observer is acknowledged by D'Arcy Thompson,[3] described to me in great detail the perfection of the whole process: the choice of the site and planning of the periphery, then the commencement within it of the web proper, the measuring off and laying down of the main radii, the insertion of symmetrical subsidiary radii, and finally the filling up of the connecting lines linking them together. He declared that both in the quality of its pattern and in the economy and ingenuity of its construction it was an *opus perfectum*, such as no geometer however expert could improve upon: indeed, over some of the details like the technique of the bridging he, a man not given to easy praise, became almost lyrical in his admiration. Yet he insisted that outside the sequence of web-making the spider gave no sign of skill: repairs to the web were botched as badly as a man's darning of a sock; and any unusual situation was met by wild and haphazard thread-laying. 'It is impossible', he said, 'for anyone who has watched the work for many hours to have any doubt that neither the present Spiders of this species nor their ancestors were ever the architects of the web or that it could conceivably have been produced step by step through random variation: it would be as absurd as to suppose that the intricate and exact proportions of the Parthenon were produced by piling together random bits of marble.'[4]

[1] Cf. Note XI of two relevant cases by H. J. Buchanan-Wollaston, below, p. 216.

[2] There is a careful but not quite complete account of the web-making in E. Nielsen, *The Biology of Spiders*, pp. 161–70, and in R. W. G. Hingston, *Problems of Instinct and Intelligence*, pp. 47–52; for a bibliography of the subject up to 1939, cf. P. Bonnet, *Bibliog. Araneorum* (1941).

[3] Cf. *Growth and Form* (Cambridge, 1942), Prefatory Note, and for Bennett's description of the Spider, my book *The Creator Spirit*, pp. 88–9.

[4] For a suggestion of the influence of a 'common subconscious' cf. Whateley Carington, *Telepathy*, p. 160 and Prof. A. C. Hardy in *Journal of the Society for Psychical Research*, XXXV, p. 235.

The problem is difficult enough when a single series of events, be it the structure of the eye[1] or the construction of the spider's web, is in question. It becomes enormously more inexplicable on the traditional lines of random variation and natural selection when we consider the cases in which an exact sequence of such events, each indispensable to the final result and each necessarily appearing at its precise place in relation to the others, has to be enacted. In such cases if there is not to be disaster there must be an interlocked and concurrent performance of a number of distinct operations. Often these have no obvious connexion or affinity. Yet each must play its part at the right moment or else the whole elaborate result is frustrated. The odds against any one of them occurring by accident are so remote as to make any theory of chance highly precarious; against their simultaneous accomplishment, the odds are astronomical. Yet such cases are in fact frequent whether we are considering questions of chemical functioning,[2] of compound organic structure,[3] or of complex behaviour. They cannot be ignored by anyone who is seriously concerned with the interpretation of nature.

A familiar example, already cited for the moral problem that it raises, and illustrating this interdependence or simultaneity can be found in the parasitism of the Common Cuckoo (*Cuculus canorus*). Darwin claimed that a preliminary stage towards a similar habit could be found in the North American Cowbird (*Molothrus ater*)[4] and a few other species. But in fact our Cuckoo is unique; and for the success of its performance a sequence of at least five distinct events, outside the run of normal behaviour and structure, has to take place. First, in order that the small foster-mother may

---

[1] The case which Darwin confessed gave him 'a cold shudder', cf. *Origin of Species* (6th ed.), pp. 145–56; *Life and Letters*, II, pp. 273–85. For a full account, cf. Sir Charles Sherrington, *Man on His Nature* (Cambridge, 1940), pp. 121–30.

[2] Cf. Prof. A. R. Todd as to the sequence and control of the changes in his address to the International Chemical Conference, New York, 1951.

[3] Cf. C. F. A. Pantin, *loc. cit.* pp. 10–12. It is disappointing that such cases are not discussed in detail by those who reject all evidence for design, e.g. by G. G. Simpson, *The Meaning of Evolution*, pp. 168–75 on photoreceptors and eyes.

[4] The cowbirds belong to a different order (Passeres), from the Cuckoos (Coccyges). The behaviour of *Molothrus* cannot represent a step in evolution towards that of *Cuculus*.

incubate it, the Cuckoo's egg has to be tiny—hardly larger than the Hedge-sparrow's or Meadow Pipit's in whose nest it is deposited. Then it must hatch some thirty-six hours before the others, so that the chick may secure all the food that comes to the nest and with it may grow from its birth-weight of four grammes to nearly twelve; so its incubation period must be abnormally short. Then the mother Cuckoo must lay her egg before the foster-parent begins to sit; if she deposits it after incubation has begun, it will not get this necessary start, and the chick will starve. Then in order to maintain this rate of growth it must get rid of the other occupants of the nest: its own share of the food is not enough to produce out of an egg the size of a sparrow's a bird the size of a pigeon. To accomplish this it must have a structure capable of ejecting eggs or nestlings. It has a wide and curiously hollowed back, a relatively long neck and legs, and wings which can be raised and held stiff so as to fence in and keep from slipping whatever is resting on the hollow of its back. Finally there is the technique of ejection. This is simple: the Cuckoo is hungry and restless: weighing three times as much as the other chicks it sinks to the bottom of the nest, squeezing them against its sides. Sooner or later one of them rolls on to the Cuckoo's back. At once, as soon as the back is touched, a characteristic act takes place: the Cuckoo drops its beak on to the nest-bottom, and splays its legs against it, and with this three-fold support lifts its back and the burden upon it. It then manoeuvres until its tail is wedged against the nest-wall at its lowest place,[1] throws back its wings to prevent a slip; keeps its shoulders well up so that its back slopes downwards, and continues to lift itself until the tail passes the rim of the nest. Then there is a backward heave and the burden is thrown off and outside the nest. The Cuckoo stands motionless for a moment; then its taut limbs relax, and it sinks down into a restless, blind, bald nestling. As it has been photographed while ejecting her young from beneath a sitting mother[2] without

---

[1] This detail is in accordance with my observations but may not be invariable.
[2] A cinematographic record of such an ejection from under a hen Redstart was made by my friend, the late Adolf Burdet, in Holland.

arousing in her any effort to rescue them, it is obvious that here as elsewhere the species victimized seems to acquiesce in the parasite's action.

It will be seen that each one of this sequence of conditions is essential to the success of the whole. Yet each by itself is useless. The whole *opus perfectum* must have been achieved simultaneously. The odds against the random occurrence of such a series of co-incidences are, as we have already stated, astronomical. Nor could a single accidental performance if it should happen establish any guarantee of its fixation and repetition. This last consideration is one to which the advocates of randomness have paid insufficient attention.

Until recently scientists, accepting the Cartesian dualism, con-fining their studies to the quantitative and mechanistic, and claiming that these limited results represented the supreme achieve-ment in man's interpretation of the universe, dismissed the evidence for design in nature on the ground that natural selection by perfecting the adaptation of the organism to its environment simulated a manifestation of purpose. Perfection of structure and pattern was reached by the elimination of those individuals and species which did not possess them; the normal standard once attained was transmitted by the appropriate genes. Those who objected were browbeaten by loud talk about mechanism and pseudo-teleology or confronted by the insistence that the only alternatives were a mysterious life-force or an intervening deity.[1]

In the last twenty years a remarkable change has been coming over the scene, and this is still so unfamiliar and in any case so important as to deserve more detailed notice.[2]

In 1932 C. S. Myers, one of the pioneers of comparative psychology and a man of outstanding ability and range of

---

[1] So, for example, H. G. Wells, Julian Huxley and G. P. Wells, *The Science of Life*, pp. 334–7; T. H. Morgan, *The Scientific Basis of Evolution*, pp. 218–54; more recently G. G. Simpson, *The Meaning of Evolution*, pp. 271–5.

[2] Of the general problem, the best discussion known to me is that by Dr Agnes Arber, *The Natural Philosophy of Plant Form*, pp. 199–211, for which cf. Vol. I of this book, p. 18. There is an excellent treatment of the case for a teleological order in G. F. Stout, *Mind and Matter*. Of French work I can only here refer to Ch. Eug. Guye, *L'Évolution physico-chimique*.

interests, in his Hobhouse Memorial Lecture repudiated the whole Cartesian body-mind position, insisted that mental activity and living bodily activity are identical,[1] and drew attention to what he called the 'directiveness' of vital processes from the level of embryonic development to that of consciously purposed behaviour He was followed in 1934 by Dr E. S. Russell in an address to the Zoology Section of the British Association on 'The Study of Behaviour'. Russell had already published an integrative or organismal theory in *The Interpretation of Development and Heredity*,[2] and has since amplified his treatment in a series of papers to the Linnean Society and in his book *The Directiveness of Organic Activities*.[3] He has here collected and arranged a large number of examples chosen from a very wide range of organic life in order to demonstrate 'the existence and importance of directive activity in the restoration of norms and the satisfaction of needs through behavioural, morphoplastic and physiological means which are functionally equivalent'.[4] From the healing of wounds to the regulation of the production of red blood corpuscles and to the balancing of the diet, and from the complicated process by which the Rhabdocoele *Microstoma* equips itself with penetrant and uniformly distributed nematocysts[5] to the equally complicated process of continuous oviposition induced in many species of bird by the stimulus of a defective clutch,[6] there is a mass of evidence irreconcilable with the traditional mechanistic hypothesis. Rejecting the Cartesian dichotomy as applied to biological problems Russell sums up his concept of the living organism by stating that its primary characteristics are the directive, creative and orderly nature of its activities in relation to maintenance, reproduction and development and to the completion of the normal life cycle primary conditions of existence are the preservation of structuro-

---

[1] *The Absurdity of any Mind-body Relation*, p. 6; he insisted that direction and purpose were universal but that in the living universe they are largely individual, in the lifeless universe only external—responsible for the history, order and evolution ultimately of both universes (p. 27).

[2] Published at Oxford, 1930. [3] Published at Cambridge, 1946.

[4] *The Directiveness of Organic Activities*, p. 80.

[5] *Ibid.* pp. 23–7, quoting W. A. Kepner, *Animals looking into the Future* (New York 1925). [6] *Ibid.* pp. 115–18, quoting my *John Ray*.

unctional wholeness or normality and integral adaptation to environment.[1] It is noticeable that in spite of his criticism of Descartes he preserves a sharp distinction between the organic and the inorganic, and does not look for or suggest any analogy between the metabolism of the living plant or animal and the chemical and physical changes that take place in the world of matter.

In this broad respect, as in many of its details, Russell's contention is expanded by the very similar work set out by Professor W. E. Agar of Melbourne in his important volume *A Contribution to the Theory of the Living Organism*. His own modesty, the time and circumstances of the book's publication, and the extent to which a shallow neo-Darwinianism dominates public opinion on the subject have combined to give this work much less influence than it deserves. But both biologically and philosophically it shows a range of knowledge, a power of thought and a wisdom of interpretation of a high order. Agar takes Whitehead's philosophy of organism as his chief guide, deals very thoroughly with the evolution of perception and its relationship to behaviour and with embryology and the building-up of the organism, and reaches a statement in terms which recognize the continuity of the whole creative process, the identity of that process with experience, and of all experience with some measure of consciousness.[2] Creativity and purpose are characteristic of the whole sequence of events.[3]

It must be confessed that in most of these recent interpretations the precise significance of creativity is not very clearly defined. Dr Agar differs from Russell and others[4] because he seems prepared to accept a panpsychist position in regard to the whole physical realm. But he does not raise the question of the relationship

---

[1] *Ibid.* p. 190. Cf. the three conclusions put forward by A. E. Boycott in 1929 in his presidential address to the Pathological Section of the Royal Society of Medicine: '(1) Structure is the hand-maid of function; (2) the organism works as a whole; (3) ends are more important than means', *Proc. Roy. Soc. Med.* XXIII (i), p. 23.

[2] For a brief summary cf. *A Contribution to the Theory of the Living Organism*, pp. 90–1.

[3] In his introduction (pp. 20–2), Agar makes it clear that he ascribes perception, causation and purpose to cells as well as to organisms.

[4] I am thinking of papers like Sir R. A. Fisher's Eddington Memorial Lecture, *Creative Aspects of Natural Law* and W. H. Thorpe, *Evolution and Christian Belief*.

of the Central Agent in the organism to a Central Agent in the universe; nor is it always easy to discern whether he rejects all 'body-mind' dualism when he speaks of a psycho-physical system and if so how far he has freed himself from its implications.

More recently it has been recognized that the evidence of design is not confined to organisms but can be found in the atomic structure of protein molecules where chain arrangements are discernible[1] and in the arrangement and control of the chemical elements out of which organisms are composed. Dr C. F. A. Pantin, whose recent paper on Organic Design to the Zoology Section of the British Association in Edinburgh 1951 we have already quoted, has drawn together and summarized a mass of details amplifying the constructional principles stated and discussed by D'Arcy Thompson, and showing that in fact the number of substances suitable for physical functioning is very limited and that some of the most specialized of them, for example, acetylcholine essential for the transmission of nervous impulses, haemoglobin for carrying oxygen, and the chain molecules of fibrous proteins for muscular contraction, have been developed and used by widely differing phyla of living creatures.

That these highly complex molecules should be evolved independently and at random again and again by any conceivable system of natural selection so as to become available for the vital functions which they alone can make possible is a suggestion which scarcely deserves mention. The theory so frequently put forward by popular exponents of natural selection, that 'man is the result of a purposeless and materialistic process',[2] that all is fortuitous until his emergence and that purpose first appears with him—a crude restatement of the Cartesian hypothesis—was always open to insuperable objections and must now be abandoned. Rather we must conclude with Professor J. D. Bernal that 'possibilities of order and function are immanent in the structure of the molecules themselves'[3] and with Dr Pantin that throughout

---

[1] Recent research in bio-physics here and in America makes this more than probable.

[2] G. G. Simpson, *The Meaning of Evolution*, p. 344.

[3] Cf. *The Physical Basis of Life*, p. 22.

he whole process in addition to natural selection there is 'an
abstract plan' manifested in the unique properties of matter and
energy and the substances in which they are expressed, and that
these substances constitute the available materials from which
living organisms draw the constituents of the structures necessary
for their functioning. How limited are the materials and how
similar the use made of them by widely different and obviously
not genetically connected creatures can be proved by a mass of
recent research;[1] and as we have seen analogies have been noted
between the mammalian brain and the electronic calculating
machine, especially in relation to the predictor mechanism which
makes possible deliberately purposive behaviour.[2]

From all of which, be it positive or negative,[3] it seems that the
old Mechanist-Vitalist alternative has become an anachronism[4]—
that we must realize that mechanism always involves purpose and
design and that Vitalism does not imply an external control
intruded into the evolutionary process. Creativity is expressed in
the properties and functioning of the elements themselves, atom,
molecule, mass; cell, structure, organism. In each and all is a
potential causality; and this, as Dr Fisher has shown,[5] is itself
creative. Probably when biologists have grown out of the fear of
being accused of following Lamarck or Bergson they will be less
anxious to insist that they are good neo-Darwinians.[6] Certainly
as the dualism of body and mind is abandoned most of the old
categories will be rejected as irrelevant, since they depend upon

[1] Pantin refers particularly to B. B. Boycott and J. Z. Young in *Soc. Exp. Biol. Symposium*, no. IV, pp. 432–53, on the similarity of nerve-networks and of behaviour (learning and perception) between octopus and vertebrate, and the complete difference of brain structure.

[2] Cf. N. Wiener, *Cybernetics*, pp. 137–55; and above, p. 50.

[3] See Note XII below, p. 218, on the evidence of Sir C. Sherrington.

[4] Yet so recent an authority as G. G. Simpson, *The Meaning of Evolution* (Yale, 1949), while professing to reject the old antithesis, constantly falls back into it; cf. his treatment of E. S. Russell, p. 127, where he says in effect 'you are not a Mechanist, therefore you must be a Vitalist: there is no alternative'. For a similar inconsistency in his thinking, cf. W. H. Thorpe, *Evolution and Christian Belief*, p. 12. Similar inconsistencies abound in the treatment of evolutionary theory by Dr Julian Huxley, cf. Thorpe, *ibid.* p. 13.

[5] *Creative Aspects of Natural Law*, passim.

[6] In their insistence on organism and purpose, their repudiation of materialism and determinism, they are far nearer to Lamarck than to the neo-Darwinians.

antitheses which will then have disappeared. We shall be thinking in terms of a single but pluralistic[1] universe in which psycho-physical organisms at different levels of development constitute a community held together by their relationship to a single integrative reality, fulfilling in spite of, or rather by reason of their individual activities a common intention, and when conditions are appropriate to it giving occasion for the appearance of the novel and unprecedented. We shall have realized the truth of Dean Matthews's wise words that 'The phrase "emergent evolution" is a transparent disguise for the idea of immanent teleology'.[2]

This idea of teleology obviously differs from that which Darwin is credited with having destroyed. It does not involve or suggest the watchmaker or the magician or a series of intrusive acts,[3] nor is it inconsistent with the operation of natural selection. It emphasizes the orderly sequence of events in the cosmos and the continuity and consistency of the creative process. It is compatible with the theism disclosed in religious experience, with the biblical attitude towards 'the works of the Lord', and with Christ's revelation of God in His relation to His creatures. What it suggests is that the ineffable whose presence we encounter in our moments of rapture is also discoverable in the texture of the universe as the *nisus* of its causality, the principle not only of its continuity but of its emergent novelty; and if so that ultimately process and reality, the time-space world and the eternal, express one and the same being. The fact that process discloses evidence of the fulfilment of purpose and also of freedom in its creatures distinguishes such a conviction from pantheism or acosmism; on this showing God is not identical with the Universe though He is its ground and source, manifested in its design and active in its operations.

---

[1] It is at least doubtful whether the ancient problem of the one and the many can be resolved at our present level without either denying the reality of process or disintegrating it.

[2] W. R. Matthews, *The Purpose of God*, p. 91.

[3] That the inventor, unlike the mechanic or engineer, is in a real sense 'indwelling' in and thus gestating his invention has been freely and authoritatively stated; this may suggest an analogy for a restated theology.

Such a process, so far as we on this earth can estimate its character, involves a hierarchy of physical events, capable of variation within strict limits and of giving rise under exceptional conditions to organisms manifesting the properties of life. These conditions are not at present reproducible by us, but it is a mistake to assume that they indicate what used to be called 'a special creation' or even a sudden and dramatic break in the series.

It is worth notice how much in the past fifty years the gaps in that series have been filled up. In the physical field the discovery of the nature and structure of the atom, the mapping and synthesizing of molecules, the disclosure by the electronic microscope of the non-filterable viruses, and the narrowing of the gulf that once separated the inorganic from the organic, have made a theory of panpsychism, or at least of the continuity and congruity of the natural order, plausible if not probable. In the psychic we have seen the former antithesis between various types of behaviour, reflex and conscious, determinate and free, tropism and autonomy, instinct and intelligence, diminished almost to the point of being resolved; and instead we have come to realize that the primitive, generalized or coenaesthetic perception, though split up into and supplemented by the activity of the separate senses, yet persists and plays a part in the normal functioning of mankind. In both physical and psychic fields we are being compelled to recognize that the minute analysis and segregation of functions, useful as it has been for purposes of description and classification, has been too often arbitrary in its methods and misleading in its conclusions; that the physiology which cut up the human being into systems, respiratory, digestive and the rest, is hardly more obsolete than the psychology which treated him as a bundle of instincts; and that the familiar dualisms of body and soul, physical and psychic, natural and supernatural are themselves becoming anachronisms. Indeed, the argument that there is in all nature a holistic principle[1] enabling both the highest development of the individual parts and their full co-operation in an ordered society seems to apply to every level from the atom to the saint; to do justice both to the

[1] For this cf. J. C. Smuts, *Holism and Evolution* and Note XIII below, p. 218.

element of continuity and to the emergence of novelty in the process; and to be congruous with the conviction that there is a hierarchy of events which finds its consummation in such a community of free individuals as could properly be called at the human level the Body of Christ and beyond it the Kingdom (or Family) of God.

We shall consider the theological significance of evolution in the next chapter when we discuss the problems of divine immanence. On the biological side the evidence for continuity, creativity and design, if taken in connexion with the data already examined from the religious experience of mankind, is compatible with an interpretation of the Godhead which Christians will recognize. It suggests the theory that there is in the whole evolutionary process a purposive urge promoting not only larger ranges of activity, fuller individuation and ultimately the emergence of personality, but a harmony in diversity, the gradual fulfilment of a plan, the integration of the several elements of the design into a complex and inclusive pattern. If this be granted, then such a pattern presupposes a model or archetype, as its 'great original' and consummation, who expresses in all its fulness the character and intention of the whole. It is legitimate and, as we have urged, necessary to associate this cosmic purpose with the infinite Being whom we encounter in our moments of fullest experience and whom the mystics and saints have made known.

This threefold hypothesis is plainly consonant with the belief that there are three modes of being in the deity, God experienced as the source and ground of all existence, God manifested in the creation and development of the universe, the educative Logos of the Greek Fathers, and God immanent in His creatures as 'lifegiver' and inspiration. The only difference between such a statement and the orthodox Christian doctrine of the Trinity is one of language; and this disappears as soon as it is recognized that 'person' in exact and careful theology does not mean and has never meant individual, nor has it implied personality in our human sense; that even if there be, as some have claimed, a 'social element' in the deity,[1] yet tritheism is always a distortion and usually a heresy; and that 'hypostasis', the term used in credal doctrine and traditionally translated 'person', can more correctly be rendered as 'permanent mode of being'. If this be understood, then we can see that the Nicene faith is not far from the theory that we have outlined, nor deserving of the criticism which it so frequently receives.

[1] For a clear statement of the two views (see Note XIV, below, p. 219) as set out, for example, by C. C. J. Webb, *God and Personality* and H. Wheeler Robinson, *The Christian Experience of the Holy Spirit*, cf. Dr L. Hodgson, *The Doctrine of the Trinity*, pp. 225–58 (though Dr Hodgson's own view seems to me very near to tritheism), and Dr D. M. Baillie, *God was in Christ*, pp. 133–40.

VIII

THE WORLD AND THE SPIRIT

THOSE Christians who have been concerned with the conflict between religion and science or even with the failure of Christianity to influence the modern world have for nearly a century pointed to one and the same defect in the presentation of the faith—to its wholly inadequate doctrine and experience of the Holy Spirit. In no other aspect of Christian thought is there so serious a difference between the religion of the New Testament and that of all subsequent ages; for in the New Testament, in the Acts and Epistles, it is precisely the presence of the Holy Spirit which determines membership in the Church and is the acknowledged source of the qualities, love, joy, peace, fortitude and the rest, which are the evidence of discipleship. In no other has there been so obvious and continuing a perversion; the gift of the Spirit, from being an abiding life 'in Christ' with God and the brethren, becomes in popular esteem first a talisman admitting to membership of the Church here and of heaven hereafter, and then a synonym for the privileges which the hierarchy is permitted to bestow, and finally a magical influence conveyed by the appropriate manual contact. If this be thought an exaggeration let the critic of it consider in the light of an honest valuation of human worth the argumentations of ecclesiastics about the fate of the unbaptized, the validity of sacraments and the doctrine of apostolic succession. For it is surely impossible to believe that anyone accustomed to weighing evidence can assert that all members of the Society of Friends are damned or even are outside the Church; that Presbyterian sacraments are not effective symbols and instruments of Christ's presence; and that the religious quality and destiny of Christians are conditional upon

148

the precise method by which the officers of the denomination to which they belong are chosen and consecrated. Yet all these contentions are logically inherent in Catholic orthodoxy.

And if it be urged in reply that in the course of the Church's growth it was inevitable that the personal devotion of its members 'in Christ' should be hardened into credal orthodoxy, and its spontaneity regulated by a return to the law, and its organic functioning handed over to a hierarchy, it is surely impossible without idolatry to maintain that these outward and visible signs are not merely the symbols and instruments of the Spirit but the essential constituents of His manifestation, the criteria of His presence, and the condition of His operation. If so, it would seem that the body is indeed a prison-house and tomb, and that we still wait for the resurrection.[1]

It is impossible for anyone who is concerned with the present position in religion not to speak plainly on this matter of truth and tradition. But to pursue it in detail would be to go beyond the scope of a Gifford Lectureship and is unnecessary for our present purpose.[2] That 'the Spirit' has been 'quenched' in the Church ever since the condemnation of Montanism; that the nature and functioning of the Spirit were never adequately discussed after the abandonment of the Logos-doctrine; that the operation of the Spirit contrary to the evidence of Scripture and the Nicene Creed[3] was restricted to the baptized and to ecclesiastical channels; and that any activity of the Spirit in nature or outside the Church is today disputed if not denied in orthodox circles;[4] these are conclusions which it is still difficult to challenge even in spite of a century of effort against them.

---

[1] A brilliant account of his own reaction to this formalizing of religion and a searching analysis and criticism of it are contained in Victor Gollancz, *My Dear Timothy*, I, pp. 108–11 and 125–8.

[2] The problem is vividly stated by R. Gardner in *Modern Churchman*, XLI, pp. 332–43, who takes Simone Weil and Albrecht Schweitzer as contemporary test cases, one unbaptized, the other unorthodox, yet both from any but the ecclesiastical standpoint manifestly saints.

[3] As now universally accepted in Christendom, not in its original form.

[4] This is the chief defect in Monsignor R. A. Knox, *Enthusiasm*; he cannot admit the presence of the Holy Spirit in Fox or Wesley—or the Montanists; similar denials are equally evident in Protestantism.

This neglect of experience and of doctrine is not due to lack of warning. When in 1873–6 H. B. Swete, afterwards Regius Professor of Divinity in Cambridge, wrote his first books on the subject,[1] he disclosed both the poverty of the Church's theology of the Holy Spirit and the importance and relevance of the problems connected with it. At the end of his life when he returned to it in his last two volumes, *The Holy Spirit in the New Testament* and *The Holy Spirit in the Early Church,* he stressed once more the need for further study; and if his own contribution was not conspicuous either for originality of treatment or breadth of interpretation,[2] at least his warnings should have been heeded. An important but somewhat conventional volume by H. Wheeler Robinson,[3] a Church Congress wholly devoted to the matter in 1926[4] and, more recently, considerable allusion to it in several books on exegetical and apologetic subjects, have emphasized the note of warning. But this has not led to anything of very serious significance. Those who have written on it while insisting upon the value of the doctrine have been chiefly concerned to confine its scope to limits compatible with the prevailing tendencies towards transcendentalism and pessimism.

Yet the need for it has obviously become more urgent with the years. It was always evident that a full and congruous doctrine of the Holy Spirit was an essential part of the structure of Christian theology, and an indispensable element in any coherent presentation of it. Unless stress is laid upon the creative energy of the Spirit in enabling the response of the creature, God's work as Creator becomes a mere operation from without, the task of a builder or an engineer. Unless the operation of the Spirit in the Incarnation is acknowledged and associated with the whole *praeparatio evangelica,* the birth of the Christ becomes merely the

[1] On the Early History of the Doctrine of the Holy Spirit and On the History of the Doctrine of the Procession of the Holy Spirit.

[2] In the second volume he ignored the basic problem of the relationship of the Spirit to the Logos.

[3] The Christian Experience of the Holy Spirit (London, 1928); the chapter that discusses the revelation of the Spirit in nature and history is suggestive but slight.

[4] Cf. The Spirit in Life and Thought, the papers read at this congress (London, 1927); and my account of it, The Eternal Spirit (London, 1926).

manifestation of a divine intruder without human kinship or affinity. Unless the indwelling of the Spirit completes the atoning work of Christ, Atonement becomes a magical gift which involves no real change in us, and no real oneness between us and God. Unless we are convinced that in some sense 'Every virtue we possess and every victory won And every thought of holiness are his alone', there can be no escape from Pelagianism and no Christian doctrine of man. Unless the whole divine activity is shared by each of the three Persons, the orthodox doctrine of the Trinity is endangered and tritheism becomes inevitable. Plainly we cannot imitate those whom St Paul found at Ephesus[1]—a group with many followers today—without gravely damaging the symmetry and completeness of the faith. Nor can we confine the Spirit's operation to the baptized or the converted, to the Church or the Churches without being guilty of the unforgivable sin which presumes to ascribe works of love and joy and peace to Beelzebub.[2]

Moreover, in the New Testament it is abundantly clear that the 'gift' of the Spirit is not only the end-product of the ministry of Jesus, but the criterion and hall-mark of membership in the Church. From the beginning of His teaching the intention of Jesus is best summarized in the utterance ascribed to Him in the Fourth Gospel, 'I am come that they might have life and that they might have it more abundantly';[3] in the selection and training of His apostles we see what significance the saying carries and how He set Himself to fulfil it. To quicken sensitiveness, to heighten vitality, to remove callousness and so to enable response to the beauty and meaning and worth of the world and a full reception of the divine inflowing—this is His first task. The range of His teaching and the patience with which He seeks for the growing-points in His hearers ('He that hath ears to hear, let him hear')[4] are characteristic of His whole approach to them; but He can use surgery as well as medicine and can on occasion challenge and rebuke in order to sting into life. If anyone denies that there is

[1] Acts xix. 2.
[2] Mark iii. 22–30.
[3] John x. 10 (A.V.) and above Ch. IV
[4] Mark iv. 9 (A.V.).

evidence of the Spirit's presence in nature he will find it difficult to explain how it is that Jesus, in bringing to life His disciples, uses not the Law and the Prophets but flowers and birds and little children, the sowing of a field, the growth of a tree, the leavening of bread and the daily work of men and women. If nature is, as Dr Barth insists, corrupt and meaningless, if natural theology is non-existent, it is strange that Jesus spent so much more time on it than on the subjects with which Christian preachers have since been usually concerned.

Beginning with the Spirit's presence in the simplest works of God, and leading His disciples from them to the unique revelation in Himself, He lets illumination produce its inevitable condemnation of His hearers' pride and sin. As they become responsive to the Spirit, so increasingly is their egotism disclosed and censured; discovering God they discover their own need, and nakedness and shame. With joy comes always humiliation, with exaltation abasement. When they are ready for it, they must be broken. Whoso loveth his life loseth it, whoso hateth his life-in-this-world, his surface sensuous life, keepeth it as life eternal,[1] *mors ianua vitae*.

This disclosure of sin in His teaching, which to Dr Barth is not only central but sole and unique, is in fact inexplicable on any incarnational principle unless it is preceded by and correlated with belief in the Spirit's presence in nature and man. For it is precisely because the disciple is given the revelation of God not only as the eternal opposite but as also the source of His own power to see and respond, that he discovers his estrangement and rebellion, and can be brought through failure to penitence. We can appreciate the significance of the Cross since we have already been led to the acknowledgment of Him who hangs on it. Only if we have caught a glimpse of Christ's Kingdom can we realize the monstrous iniquity that has denied and forsaken its King. Only because we know the earth to be so constituted that seeds grow in it, can we realize and ultimately accept and rejoice in the analogy between the Crucifixion and the corn of wheat that dies in order to bear fruit.[2] If in spite of their Master's teaching the disciples, even after

---

[1] Cf. John xii. 25. [2] John xii. 24.

His resurrection, still expected that God would act for them instead of acting in them,[1] and were inevitably rebuked for so doing, it is strange to find theologians of today repeating a similar error and affirming that we can acknowledge our emptiness although we have never known what it is to be filled. The process of illumination and judgment by which the disciples were prepared for Pentecost repeats the basic religious experience of adoration and abasement, and is effective just because in each moment the Holy Spirit is operative both by life imparted and by life laid down.

For those so disciplined there is individually and collectively the promise of power. The 'explosive event' which released the gathered energy may well have been the commission to teach all nations.[2] The sensitiveness which Jesus had imparted and trained came to its fulfilment as love cast out fear and enabled freedom. The vitality which He had inspired displayed itself in the revelation which changed history and in the passion and permanence of the Scriptures in which that revelation is described. Today and in spite of the scepticism of two centuries and the calamities of two world wars,[3] the inspiration abides and renews its influence in the succession of the saints; and the doctrine remains essential to Christendom and its first point of contact with the scientist and the philosopher.

If the doctrine was always essential, two recent developments of thought have made its recovery urgent. The first is our sense of the continuity and purpose of the creative process; the second is our concern with psychological and sociological analysis. The first links inspiration with creation: the second links it with incarnation.

Whatever be thought by the strict and conventional biologist of Bergson's *Creative Evolution* and the subsequent cult of the life-force, it was plainly a timely and brilliant attempt to lift the

[1] Acts i. 6–8.

[2] For the importance of such an event and the flash of insight that accompanies it, cf., for example, Sir J. Marchant, *A. R. Wallace*, I, p. 116 and Dr Rosamund E. W. Harding, *Towards a Law of Creative Thought* (London, 1936), pp. 139–63.

[3] It is a truism of neo-orthodoxy that in this period mankind has become secularized and progressively more sinful. For this, so far as we in this country are concerned, cf. the wise and well-informed opinion in B. S. Rowntree and G. R. Lavers, *English Life and Leisure*, especially pp. 366–74.

story of evolution out of the dreary materialism into which the later Darwinians had been forcing it. Here was an interpretation in organic terms which, if it did not wholly escape the charge of poetic personification in regard to the *élan vital*, at least accepted the testimony that 'one does not come by studying living things for a lifetime to suppose that physics and chemistry can account for them all'[1]—an interpretation which disclosed a remarkable analogy between the method and course of evolution and the operation of the Holy Spirit.[2] Here was abundant testimony to the element of purpose and successful striving in the advance of life such as is now fully recognized by exponents of natural selection: a record of a progress often obstructed and side-tracked, always conditional upon the ability of the organism to adapt itself to its environment, yet continually disclosing fresh marvels of exact and intricate achievement; a story in which the future seems to belong not to the predatory nor to the immune but to the sensitive who live dangerously. In his own inimitable style and with a mass of detail largely borrowed from the insect studies of Fabre, Bergson took up the interpretation of nature from the point at which Cudworth and Ray had left it; if he did not make an adequate allowance for the value of the intervening mechanistic period, his eminence as a philosopher and man of letters did much to convince the world that the confident materialism which dominated biological studies was incapable of explaining the behaviour or even the growth of insect, bird or mammal, let alone man. He was perhaps the first to show how readily scientists of repute could close their eyes and minds to facts which did not fit their theories, and to bring back into the study of nature the concept and language of creativity. What has happened since has, as we have seen, replaced his poetry by the prose of closer observation and more exact statement. Theology can safely take account of this when it resumes its task of interpreting nature and history in terms of the 'Acts of the Holy Ghost'.

[1] D'Arcy Thompson, *Growth and Form*, p. 14.
[2] This analogy was discussed in my chapter on the Holy Spirit contributed to *Faith and Freedom* (London, 1918).

So stated the position is open to immediate criticism. We shall be told that it merely applies the language of religion to the theories of the Vitalists, and baptizes the *élan de vie* or life-force with the name of the Holy Spirit. Such an objection would have much to support it, did it not suggest an acceptance of the dualism which Professor Ryle condemns by his gibe at 'the ghost in the machine'. It is difficult, as every theist knows, to avoid ascribing to God what the first of the Thirty-nine Articles explicitly denies to Him, 'body, parts, or passions'; for not only are the languages of the Bible lacking in any abstract vocabulary, but few of us can conceive and still fewer express extra-sensory events; and God, as Professor Tillich firmly insists, is properly beyond predicates and analogies. Nevertheless, it must be attempted.

We are not contending for the sort of overruling control suggested in the traditional teleology nor for the vitalistic element symbolized by breath or impulse, but for a quality inherent in the stuff of the universe, a creativity or *nisus* manifested in the whole and in every particular, a concreteness or holistic principle whose effect can be seen throughout the process of causation. At the very opening of the modern age Francis Bacon indicated a similar conviction in the famous passage in the section 'Silva Silvarum' of his *Natural History*: 'It is certain that all bodies whatsoever, though they have no sense, yet they have perception; for when one body is applied to another, there is a kind of election to embrace that which is agreeable, and to exclude or expel that which is ingrate;...sense is but a dull thing in comparison of it:...this perception is sometimes at a distance,...as when the loadstone draweth iron; or flame naphtha of Babylon....'[1] So he drew attention to the principle of attraction and repulsion, which operates in the whole universe and gives rise to the unity and diversity which was the basic problem for the thinkers of Greece, and to the individuality and community of our own social nexus. This principle, along with that which we know from its manifestations as value and describe in terms of beauty, truth and goodness, seems characteristic of the nature of things. Natural religion

---

[1] *Natural History*, IX, I, quoted by Whitehead, *Science and the Modern World*, pp. 60–1.

can hardly go further than to acknowledge them with what Samuel Alexander taught us to call 'natural piety' and to trace how from level to level of existence they attain fuller, more complex and more universal significance: they constitute for some of us the evidence for the immanence of the divine and illustrate for the Christian what he knows as 'the operation of the Holy Spirit'. In the light of them we may claim that it was a true instinct which led the early Greek Christians to describe the creative work of the divine Logos in terms, not of carpentry or engineering, but of education.

The objection that there is no specific assurance in Scripture of such an indwelling of the divine in the sub-human world is by no means established. The present exaggerated emphasis upon the total transcendence of God as wholly other than and estranged from His creation is reached by an ignoring of much of the evidence and by an ingenuity of exegesis in explaining away what cannot be ignored. As we have already shown, it is impossible to extract from Judaism or from St Paul[1] the dualistic determinism of Calvin and of Augustine's latest phase.[2] The Old Testament continuously appeals to 'the starry heavens above and the moral law within'[3] as declaring the 'glory' and nature of God; Jesus explicitly bases His gospel of God's Kingdom upon evidence and similitudes drawn from the natural order; the claim made for Him as the incarnate Lord involves the corollary that humanity is *capax deitatis*; the concept of the Church as the body of Christ affirms that an indwelling in mankind, individually and collectively, of the Spirit of God is integral to the divine purpose. That such indwelling is not conditioned by any ritual or moral condition that we can adjudicate upon is proved by the crucial case of Cornelius: 'Can any man forbid the water', said St Peter, 'that these should not be baptized', of alien race though they are, 'which have received the Holy Ghost as well as we.'[4] Nor is there at any point in the New Testament justification for the belief so often

---

[1] Cf. Vol. I of this book, ch. II.
[2] As shown in the *De Civ. Dei* and still more in the controversy with Julian of Eclanum.
[3] Nowhere more clearly than in Psalm xix.   [4] Acts x. 47 (R.V.).

ffirmed today that inspiration, the indwelling of the Spirit, and
ncarnation, the indwelling of the Son, belong to different levels
of religious reality: on the contrary 'I live; yet not I, but Christ
iveth in me'[1] is the proper Christian confession.

The fact is that if we are to see the creative process as a whole
and culminating for us in Christ we shall regard it as at every level
reflecting in its own measure something of the quality of deity:
rom atom and molecule to mammal and man each by its
appropriate order and function expresses the design inherent in it
and contributes, so far as it can by failure or success, to the fulfilment of the common purpose. We can refer to it in three main
errestrial phases, as a preparation for the organism, as a process of
organic individuation, as a culmination in a community of persons,
and can interpret these phases as due to the continuous *nisus* of the
indwelling Spirit. If so, then it is surely congruous that at a
definite stage in the process, as the partial reflexions of the divine
reach their human fulness, they should be consummated in the
perfect image of God; and that thus the goal of the whole adventure should be interpretable in terms of the attainment by mankind of its true stature and significance, the stature of the Christ
and the significance of the family of God. The cost of the process,
n terms of error and frustration, suffering and pain, sin and
rebellion, can only be appreciated by those who have themselves
experienced heartbreak and dereliction. Even for them the effort
o hold together a full acknowledgment of evil and a conviction
of the continuity and victory of good demands a range of
sensitiveness and a sense of proportion only attainable by the
saints. Those who have shared the Pauline experience and learned
that the true symbol of reality is neither power nor wisdom but
a Man on a Cross have a clue to the resolution of the paradox. If
Christ crucified be the one perfect manifestation of the Godhead
to us, then we shall expect to find foreshadowings of it at every
preliminary stage of the creative process. These will necessarily
be conditioned by the limitations of the level at which they are
disclosed: we cannot find in the star or the stone what we find in

[1] Gal. ii. 20 (A.V.).

the plant or the bird. Wheeler Robinson[1] is right in recognizing that this 'self-emptying' of the divine Spirit is a kenosis similar to that of the Word when he became flesh and dwelt among us.[2]

The second event which specially challenges Christians to examine and restate their doctrine of the Holy Spirit is the development of psychological and sociological studies. With the latter of these we shall be concerned when we consider the collective aspect of the Spirit's influence. The former, which for all its vagaries has given us new and revolutionary insights into the character of what is conventionally called the soul, indeed into the whole of our human nature and relationships, affects the whole field of knowledge and of experience. In previous chapters we have discussed this field in some detail, but plainly the precise problem as to what is meant by inspiration must be considered if we are to discuss or interpret our belief in an indwelling deity. It is disappointing that, although much attention has been given by Christians to psychiatry and its use for moral and pastoral problems, there have been very few serious efforts even in America to study the doctrine of the Holy Spirit in the light of psychological knowledge. In the exegesis of the New Testament, for example, where a considerable confusion between the psychic and the spiritual is manifest[3] and where an exact study of the records and vocabulary of inspiration is obviously of great value, there has been singularly little work of importance.[4] The theological climate of the last twenty years has been very uncongenial to any effective belief in a divine indwelling.

If, as we have indicated, such indwelling is an essential element in a Christian theology, it is best to begin enquiry into it at its most intelligible level, that is, with ourselves and our capacity for inspiration. Here we have already seen that there is an abundance of testimony not only from the saints and mystics of religion but

[1] Cf. the interesting discussion of this in his *Christian Experience of the Holy Spirit*, pp. 85–90.

[2] For the kenosis in Christ and in Creation, cf. above, Ch. VI, p. 128.

[3] Notably in the estimates of the value of speaking with tongues as between Acts ii. 4–13 and I Cor. xiv. 2–28.

[4] An exception should perhaps be made on behalf of Dr W. D. Davies, *St Paul and Rabbinic Judaism*, for which see Note xv below, p. 220.

from artists and musicians, poets and thinkers, scientists and men of action who have at certain moments and sometimes almost regularly found themselves enlightened, quickened and constrained to vision and achievement of which they were normally incapable and who can only describe their experience in terms of possession or compulsion as if by a power not themselves nor their own.[1] It is plain that, in certain cases at least, they painted or composed, wrote or acted at a level far higher than normal, and often in a fashion unexpected and inexplicable: they are impelled and controlled, and it is given to them what they shall do or say. Such experiences seem usually to come when the individual has reached a measure of concentration but is not at the moment actively striving; when he is sensitive but not fretful, alert but receptive; when he has suffered and been broken, and sometimes indeed while he is still in agony: they come with a sense of peace and fulfilment and creative power; and though their coming humiliates and distresses, it yet accomplishes what the experient knows that he could not have achieved unaided.

It is natural to think of such inspiration in terms of the great masters who have left on record their evidence of it. But in fact a similar influence is widely if not universally acknowledged not only in the general practice of prayer but in the normal dealings of men and women with one another. That human beings are intimately connected at the subconscious level of their existence and so are exposed to mutual influence by more immediate contacts than sense-perception seems abundantly demonstrated. With our solidarity and its fulfilment in community we shall be concerned in the next chapter: that as individuals the linkage between us is not confined to the conscious exchange of sight and hearing, taste and smell and touch, is manifest from the mass of evidence that establishes the widespread occurrence of clairvoyance and telepathy; but our ordinary intercourse demonstrates it when once the attempt to explain all relationships in terms of sense-

---

[1] For this and for a large number of detailed examples of it, cf. Dr Rosamund E. M. Harding, *An Anatomy of Inspiration* (3rd ed. Cambridge, 1948), pp. 15–18. The whole book is a valuable and scholarly contribution to the subject.

perception has been abandoned. The sympathy that makes an immediate impact in a time of bereavement is not a matter of our friend's looks and words: indeed, in the deepest contacts such aids are needless. The help that we draw from another's speech is often in inverse proportion to the fulness and fluency of his utterance. Our greatest comfort comes often inexplicably until we discover that at that very time someone was writing to us or praying for us. And we give in the same way—not when we are feeling clever and self-conscious and flattered by having our opinion invited, but when, faced with another's need, acknowledged or unspoken, we forget ourselves and our conventions and let that need drag out of us whatever we have of compassion and experience. Probably we say very little, and that haltingly and ashamed; but what passes between us has an immediacy and an influence that no clever eloquence could achieve.

It may perhaps be permissible to illustrate this point by a paradox which must be familiar to every preacher. On the occasions when he is 'at his best', when his thought flows clearly and his words give eloquent expression to his message, when a close relationship is established between him and his hearers and they respond quickly and sympathetically to his slightest change of mood, he is apt to discover that though they go away pleased and interested nothing of any importance has in fact occurred. He and they have had a pleasant meeting and that is all. But on occasions when he has seemed quite unable to express the experience that haunts him, when words are hesitant and commonplace, when speech is an effort, almost an agony, and he comes away feeling exhausted and ashamed, having 'let down' God and failed to help men, he gets evidence that in fact a real experience has been made possible, that though his phrases are not remembered nor his arguments discussed his hearers have found a communion not with him but with God. In this latter case he realizes that the cause of his inability was that he too had caught a glimpse of the invisible, and that though he failed, inevitably, to express it, yet the failure was a greater and more effective ministry than any glib and easy success.

It is of course the fatal error of all behaviouristic theories of human emotion, from the James-Lange hypothesis to the materialism of J. B. Watson and even of Professor Gilbert Ryle, that they reverse the true order of percipience. Living organisms possess awareness and some power of impact at a level of being at which sense-perceptions have not yet received their appropriate instruments or become specialized: perception even if it cannot be precisely located or defined remains during and after their development; sensitiveness is prior to sense-perceptions and cannot be fully analysed into them. It is plain that mankind by reliance upon sight has not only impaired its other sense organs but atrophied certain perceptions which insects and birds manifestly possess. Work like that on bird migration reveals to us the inadequacy of the attempts to explain its phenomena in terms of our human senses; and Professor Rhine's evidence demonstrates that perception can take place under conditions which exclude each and all of these senses. For interpretation and communication, sense organs and their mechanisms are invaluable. They scale down and define and standardize our ineffable experiences and enable precision in comprehension and response. Man has gained enormously from the intellectual activities which derive their symbols and content from the senses; he can examine and analyse, record and retain, calculate and plan: he lives, as we used to say, 'not by instinct but by reason', and progressive achievement and all the gains and losses of human, as opposed to animal, existence[1] are the consequences. We have already argued that his peculiar self-consciousness is correlated with his capacity for adoration and that of this experience his characteristic capacities, aesthetic, intellectual and moral, are the expression and outcome.

Our present concern is to maintain that, just as an encounter with God is the primary experience of humanity, an encounter which man must then endeavour to fix and express, so within himself at a deeper level than his world of formulated perceptions

[1] So crude a contrast needs much modification. Animal sense-perceptions and means of communication have of course been developed long before the human level was reached and have prepared for it.

is an urge which corresponds to the divine and may properly be regarded as 'of one substance' with it. We have already argued that, if God is to be conceivable and revealed to us, there must be, alongside the Godhead who is beyond existence—the universal subject—the Godhead manifested and operative in the creation. If when thus revealed He is to be known to us, there must also be the Godhead indwelling in us, the 'germinal Logos', the 'Inner Light', the image in which we are made and which the Fall has not wholly effaced, the Spirit of God, the Spirit of Christ, the Spirit the Holy One.

Whether the gift of the Spirit belongs by birthright to all men or is bestowed only upon some, is a matter on which no one perhaps is competent to judge: it is certainly a matter on which there is much confusion. It would seem to be linked with the similar problem of immortality: are all men to survive death or is such survival conditional? Those who would insist that the gift of the Spirit is, by Scripture and tradition, exceptional and that the unbaptized or the non-Christian do not possess it are also usually those who insist that nevertheless man's spirit is deathless and abides everlastingly even though it be in hell—a conclusion which seems difficult to justify unless there is eternity in evil. It would seem more scriptural and more consistent to believe with the earliest Christian thinkers that all men possess 'the seed of the Word'; that all can, if they will, choke it; but that, if it is duly acclimatized, it produces a quality of life over which death has no power. This quality is characterized by sensibility, integrity and above all by the distinctive love which neither exploits nor sentimentalizes its object, the love for which Christians had to employ the new word, *agapé*.[1]

That the operation of the Spirit is discoverable first in an intensified awareness, such as accompanies and enables communion with God, and in a heightening of human perception and vitality, indicates that it affects the personality as a whole and

---

[1] It is well known that though the verbs ἀγαπάω and ἀγαπάζω are not uncommon in classical and secular writings the noun ἀγάπη is first found in the Septuagint, and only in Jewish and Christian literature.

thence flows out, so to speak, into its several and more specialized elements. Recipients of it differ widely in the extent to which they dramatize it in visual and auditory images. To some, visions and voices are the familiar accompaniments of inspiration. They can honestly claim to have seen and heard where others would speak less concretely of an impulse or a constraint. In any case our analytical methods are not capable of defining with precision the points at which inspiration and response are separable. St Paul can state plainly 'I live; yet not I, but Christ liveth in me'[1] or 'speak I, not the Lord':[2] but when he claims to 'sing with the spirit'[3] it is uncertain whether it is his own individual spirit[4] or the Spirit of Christ. So we, though we may be sure after the event that we were 'confirmed of God'[5] and given a mouth and wisdom[6] not our own, yet at the time will certainly not be conscious of the power working in us and may well be merely aware of our own complete ineptitude for the task laid upon us.

There is here plain evidence of the distinction between the Spirit and our own individuality; and this is our answer both to the pantheism which absorbs all in God and the Pelagianism which asserts man's independent worth. In our richest experiences there is always the familiar contrast. We are enraptured, illuminated, inspired, but we are also convicted of futility, blindness, isolation; and the measure of achievement is conditioned by the measure of humiliation. The experience of the saints who, as they manifestly grow in grace and power, yet become correspondingly conscious of their sin, finds its repetition in us all. We cannot presume to say what the Spirit works in us or to claim that we give Him free course. But we can and must acknowledge that if any good results from us, it is not our merit but His influence that is responsible. There obviously is and must be some mutuality in the relationship. We are not robots nor chessmen to be 'tossed to and fro' like leaves in the wind. But whatever be the measure of our ability to respond we shall realize that it gives us no ground

[1] Gal. ii. 20 (A.V.).
[2] I Cor. vii. 12 (A.V.); cf. also vv. 10, 25, 40.
[3] I Cor. xiv. 15.
[4] As it is plainly in Gal. vi. 18.
[5] I Cor. i. 4–8.
[6] Luke xxi. 15; cf. Mark xiii. 11.

whatever for self-assertion or pride. At best we are unprofitable servants.

Yet when this is said there is plainly a difference between such a confession and the inverted Pharisaism which glories in the total depravity of mankind and ignores or denies the indwelling of the Spirit. Those who from Augustine's time onwards have insisted that the good works of the heathen are evil, that the unbaptized are damned and that outside the Church (by which they usually mean their own religious institution) there is no salvation, not only assume judicial functions to which no human being can lay claim but explicitly reject the plain teaching of Jesus.[1] But, in spite of that, whenever the state of the world suggests insecurity, the contrast between natural and supernatural, between the secular and the heavenly citizenship, is emphasized, and men proceed to magnify the majesty of God by denouncing the wickedness and worthlessness of His works. Man left to himself, nature forsaken by God, would, if such dereliction were conceivable, deserve such condemnation; but we who have seen His rainbow and know His saints,[2] and who in our glimpses of beauty and truth and goodness have sensed His presence, cannot lightly renounce the Creator or banish the Spirit. 'God so loved the world' wrote the Fourth Evangelist:[3] when Augustine omitted those words from his exposition of the gospel[4] he revealed the defect of his understanding of Christ's religion.

Moreover, those who thus magnify the sin of man magnify also his status. Much that is written in times of pessimism like the present imputes to Satan and his human subjects a power in rebellion which has not only defied God but virtually dethroned Him from His world. That man can deny and resist and crucify the Christ is the measure of God's love for him and of the cost of bringing into existence creatures possessed of individuality and

---

[1] Matt. vii. 1; John iii. 8.

[2] It is not improper for me to mention as saints known to me Beatrice Hankey and Florence Allshorn, Bertram Keir Cunningham and Alexander Wood.

[3] John iii. 16.

[4] In Tractatus XIII of *In Johannis Evang.* cap. 3, he passes from *v.* 15 to *v.* 17; I owe this striking fact to my colleague Professor John Burnaby.

freedom. But to exalt man so as to assume that his posturing and pride are evidence of cosmic apostasy or a pre-cosmic fall seems only an example of the same self-exaltation which accredits us with the power to measure all things and enunciate infallibilities. Even a pope cannot define the eternal.

That the abundant life which is the primary evidence of the Spirit's presence expresses itself not only in a general increase of activity but in special accomplishments, artistic, intellectual, moral and physical, can be seen from the biblical references to His influence. Bezaleel the craftsman and Samson the athlete, Solomon the sage and Isaiah the prophet—these are an earnest of the day when the seven-fold Spirit of the Lord shall rest upon the scion of Jesse[1] and when the Lord will pour out His Spirit upon all flesh,[2] when His Wisdom and His Word will have free course in the world, and mankind will walk in the light of open vision. Yet in fact when the promise was fulfilled and the work of Jesus made possible a 'new age of the Spirit', the effects were so unprecedented that the Fourth Evangelist could say of previous times 'the Spirit was not yet given; because Jesus was not yet glorified'.[3] The new title 'the Spirit of Jesus' and the doctrine of the double procession, 'Who proceedeth from the Father and the Son',[4] are further proofs of the extent to which the embodiment and manifestation of the Spirit in Christ enlarged and intensified the inspiration. Plainly the vitality of the Apostolic Church, the love and joy and peace and fortitude[5] which are the proofs of the Spirit's indwelling, and which brought the disciples of the crucified Jew in a single generation to the court of imperial Rome, reveal a quality of passion and power such as have seldom since been recovered. Though this was largely the impact of the community rather than of individuals ('See how these Christians love one another' is the characteristic testimony to it), yet the evidence alike of the graffiti in the catacombs or the Letter to Diognetus, of

[1] Isai. xi. 2.   [2] Joel ii. 28.   [3] John vii. 39 (R.V.).
[4] The *Filioque* clause inserted in the Western version of the Nicene Creed is still the formal cause of separation between Catholic and Orthodox; but in fact it does not denote great difference in doctrine.
[5] Cf. Gal. v. 22.

165

the martyrs or of the missionaries proves how various and widespread, how valiant and revolutionary were its effects. Where there has been a similar experience of life in the Spirit as in the days of George Fox or John Wesley, results comparable in quality have been freely and victoriously achieved. But if this is admitted, it must be recognized how unexpected have been some of these manifestations and how closely akin to similar events in non-Christian circles, so that any suggestion that the Spirit works only in the Church or is confined to those who have received any particular ritual or ecclesiastical preparation would seem to be false to the facts. Here as elsewhere the scribes of the tradition are quick to assign such works to the Prince of the Devils; in so doing they were wrong once and may well be wrong again.

IX

THE SPIRIT AND COMMUNITY

If the gracious gift of the Lord Jesus Christ made inevitable a new concept of the nature and name of God, it also enabled for those who came to a full confession of it a new relationship with their fellows, a fresh experience of community, a creative fellowship such as the world had never previously known.

It is not altogether fanciful to suggest that in the threefold temptation which was the prelude to His ministry Jesus had seen and rejected the three types of human society which then as now drew men into partnership—those based upon economic, or political, or religious obligations, and represented by the friendly society, the state, and the sanctuary. Rome had fostered plenty of clubs for the provision of food and funerals;[1] she had established dominion over the kingdoms of the world; she patronized sacred fraternities attached to shrines and mysteries, from her own Vestals to the devotees of Cybele. She had exploited all three methods of rule, 'bread and the games', the marching legion and the deification of Caesar. Jesus might have gathered followers under any one of these: the relief of poverty and hunger, the gain of power and freedom, the fulfilment of Messianic expectations, these were laudable objectives; but to Him they were concessions to Satan. He chose instead another sort of community which, binding its members by a common loyalty for an impossible task, should lift them free from the wastage of friction and self-interest and unite them into a single and articulated organism which should embody the Spirit of God and express in its activities His own

S. Dill, *Roman Society from Nero to M. Aurelius*, pp. 251–86, gives a vivid and full account of these multitudinous *collegia*.

continuing work. For such a community the family was the natural analogy.

We have seen how He trained the individual disciples by enlarging and integrating their sensibilities, by challenging and breaking their self-esteem, and by assuring them of His forgiveness and trust. From the first He trained them as a group, selecting them as Apostles,[1] keeping them with Him, restraining their individualism and rebuking their pride of place. Though they seem to have had certain differences of duty and though on special occasions 'the Three' represented the rest, he that was great was minister, the first were the last, and the self-important were the most apt to betray. Thus they were guarded against the danger, that besets the mystic, of regarding himself as a unique and specially favoured individual, and religion as a solitary communion between himself and his God. Jesus by example and precept combated in them the temptation to Pharisaism—even to the extent of appealing to the awful impartiality of nature[2] as proof not of the indifference but of the love of God. Those who represent the Church as the 'new Israel' are apt to impose on it an exclusiveness which its Founder plainly repudiated. In His community the three basic distinctions of race and class and sex were to be done away, as His great apostle immediately recognized; the members were to constitute a single human organism, 'one man',[3] 'the body of Christ'. Nowadays such a metaphor takes on a fuller meaning if, as W. E. Agar writing of animal life in general puts it, 'The organism is a nexus of living agents of which at least the cells and the Central Agent of the organism as a whole are subjects'.[4]

For this solidarity they were prepared by a threefold discipline. As their judges afterwards said, 'they had been with Jesus', learning from Him to know and love God and one another and to see such love perfectly expressed by Him in a quality of personality and a way of life. As they themselves realized, they had been 'crucified with Him' and so gained the freedom of those

---

[1] The term is of course one of function ('missionaries') not of status.
[2] Matt. v. 45 (R.V.), 'he maketh his sun to rise on the evil and the good'.
[3] Gal. iii. 28.
[4] *A Contribution to the Theory of the Living Organism*, p. 57.

who have passed through death into life. Then the overwhelming experience of forgiveness, commissioning, and renewed discipleship accomplished their welding into a solid community of which it could be said that 'the multitude of them that believed were of one heart and of one soul'[1] and for which the inevitable analogy was that of the 'one body and one spirit'.

In these days when St Luke and the Acts are being assailed on all sides it is a commonplace to dismiss their picture of the earliest Church as utopian, the nostalgic dream of a golden age that haunted the Greeks. Some reaction against Ramsay and Harnack was perhaps inevitable—though it is noteworthy that the account of Jesus and the beginnings of Christianity given in the volumes with that title[2] represent Him as so commonplace,[3] and it as so questionable,[4] that their effect upon mankind becomes an inexplicable miracle. Fortunately, the Lucan valuation of the Church is supported by the one author whom these scholars find it difficult to reject: St Paul, whose difference from the author of the Acts is the first count in the case against St Luke,[5] is in this respect in agreement with him—indeed, goes beyond him, both in the great hymn to love and in the constant insistence upon the organic and divine life of the Christian community.

For St Paul, the belief that the Christ is formed like an embryo within the body of every Christian goes back to his letter to the Galatians.[6] In the first letter to Corinth the idea has been enlarged: the Church like a body is one but has many members; and every Christian who is 'in one Spirit' is baptized into the one body. The members of it differ in function as foot and hand, ear and eye; all

[1] Acts iv. 32 (A.V.).
[2] *The Beginnings of Christianity*, edited by F. J. Foakes Jackson and Kirsopp Lake; this suffers partly from the faults of all composite books, partly from the limitations of its editors.
[3] *Ibid.* I, pp. 267–99, the only account known to me which makes Jesus merely dull.
[4] *Ibid.* I, pp. 301–3 etc. The preface of vol. II, p. vii, tries to counteract this: 'great histories are evoked by great events.' But this volume, like its predecessor, suggests a doubt whether its authors, with two exceptions, regard Acts as history or the events as great.
[5] The critics transformed Paul into a Calvinist and then condemned Luke for not describing him as such.
[6] Gal. iv. 19; this, if not actually the earliest of his letters, is certainly earlier than any except those to the Thessalonians; cf. also I Cor. iv. 15 and II Cor. iv. 10.

are needed, the weak and less honoured as much as the rest; for God has fashioned it; and all the parts are linked together by shared suffering and shared joy.[1] The same idea is taken up in Romans (xii. 4, 5) and, with Christ as the head of the body, in Colossians (i. 18 and ii. 19); it finds its fullest and most familiar expression in Ephesians (iv. 4–16). Nor is the concept of the body of Christians confined to this metaphor. St Paul's most characteristic phrase, 'in Christ', to which A. Deissmann so rightly drew attention,[2] not only discloses the source and character of his own integration ('I can do all things in him that strengtheneth me')[3] but indicates that the Christian Community is integrated in precisely the same way ('Christ in you, the hope of glory'and 'every man perfect in Christ').[4]

That neither St Paul nor the author of the Acts is blind to the defects of Christians or slow to draw attention to them is obvious enough. But the zest with which champions of ecclesiasticism insist upon the failure of the early communism of the Church of Jerusalem, upon the story of Ananias and Sapphira or the jealousy between Jews and Hellenists, must not lead us to minimize the novelty, the efficacy and the too brief splendour of the fellowship originating at Pentecost. To infer from the Matthaean parable of the wheat and the tares that the Church has always been a mixed society and so to conclude that its present quality is apostolic is to ignore the fact that the original community produced the New Testament, carried the gospel in one generation to the palace, and gardens, of Nero and gave to the world a new revelation of human and divine love. The possession of an integrative loyalty, the experience of a shared bereavement, the gift of forgiveness and of trust were a preparation which subsequent ages have not found it easy to perpetuate; in consequence the organic life of the family of God has too often deteriorated into a lower type of association, legal, hierarchical and conventional.

In this process of integration an essential element is supplied by

---

[1] I Cor. xii. 12–27; he had already used similar language in vi. 15.

[2] Cf. his *Paul*, p. 140. He claims that it occurs 164 times in the Epistles or 155 times if the Pastorals are omitted.

[3] Phil. iv. 13 (R.V.).   [4] Col. i. 27, 28 (R.V.).

the 'explosive event' as we have already called it,[1] which gives the release of urgent action to the accumulated resources of aspiration and passion. As we all know, to arouse emotion without providing for it any means for its fulfilment is to invite frustration and to risk embitterment. The dream unrealized becomes a source of disintegration: at best it provides an escapism, at worst it results in rancour and rebellion. For the disciples of Jesus, His readiness not only to pardon but to commission was an indispensable stimulus to the manifold activities in which their loyalty was fulfilled, their forgiveness ratified, their power expressed, tested and increased. The very magnitude of His demand, 'Go ye into all the world', guaranteed their response: men will give their all to the attainment of the impossible; and in the common adventure they will seal the instrument of their freedom from self-seeking, and experience the solidarity of a corporate service. The 'doing of the work' is, as the Fourth Evangelist proclaimed, the condition and nutriment of their fulness of life. To that extent at least Christianity is wholly existentialist: community is realized in shared achievement. It is in dealing with concrete situations that individual and community discover the answer to their problems and learn of the doctrine.[2] Christian theology and culture draw their raw material not from the study nor the shrine, but from the contacts of the market-place and the home.

This community was the new event, as C. A. Anderson Scott was perhaps the first to point out,[3] which gave its peculiar significance to Whitsuntide. The gift of the Holy Ghost was not primarily an uprush of religious excitement culminating in the ecstatic utterance of 'tongues', nor even the rapport which made such utterance intelligible and, as men thought, native; it is unfortunate that this common psychic phenomenon should have made such a vivid impression on the author of the Acts. Pentecost was the birthday of the Church, the 'coenonia'—a word like 'agapé' hard to translate and linking with communion,

---

[1] Cf. above p. 153. This *coup de foudre* is discussed by S. De Sanctis, *Religious Conversion* (Eng. trans. London, 1917), p. 65, and E. Underhill, *Mysticism*, p. 179.
[2] John vii. 17. [3] In *The Spirit* (London, 1919) edited by B. H. Streeter, pp. 136–42.

community and communism; hard to translate because it represented a new type of participation and association for which we have even now no completely satisfactory title.[1]

It is indeed not much to the credit of psychology that, relatively speaking, so little work should have been done upon the character and constitution of human collectives and that such work is in the main so unsatisfactory. This is the more remarkable because for the past twenty years in Britain and the Western world generally 'community' (this name is the least inappropriate for the society in which each member finds himself wholly co-operative in impulse and action) has been a thing of quest and a word of power. All over the distressed areas and not least in this country little groups of men and women, brotherhoods, fellowships, guilds, colleges, fraternities, orders, have sprung up and experimented with the difficult business of forming a society which should be economically self-sufficient, domestically neighbourly and constitutionally co-operative if not communistic. So much enthusiasm, and effort, and sacrifice have been put into these ventures that there is available a mass of material from which to discover the conditions which make for their success.[2] Unfortunately the much publicized schools of sociology do not seem to have produced any very profound investigation of the fundamental human problems, largely because like the psychologists they hesitate to deal with its religious elements. So we still await any clear and detailed exposition of the differences between the various types of association and of the conditions which make possible a truly creative fellowship.

Meanwhile the indiscriminate eulogies of democracy and of the multifarious systems masquerading under that title add confusion to the subject. It is no part of our task to examine the evidence which led a distinguished student of political philosophy to maintain that democracy might remain our ideal provided we recognized that it had never yet been realized on the earth. But

[1] There is a full discussion of the term and of the evidence both of the Acts and of St Paul in L. S. Thornton, *The Common Life in the Body of Christ*, pp. 66–95.

[2] Cf., for example, L. Stubbings, *Community in Britain* and the letters of Max Plowman, *Bridge into the Future*.

few would contend that in its present form it is either practically efficient or morally edifying; and if its critics are asked to justify their condemnation they would point not so much to its faith in what Dean Inge called 'the plenary inspiration of the odd man' as to its method of government by committee. In theory it may perhaps appear that to submit our problems to a representative conference attended by delegates from all the parties concerned would give us full evidence, fair debate, and a just decision. In fact, so long as the members are loyal to those whom they represent the result must inevitably be a compromise and probably a rather low highest common factor—something less adventurous, intelligent and effective than any of the members would achieve by himself. It is only too often true that the wisdom coming out of such a committee is in inverse proportion to the number of wise men constituting it: if it never displays quite the ferocity and foolishness of a crowd, it cannot of itself rise to the level of creative partnership in which results wiser than the sum-total of the members' individual wisdom can be obtained.

For the democratic world there is probably nothing more vital than to discover how to transform its traditional groupings, the crowd and the committee, and to release in them (and perhaps even in the cabinet or its equivalent) the resources of power which a fellowship can under its best conditions display; and this should be a matter in which Christian experience is of value.

Broadly speaking it is obvious that the three chief types of human association, the crowd, the committee and the community, correspond to the emotional, the intellectual and the personal levels of activity. The crowd, though owing something to the herd-instinct and, to that extent, deserving the comparison with Galton's ox,[1] is not necessarily so animal in its passions as its political and psychological critics have tended to insist.[2] Its

---

[1] For this cf. Sir F. Galton, *Inquiries into Human Faculty*, p. 72, an example of gregariousness quoted as a type of fellowship by nearly all the treatises on group-psychology without any question of its validity.

[2] Much of the older literature (G. LeBon, *The Crowd*; W. Trotter, *Instincts of the Herd*; W. McDougall, *The Group Mind*) is heavily biased; I discussed this subject in *The Creator Spirit*, pp. 169–203.

members plainly relax the control which the higher centres of the brain normally exercise; they give full freedom to their feelings; they generate a mass-emotion which may easily become almost irresistible in its force; they are highly suggestible and at the mercy of the demagogue or the evangelist; under the influence of the one or the other they can perpetrate diabolical cruelties or see heavenly visions. But when this is said, there remains testimony to the underlying solidarity of mankind which our Western egoisms and individualism have obscured and corrupted. Gregariousness and fellow-feeling are native qualities, not necessarily more depraved than snobbishness and self-assertion.

The committee plainly represents association on the intellectual plane for the deliberate discussion of particular tasks, policies or problems with a view to the appropriate form of agreed activity. As such it is easy, in these days when the revolt against reason is an open road to popular esteem, to decry it—on the wrong grounds and often for the wrong motives. If there comes a point at which we must recognize the limitations of logic, we dare not, at our peril, lightly assume that that point has been reached or give up the effort to make our intellectual formulation of the problem complete and consistent. Human reason drawing its symbolism mainly from the phenomenal world for purposes of illustration, interpretation and communication is, as we have fully acknowledged, imperfect for the transmission both of the most abstract and of the most intimate experiences: other media, aesthetic and personal, have to take a share in providing and sharing information. But the amazing achievements of man's most familiar characteristic must not be minimized because his specific name does not solely express his capabilities. Wisdom remains preeminent and its intellectual elements are unique and indispensable. The committee falls short, not because of what it has, but because it is often so constituted as to prevent its attaining the one thing 'more excellent'. While its members are merely an aggregate of individuals, they will almost certainly remain self-conscious and 'on guard', debating rather than consulting, bargaining when they should be co-operating, and at the mercy of cleverness and ntrigue, if not of the usual alliance between chairman and secretary.[1]

It is sufficiently obvious how such an association differs from the creative fellowship of which democracy should be capable, and which most of us have seen foreshadowed in the simple activities in which a common ideal, a common task and, in consequence, a real unity of partnership and affection integrate the team into an effective whole. A great Oxford rowing blue, a member of the crew which first beat Cambridge after being led at Barnes Bridge, once said to me that his favourite illustration of the Kingdom of Heaven was a racing eight at the moment when every man was 'all out' and the boat was moving in perfect rhythm and unity; he added that to produce such a moment at its best the friendship of the members was an essential element.[2] A similar example can be found when a football team 'finds itself' and plays as if a single organism were in control—plays so that every man is always where he is wanted, and every pass comes to hand, and every move is anticipated: here also I am convinced that friendship plays a large part in the result.[3] If such instances seem trivial they can easily be supplemented. Those of us who have been in a good battalion on the eve of an attack will know how intense is the fellowship then manifested[4]—so strong that the aggressive are controlled by it and the frightened can lean upon it securely, and every man 'plays up' to his neighbours and to the common need. But the same integration and sensitiveness, the same mutuality, spontaneity and creativity are found in fullest measure when a shared vision of God, a shared experience of service, and the consequent release from all self-concern accomplish a similar solidarity to that manifested at Pentecost. At such

[1] 'L'état c'est moi' is normally true of him who arranges the agenda.
[2] I have been savagely criticized (*Church Times*, 2 May 1952) for using this analogy, but there is good biblical authority for illustrations from athletics, e.g. I Cor. ix. 24-7; II Tim. iv. 7; Hebr. xii. 1.
[3] This result is rarer in other games than in rowing—which is one reason why some of us believe that rowing is the most richly educative of all athletic events.
[4] My own experience was with the 1st Berkshires on the eve of the fight in front of Oppy Wood in April 1917 and again in the sugar factory outside Bourlon Wood on 30 November.

times 'the body having many members' is reborn; and all the energies usually wasted on maintaining our self-respect, keeping up appearances and putting our neighbours in their proper place, on all the trivialities of our pride, are available for the common purpose and fused into the life of the community.

And as with the individual so in the common life thus integrated there is manifested and operative, when the necessary conditions are fulfilled, the inspiration which we have learnt to recognize as divine. The illumination that gives his message to the prophet and the seer; the sensibility that establishes an immediacy of awareness and response; the affection that is too intimate and appreciative to exploit its object or to sentimentalize over it; so do light and life and love, God in action, work in us to constrain and to energize and to unite. As the several members find each its proper function in the economy of the whole, their fellowship develops a spontaneous co-operation in obedience to the creative guidance of the indwelling Spirit; each individual unit finds his freedom in the voluntary service of the whole, the whole is possessed of the full powers and resources of its constituents. To describe it as 'one body and one Spirit' is no exaggeration; and available for it are the resources of God. Sensitiveness integrates the community as the barriers of individuality are transcended; creativity inspires it as it gains release from fears and selfish ambitions; power without limit is at its disposal when there is no longer the wastage of inward conflict and when the Spirit of Christ is given free course.

Under what conditions can we expect such collective integration to take place? Traditional religion will answer that it is the act of God, that just as the Apostles waited in Jerusalem for the coming of the Spirit at Pentecost so we cannot foretell, much less hasten, the attainment of inspiration. Such a claim, so far as it asserts the divine initiative, is manifestly true; in inspiration as in creation and redemption God is the agent. But it may well be questioned whether the implicit suggestion that He acts arbitrarily and intrusively is equally true; indeed, it is surely unworthy of the divine. God's love is always pressing in upon us, manifesting tself continuously in the whole course of nature and history by the beauty and order and goodness of the world. If creation is what we have claimed, an adventure in the evolution of life, individuality and community, then the divine initiative in respect to it must be voluntarily conditioned by the response of the creature. If God is love, He cannot treat his children at any stage of their development as if they were less than persons. To that extent in creation as in incarnation He 'empties Himself of His Glory';[1] and can only accomplish His will if we can say 'Behold the handmaid of the Lord; be it unto me according to thy word'.[2] That the universe is so ordered that in the last resort His word prevails in it; that in our rebellions we discover sooner or later that 'all things betray thee, who betrayest me';[3] that ultimately 'all things work together for good to them that love God'[4] and will not work on any other terms: these things warn us of our inability to defy or to bargain—even though love does not deny us the power to do so.

If our response is necessary, it is important that we should consider the sort of invitation that comes to us. How does the love that presses in upon us make itself known? Here again the tradition replies that there are certain clearly recognizable channels of revelation—for Christians Christ, the Scriptures and the Church, however this be defined; if we pay heed to these, all will be well. In pursuance of this belief the revelation has been formulated, prescribed and enforced by the dogmatic, disciplinary and liturgical systems; a complete legal and authoritarian scheme is available; and this has its authorized exponents and administrators. In consequence passive acceptance is the only necessary condition; and the Christian is not under grace but under law!

To say so is to make plain in a sentence the contrast between the religion of the New Testament and Catholic Christendom. To St Paul, brought up under a similar system of law and tradition, the whole ethos of Christ's way of life was the personal relationship between the believers and the Lord, the freedom and

---

[1] Cf. the famous phrase in Phil. ii. 7 (R.V.). [2] Luke i. 38.
[3] Francis Thompson, *The Hound of Heaven*. [4] Rom. viii. 28 (A.V.)

spontaneity and adventurousness of discipleship, and the reliance not upon external precept but upon inward constraint. The difference was that between a walk along a strictly fenced path where every stage is marked and no wayfarer can go astray and an expedition over unmapped country with a companion who knows the lie of the land—the one as dull as a treadmill, the other a voyage of discovery.

But if so, how does the guide communicate his advice to us? How is the message revealed? Plainly the channels of revelation, in the narrow sense, are of unique and primary value; but equally plainly they do not stand alone. They are representative not exclusive, representative of a vast number of other revelatory sacraments through which the life and will of God make contact with us. All beauty, all truth, all goodness are the signs of His presence and, potentially at least, the instruments of His purpose; and we, to the extent to which we are capable of realization and response, as in some sort 'made in His likeness', can perceive and appreciate and accept his gifts. The heavens declare the glory of God;[1] the earth is full of His goodness;[2] so is the great and wide sea also:[3] thus the ancient Scriptures anticipate the poet's words.

> I but open my eyes—, and perfection, no more and no less,
> In the kind I imagined, full-fronts me, and God is seen God
> In the star, in the stone, in the flesh, in the soul and the clod.[4]

Hence the need in the full-grown man of the widest possible range of interests, so that he may dismiss nothing as common or unclean that God has cleansed,[5] and may be attuned to join the chorus of his fellows in the great *Benedicite* which rises continually from the creation. Unless he has sufficiently varied appreciation to realize something of the full scope of being and to see his own particularity in relation to a large whole, he will lack the sense of proportion essential to any co-operative venture, the humility necessary if he is to join with others in a complex society, the sympathy which rejoices in their part in the joint adventure. He

---

[1] Ps. xix. 1.   [2] Ps. xxxiii. 5.   [3] Ps. civ. 25.
[4] R. Browning, *Saul* XVIII.   [5] Cf. Acts x. 14, 15.

will not understand, as St Paul put it, that the eye and the ear not less than the hand and the foot are parts of the body; and that he has no monopoly in its service.

With this versatility of interest there must also be a conviction of the central purpose which underlies and integrates the functioning of each and all. By itself a wide range may only mean dilettantism, the mania for collecting experiences, the Athenian desire 'either to tell or to hear some new thing'.[1] To arrange the several pieces in the proper pattern, to discover the place of each in the hierarchy of the whole, to 'prove all things; hold fast that which is good'[2] must demand a discriminative sense of values and standards which only a clear ideal and criterion can supply. At present when in large areas of aesthetic and intellectual life there is a deliberate rejection of such an ideal, it is the more important to maintain that in its absence the alternative is an anarchic and individualistic relativism, or else obedience to an arbitrarily imposed ideology. Certainly there can be no integration either for the individual or the community unless in loyalty to a perfection which satisfies and unifies and therefore energizes. For us human beings, as we have claimed, only perfection in terms of personality, only the Christ, can quicken admiration into love, and so exercise upon us the one alchemy that can truly transform.

Such a claim may well seem to confine the possibility of entrance into a creative fellowship to the company of the saints; and indeed, though according to St Paul all those called to be Christians are saints, that company is a small one. Nothing is gained by pretending that those who represent the full religious achievement of mankind are numerous or ordinary: now as of old they stand out from the rest of us. But it is also true that if we define the fruit of the Spirit not in terms of ecclesiastical eminence or of orthodoxy and Church attendance, but of love and joy and peace and fortitude, we shall realize that there is in fact among men and women of all races and many faiths an exceeding great multitude of those whose lives testify to their worth. When Bernard Bosanquet wrote 'it seems well within the mark to say

---

[1] Acts xvii. 21 (R.V.).   [2] I Thess. v. 21.

that a careful analysis of a single day's life of any fairly typical human being would establish triumphantly all that is needed in principle for the affirmation of the Absolute',[1] he indicated the same claim that in the ordinary folk of our daily experience there is evidence of a sensibility, a kindliness, a courage and a sympathy as moving as it is genuine. Anyone who has suffered, or who has had work to do which depended upon the help of others, will have been constantly amazed at the plain proofs of their loyalty to their ideal and their unselfish service. At a time when we are so constantly reminded by some theologians of the total corruption of human nature and by some politicians of the devilry of one half of the race and the selfishness of the other, it is necessary to keep a sense of proportion and to learn the danger and the sin of our exclusiveness.[2]

A wide and ordered sensitiveness to the manifold splendour of God should ensure release from self-esteem. For the best it is enough; they grow up naturally into an increasing spiritual stature without the violence of sudden conversion or the shock of gross betrayal. But for most there is need of the bitter experience of failure if they are to be schooled into a reasonable humility. They must be broken that they may be emptied of pride and given the indispensable gift of a sense of tragedy. Spiritually they must have passed beyond death if they are to reach any maturity of life. The marks of their passage are thereafter plain for those who have eyes to see; and the effect of it is an emancipation. Such folk are no longer wholly earth-bound: being no longer self-centred they can develop an immediacy of contact with God and their neighbours, partly by the quickening of their conscious perceptions but partly, and perhaps more fully, by the establishment of a general awareness which cannot be analysed into ordinary sense-impressions. They have gained admission to a level

---

[1] *Individuality and Value*, I, p. 377.

[2] Cf. Simone Weil, *Waiting upon God*, p. 28, 'There is an absolutely insurmountable obstacle to the incarnation of Christianity. It is the use of the two little words *anathema sit*'; and D. G. Marcel, *The Mystery of Being*, II, p. 172, 'We must fight in ourselves without respite against that spirit of exclusiveness of which theologians afford such distressing examples'.

of sensitivity which most of us only experience on occasion and appreciate by analogy. They are seised of a permanent relationship to their environment which enables an immediacy of insight and response. They live in the 'blessed community'. The rapport of a speaker with his audience when he has lost his self-consciousness and it is in tune with him, the intimacy of a conductor with his orchestra, the creative fellowship of a group that has found its unity, these illustrate the mutual incorporation of the members in such community; and for it the stages that we have been describing are the normal preparation.

That such a community if it is to respond adequately to its environment and opportunities will do so through particular members is obvious; it is equally obvious, if we take the earliest Church as our example, that fitness to act is determined rather by capability than by office. Those who show that they possess the appropriate gifts become thereby responsible to the community for their exercise; and this qualification is then recognized and officially sanctioned. Whatever the precise stages in the development of the ministry, it is clear that functions necessary to the well-being of the community were speedily discovered and discharged in accordance not with a predetermined plan but with the requirements of concrete situations; that these functions soon became standardized and were, more slowly, appropriated to special officers; and that by the early part of the second century the orders of bishops, presbyters and deacons were taking shape. When it was maintained that the sacramental acts of these officers were not impaired by their moral depravity,[1] and when their duties became rather legal and administrative than personal and spontaneous, it was plain that the 'body' was ceasing to be an organism and was becoming an organization. From this example it would seem to follow that, though a constitution and officers may be necessary, the community must see that stress is laid upon function not status and that duties are kept as elastic and informal as is consistent with efficiency. Right personal relationships are

---

[1] It is difficult not to admit that the *ex opere operato* doctrine of the sacraments involves a magical or at least a sub-personal theory of grace.

essential: to know as a priest what one must deny as a man is to be put in a false position; indeed, any divorce between person and office must be regarded as dangerous to the community. We must live under grace not under law.

Here arises a problem which is hardly yet recognized but which is already becoming urgent. From both sides of its ancestry, from Israel and from Rome, Western Christendom has inherited a civilization based upon a strict system of law. It has too seldom been recognized that the lawyers' maxim 'Hard cases make bad law' is incompatible with the Christian conviction that every case is a hard case. Yet if each particular person is to be regarded as potentially a child of God, he can never be treated as a mere type, an example of a class, a generalized law-breaker without denial of his individual worth. If we are to follow the way of Jesus we cannot lump[1] human beings together as a purely legal attitude must do; indeed, to do so is only too often to divorce law from justice. With our fuller knowledge of psychology this truism is being underlined; and in spite of the protests of the profession judges are being constrained to adapt general statutes to special circumstances by decisions which not only constitute a growing mass of case-law but increasingly invalidate the meaning and maintenance of the law as drafted. The prophet of old declared that the law of the Lord was simple, 'precept upon precept; line upon line'; he could not have so referred to the present chaotic condition of the law in Britain and America where judge-made verdicts have constantly changed the plain meaning of the act, and must inevitably do so if law is to serve the interests of justice and the punishment is to be made to fit the crime. For the Church,[2] almost as clearly as for the State, the entanglement with law is a matter of serious perplexity.

It would be an evasion to ignore the urgent and universal dilemma caused by the acceptance in Christendom of the moral standards and traditions of a non-Christian society. All of us who

---

[1] Cf. 'The poor in a loomp is bad', Tennyson, *Northern Farmer. New Style.*

[2] Witness the recent pronouncements of the Pope on the subject of family limitation and of the duties of doctors in childbirth.

have realized the immense development, in the past three centuries, of social evils for which no one individual or group is responsible, and which only collective action can effectively remedy, must be concerned with the simple question, 'how is it possible to live Christianly in a society ordered on lines sub-Christian or anti-Christian?' We must admit that, whereas not long ago men of strong character and sincere conviction could escape from the social nexus by emigration or isolate themselves from it in an independent community,[1] no one of us can do so today: even a Bruderhof in Paraguay needs the financial support of the worldling. So it has become essential to discover how reform can be made effective, and, as a preliminary, what are the most serious and remediable compromises. There can be little question that, while every aspect of our corporate life supplies instances of the conflict between religious and conventional standards, there is no issue so typical and so obvious as that which concerns our attitude towards modern war. In no other are the factors so easy to analyse or so generally familiar; in no other are the irony and the crisis of our time more evident.[2]

Whatever may have been the case in days when warfare, however savage, had about it something of the character of a tournament and when the Church strove to prescribe regulations for the protection of non-combatants and the observance of standards of conduct, the advent of new weapons and particularly the use of chemical and bacteriological techniques, of obliteration bombing, of nuclear fission and the so-called hydrogen bomb for indiscriminate massacre, has produced a situation in which there can be no pretence of a just war in the traditional meaning of those words and small possibility of reconciling warfare with any religious or moral valuation of mankind. When, under the influence of conflict, the order was given for the destruction of Hiroshima excuses might be found for the decision—even though those publicized were apparently not valid. But when in quiet

---

[1] Two centuries ago the great households and estates even in England were virtually self-sufficing: a 'New Harmony' was not utopian.

[2] The brief summary which follows is based upon my Paine Lectures, *The Theological Basis of Christian Pacifism* (New York, 1951).

conference Christian leaders decide that it is permissible to defend their own way of life by annihilating human communities indiscriminately it is obvious that by so doing they contradict the basic Christian beliefs about the nature of God, the revelation in Christ, the means of overcoming evil, and the sources of human well-being. If God is love and each individual person precious in His sight, we cannot go behind Abraham's plea for Sodom and treat cities as we treat cockroaches in our kitchens or ants' nests in our gardens. If Christ chose neither to fight nor to flee but to be crucified, and so accomplished the overthrow of sin, we cannot repudiate His example, do evil that good may come, and insist that self-preservation is our primary duty.

If life is sensitiveness and its goal the blessed community, then to make a lethal chamber of Hiroshima is as monstrous as to set up such a chamber at Belsen—indeed, it is perhaps more evil; for at Belsen torture and death were at least not wholly reckless and indiscriminate. Is there anything in Christian history—or indeed in history anywhere—more terrible than that commissions of our Christian leaders should have published vindications of such actions?[1] If we are to be honest, we must face both the splendour of life and its shame, and look not at others only, but at ourselves. In our human scene and in this twentieth century after Christ the basic experience of illumination and abasement, the *mysterium tremendum et fascinans*, repeats itself on a world-wide scale. It is against such an apocalyptic background that our adventure is set.

[1] It is only necessary to refer to Dr R. A. Knox's mild protest *God and the Atom* (London, 1945), pp. 61, 124; and the Reports of the two British Commissions, one appointed by the Christian Frontier under Dr J. H. Oldham and the other by the Church Assembly under Dean E. G. Selwyn.

X

ETERNAL LIFE

PARTICIPATIO legis æternæ in rationali creatura lex naturalis dicitur:[1]
so St Thomas Aquinas had written, and so a sacramental and
incarnational philosophy must maintain. We may admit that
according to the usual reckoning natural religion ceases with the
things that are seen and temporal, while the unseen and eternal
belong to the supernatural or revealed: but plainly any religion
which ignored the question of immortality and confined itself to
this world would hardly deserve the name; and for those of us
who refuse to cut up our experience into body and spirit, natural
and supernatural, such an omission is impossible. It would be
false to the universal testimony of the mystics in all religious
traditions, false to the evidence of anthropology and history, false
to poetry and philosophy, to the seers and sages, to omit the
problem of man's destiny in the hereafter or at least of his eternal
relationship here and now. This is particularly important in these
days when the eschatological element in religion is so generally
and yet so confusedly emphasized.

It is unnecessary to repeat or to enlarge upon the claim that the
fundamental human response to the universe is an awareness of an
existence which is permanent, unitary and inclusive, which at
once welcomes and judges us, catching us up into adoration and
communion and at the same time convincing us of our solitariness and our shame. To give expression to this experience in
appropriate cultus and creed and code is the task of the world's
religions; and the understanding, verification and amendment of
our interpretation of it is the province of theology. To know in

[1] *Summa Theol.* I, 2, Q. 91, 2.

faith[1] the reality disclosed by it, to live eternally to the fullest possible degree;[2] and to conform all our activities to this eternal relationship, this is our supreme human obligation. It has been our purpose to show that this relationship can be interpreted in terms of the Christian revelation in a manner compatible with our present scientific outlook.

There is no need to discuss in detail the place of eschatology in the Christian Scriptures or tradition. The general Jewish view had been shaped in Maccabean times and by literature of which the Book of Daniel was typical. It set this age in contrast with the age to come, looked for the advent of the new age by the agency of the Messiah and on 'the great day of the Lord', and expressed its effects under the familiar images of the last judgment and the Messianic banquet and kingdom. Such ideas are plainly traceable in the Synoptic Gospels and, since Schweitzer, scholars have increasingly emphasized their importance. They have always supplied the main outline of traditional teaching on the subject both for Catholic and for Protestant Christianity. Over details such as the occasion of our resurrection, the idea of purgatory, the millennial reign of Christ, the pains of hell and the joys of heaven, beliefs differed; they agreed that the eschatological state did not begin until after the death of the individual, unless the Second Advent came during his lifetime.

Of the influence of such expectations from the third century until recent times there can be no question. Dante's great poem, the sculptured 'dooms' at the west doors of churches, the ceremonies of Advent, the language of funeral services, and the contents of many sermons and hymns testify to the universal importance of the subject and to the deep interest in all its imagery. The development of chantries and masses for the dead, of pilgrimages and pardons, of saintly intercessors and grants from the treasury of merit—all this apparatus tended to transform Catholic piety into a prudential investment. The Reformers who protested nobly

---

[1] 'Faith is not a bundle of mere spiritual truths, but a condition of soul which I should describe as eternal life', Mrs Mary Benson, quoted by M. H. Watt, *The History of the Parson's Wife*, p. 155.

[2] ἐφ' ὅσον ἐνδέχεται ἀθανατίζειν, Aristotle, *Eth. Nic.* x, 7, 8.

against the sale of indulgences and less nobly against the doctrine of purgatory did little more than prune the secondary growths off the eschatological thicket; there was no root and branch treatment, and their attention to the horrors of everlasting torment, intensified by the removal of all means of alleviation and by the development of the doctrine of predestined damnation, did much to replace and even to extend the area of danger. For both parties the fear of judgment often appeared to be the master motive in the religion of Jesus.

That the result gave a high seriousness and sense of responsibility to those who were thus trained to fix their eyes upon the great white throne, and weigh every action by the sentence of guilt or acquittal then to be passed upon it, is familiar to the elderly among us whose childhood was spent in contact with Victorian puritanism. That it gave an urgency and poignancy to the preacher's message and to the missionary cause in heathen lands is obvious from the literature and records of the religious societies. Christians were convinced that their everlasting destiny depended irrevocably upon the quality of their lives here and now, and disciplined themselves accordingly. Under such penalties for so great a reward much was, and in some quarters still is, achieved. It is hardly fair to press the question whether either means or results had much connexion with the life abundant or the self-surrender, with the humility or the joy, of the Christian religion.

Few ideas so powerful, so ancient and so widespread can ever have disappeared more rapidly than this traditional eschatology. When a hundred years ago F. D. Maurice was deprived of his professorship at King's College, London, for maintaining the Johannine view of eternal life, no one could have foreseen that before the end of the century educated opinion would have swung over to the position for which he had been condemned; that belief in everlasting torment would have disappeared; that judgment would have been interpreted as a process working here and now[1] rather than a verdict delivered after death; that immortality would be understood rather in terms of relationship[2] than of duration;

[1] Cf. John iii. 19.　　　　[2] Cf. John xvii. 3.

and that the Second Advent of Christ would be pictured not as the descent of the Judge at a particular date and with the traditional imagery of trumpets and angels but in the language of the building up of the body in which Christ's Spirit was even now in some measure active and incarnate.[1] With this change, and contributory to it, came the development of the social conscience among Christians, with its emphasis upon the relevance of religion to this life in its secular as well as its ecclesiastical aspects; and the tendency to claim that Q, the document common to the First and Third Gospels and containing the Lord's Prayer and the Sermon on the Mount, was at once the most ancient in its dating and the most modern in its teaching of all the records.[2] Eschatology fell into the background to such an extent that, when in 1906 Dr Albrecht Schweitzer's *Von Reimarus zu Wrede* and in 1910 its English translation *The Quest of the Historical Jesus* were published, the world of Christian scholarship was shocked and shaken.

None of us who were working at New Testament theology in those days will forget the impact of that astonishing *tour de force*. It is easy—it was even easy at that time—to point out that the series of alternatives, by which scholars were set in antithesis and the issues narrowed, was artificial and arbitrary; that the method of 'entweder—oder', 'either black or white', is grossly misleading; and that the schema was simplified by the omission of some of the most important authorities. It was equally easy to show that the evidence for Schweitzer's own interpretation was neither representative nor reliable, that his theory rested upon texts peculiar to St Matthew and therefore upon the least authentic element in the Synoptic material, and that the crucial verse, 'Ye shall not have gone through the cities of Israel, till the Son of man be come',[3] which was the clue to his whole reconstruction, could only bear his significance if it were demonstrably spoken at the precise time and in reference to the particular journey. On the

---

[1] I.e. in the ideas of Ephes. iv. 4–16, rather than of I Thess. iv. 16, 17.

[2] The debate as to the primacy of Mark or Q had a theological as well as a historical importance; for the two sides, cf. A. von Harnack, *The Sayings of Jesus*, and F. C. Burkitt, *The Gospel History and its Transmission.*

[3] Matt. x. 23 (R.V.).

broader issue we could make an overwhelming case for the view that eschatology did not play so large a part as he supposed; that its language and ideas were by no means so uniform or so literally accepted as his theory demanded;[1] and that in the New Testament itself there was abundant proof that apocalyptic language and eschatological ideas, if sometimes used as cryptograms, were in many cases no more than vivid and even traditional metaphors. Yet in spite of our criticisms the power, originality and insight of his last two chapters could not be gainsaid or dismissed. Here was a way of life interpreted clearly and vividly of which in our sheltered mechanized world we had no personal knowledge but which, in its realistic presentation of existence 'in the realm of ends', opened up possibilities of experience which might well be valid. Those chapters were for us an apocalypse.

So indeed it proved. For while we were still arguing and denouncing, our world was plunged into war; and for the front-line soldier high explosive brought eschatology into the centre of his experience. We had been exhorted 'to live each day as if thy last' and had on occasion taken the exhortation to heart. But death is an event which even cowards cannot really face in imagination or at second hand. Life in its presence is liable to undergo unprecedented experiences which demand a drastic revision of religions and philosophies. That is why those who have come to terms with it—who have passed its great examination—carry a certificate which their colleagues can recognize. Those who are not so certificated ought not to be encouraged to write about eschatology; in too many cases they do not know what they are talking about.

The immediate effect of living with death is to escape from the world of prudential investment, of securities and safeguards, of calculation and anxiety, of compromise and complacency into

---

[1] This is a warning which still needs repetition. For many modern scholars the word eschatology seems to have a hypnotic effect; to their readers their use of it is ill-defined, inconsistent, bewildering. For a striking instance of this confusion, cf. Bishop F. R. Barry, *Recovery of Man*, p. 67 (of the premundane fall), 'there cannot be any event outside the time-process', and p. 108 (of the consummation), 'it is not to be sought in this world of time'.

a world of immediacy and peril where there can be 'no thought for the morrow', and where each day is a special gift unexpected and delightful. The shock of the change may be too much for us. Many dare not or do not face it and never enter the new world. Many are broken by the terror of it. But for those who pass beyond the gate there is a freedom, a simplification, a spontaneity such as they have hardly glimpsed or imagined. They are no longer earth-bound; they live in the present and, for many of them at least, in the heavenlies. They discover the beauty and order and goodness of the earth just because they have ceased to possess or exploit it. That is why for some of us Flanders poppies—with cornflowers and daisies, the tricolour of the trenches—are the flowers of remembrance and reminder.

In such an experience the language of apocalyptic becomes inevitable. Nothing less than the turning of the sun into darkness and the moon into blood, than the rolling up of the heavens and the shattering of the earth can do justice to the agony and ecstasy of what happens when we pass out of death into life. To take such language literally, to argue about its precise symbolism, to treat it as a prophecy of an Advent whose date can be calculated and whose details have been revealed is not merely to translate poetry into prose, it is to misconceive and misuse the whole significance of what has been written. If eschatology only means living in preparation for certain events after death, it will produce caution and legalism and a calculating priggishness; and its servants will remain to that extent in outer darkness. If it means life here and now in the realm of ends, it is a foretaste of eternity; it is walking in the light; it is deliverance from self-pity and self-esteem; it is, at its best, to walk like Adam with God in Eden, or to keep vigil like the disciples with Christ in Gethsemane.

Such emancipation, though for many of us achieved first by the presence of death, is not necessarily associated with that particular experience. Men and women differ widely in the degree to which they are earth-bound. Some, indeed, seem always to live in a measure of freedom; others find release in a great love, or like Nietzsche in creative art, or like Socrates in philosophy.

Others need the agony of bereavement or of mortal pain or of humiliation and calamity to set them free. The experience, like that of conversion, to which it is manifestly akin, takes many forms. In essence it is the same. In its fullest manifestation it is that eternal life which Jesus possessed and imparted.

For if on its negative side it is deliverance from contingency and transience, it is on its positive side entry into a realm of life and personal relationships. There is in it a vivid awareness not only of the presence and needs of others, of those with whom whether they be absent or at hand, living or dead, we have established permanence of kinship, but also the thrill of contact with a world tinglingly alive, a presence that inspires and sustains. In the resultant community of life with life, the personal with the personal and super-personal, all the manifold facets of the physical environment, all the varied objects of sense perception take their place as subsidiary, as the symbols and instruments through which we manifest and communicate, interpret and understand, enjoy and increase our relatedness.

In consequence it is wholly a mistake to suppose that such emancipation involves a dreamy other-worldliness or an indifference to present duties and opportunities. In all the strange byways of hagiology there is perhaps nothing more perverse than the presentation of the Fourth Evangelist as an effeminate and beglamoured visionary. Whether or no he was the beloved disciple, the author of that tremendous Gospel was no enraptured sentimentalist. Whether or no he was the son of Zebedee, he was very certainly Boanerges, 'a son of thunder'. In no book of Scripture is there more insistence upon activity and the doing of works. In none is there a greater vigour and violence of praise and of condemnation. He is intensely alive just because he is living in the knowledge and love of God. He can disclose the true significance of events to the measure in which he sees them in the light of the eternal. He has written the most mysterious and the most meaningful of books, inasmuch as he has, more clearly than others, integrated the permanent and the ephemeral, the things of earth and the things of heaven. In this respect he, more than any other, can help us to give meaning and reality to the belief that, in Christ, God and man are indeed one.

Nor can the activity and practicality of those who are living eternally be dismissed as peculiar to the saints.[1] History has too often been changed by dreamers whose dreams came true for us to doubt that the familiar process of integration and sublimation releases energies whose efficacy is unpredictable and unprecedented.

But the peculiar ethical characteristics of that way of life, though they ought to be familiar to every student of the New Testament, are still seldom recognized or taken seriously.

When Adolf von Harnack expounded the famous epigram, 'Marcion was the only Christian of the sub-apostolic age to understand St Paul, and he misunderstood him',[2] he drew attention to this precise issue. St Paul had insisted as a matter of primary importance that the acknowledgment of Christ involved a total change in the whole quality of our moral life and conduct. 'We are not under law, but under grace' meant for him that we must no longer regulate our conduct by obedience to formulated rules, no longer walk the road between fences and by a map, but would live 'in Christ', in perpetual contact with one who would accompany and guide us. This meant a revolutionary change. All the elaborate business of scribal religion which had classified and codified and commented upon the Law so as to provide an appropriate ruling for every possible perplexity, which had assumed that human affairs could be thus reduced to categories and settled by statute, was now an anachronism. Its value for the education of the race, its interest for present study need not be disputed. But as a means to fulness of life, to the freedom and creativity and adventuring of the full-grown man, it had failed and been superseded. Henceforward the Spirit of Christ, continually present with and in the Christian both as individual and as member of the community, enabled men to live always on the level of personal relationships and in the presence of God. Marcion

[1] It has often been demonstrated, for example, that St Francis attained not only the stigmata but the foundation of his Order, and that St Theresa along with visions and levitation controlled a great community with singular efficiency and wisdom.

[2] *History of Dogma*, I, pp. 267–86.

was alone[1] in realizing the novelty and scale of the change. He made the mistake of supposing that it involved the total rejection of the Old Testament and the wholesale repudiation of the Church's connexion with Judaism. He thus allied himself with the gnostic schools that denounced the God of Israel as an enemy and made it essential for Christians who had any sense of history or any appreciation of the spiritual value of the *preparatio evangelica* to oppose him. In consequence the element of real importance in his teaching, the Pauline insistence on freedom and on life in Christ, was never fully appreciated until the Reformation, and even then the belief in the infallible authority of the Scriptures prevented faith from being fully personalized. 'Belief in the Bible' kept ethics on the legal plane.

The result has too often been to encourage the ancient dualisms and to destroy the possibility of making life 'all of a piece'. The personal surrender and communion of faith, the gracious relationship of the believer with God in Christ, is patched on to a course of conduct dictated only too often by enlightened self-interest and producing all the perils of Pharisaism. Instead of living in one world, God's world, the Christian sees himself as the 'Great Amphibium' whose business it is to spend most of his time in secular activities where certain rules mostly of a negative kind are provided by the Church for his guidance, and to maintain a secret sanctuary of the soul, a place of regular but occasional prayer, a mount of vision to which he can escape and in which he can find God. He is a denizen of two different worlds and must be ready to adapt himself to both environments.

It might have been expected to be, and to some extent is, the fact that the recent emphasis upon eschatology, particularly upon what Professor C. H. Dodd has taught us to call 'realized eschatology',[2]

---

[1] The extent to which Clement of Rome, even though writing to the Corinthians and reminding them of St Paul, totally missed the Pauline gospel is well stated by C. A. Anderson Scott, *Romanism and the Gospel*, pp. 22–8.

[2] Cf. especially *The Parables of the Kingdom*, pp. 197–206; and previously *The Gospels and History*. Theology owes a great debt to Professor Dodd for having demonstrated that the apocalyptical eschatology of the Synoptics is not inconsistent with belief in the Kingdom here and now, or with the later Pauline and Johannine interpretations. It is

has helped forward the task of integrating the temporal and the eternal, of enabling a single and coherent way of thought and life. Unfortunately, eschatology has been generally interpreted in its crudest form so that the traditional dualism of body and soul is reproduced by the contrast between this world and the world to come. When, for example, it is stated that the records of the New Testament are 'superhistorical' or 'eschatologically conditioned', this is often equivalent to saying that their factual accuracy as authentic records of the teaching and deeds of Jesus is unimportant and to suggesting that what is factually false or fictitious can be eternally true. Such an argument would seem to destroy the plain significance of the Incarnation, the claim that in the physical life of Jesus is manifested the eternal life of God. It must mean that the impact of Jesus, interpreted and amplified by the fancy of men for whom history was unimportant in comparison with edification, conveys to us an eternal reality which the facts did not themselves convey. No one will dispute that such a process of fuller understanding took place and that it need not lead to a disparagement of the importance of historicity or an abandonment of the task of scrutinizing, criticizing and, if necessary, rejecting the records; but, as understood by many who write glibly of eschatology, the argument leads only to a confusion between fact and fancy and even a belief that the temporal and the eternal, the historical and the religious, have no necessary connexion. And not only so, but eschatology has been used to import into the record a heightening of the other-worldly reference, a dramatization of the conflict between the powers of this world and of the world to come, a stress not only upon God's judgment but upon our right to see ourselves as His agents in enforcing it. If eschatology means Armageddon, the final conflict between good and evil, and the overthrow of Satan and his host, then it can only strengthen the present tendency to divide humanity into two camps and to commit Christendom to an atomic war as to a new

indeed evident that the traditional eschatology—a literal Second Coming, not immediate but in fact indefinitely postponed—destroys the whole significance of the Gospel of the Kingdom. Cf. Note XVI below, p. 221.

Crusade. To weaken the sense of history so that we prefer our beliefs and wishes to the facts, and to visualize our struggles in terms of the war in heaven so that we can treat our enemies as subhuman and devilish, this has been to very many the chief effect of a thorough-going eschatology.

In this connexion it is significant to note that the use of apocalyptic language and supernatural imagery, though often and appropriately employed in times of crisis and convulsion, is also the regular habit of writers who are in revolt against the realism of science or the sanities of reason. The extravagancies of the Book of Daniel owe something to reaction against the impact of Hellenism which had tended to substitute philosophy for prophecy; the Revelation of St John the Divine represents a type of imagination poles apart from that of the Fourth Gospel, and in some sense a protest against it. So too the art and poetry of Blake are an indication of the extent to which scientific rationalism was driving religion into this twilight borderland of dissociated fancy. The scorn of nature which plays so large a part in the writings of Mr C. S. Lewis and to some extent also of Charles Williams and Dr T. S. Eliot, as well as of contemporary artists from Picasso to Walt Disney, may give evidence of a similar dread of the machine. The manifest dualism of neo-orthodoxy is the theological representative of the same trend.

It is of course obvious that a similarly apocalyptic background gives its peculiar character to Marxist Communism and has transformed the dreary economics of *Das Kapital* into one of the great fighting religions. The sovereignty of the proletariat takes the place of the Messianic kingdom; Marx is its prophet; Lenin and Stalin its Messiahs; the Comintern its Chosen People; the approaching collapse of Capitalism its Day of the Lord. If its vision of the New Heaven and the New Earth is less clear, if indeed it has little concern with the morrow of the revolution, that is the penalty for its atheism. But if it has no abiding end or positive objective, it has at least an immediate enemy, and a strong conviction that Armageddon is at hand: and for a war whether on earth or in heaven hate can be a more powerful incentive than love. In Marxism, as in traditional Apocalyptic, a clean-cut dualism, a picture of the world in black and white, is essential.

An illustration from current affairs will illustrate the evil effects which too frequently follow from this double status.

When in the spring of 1951 Bishop Otto Dibelius spoke with the Archbishop of York at a mass-meeting in London, he told his audience that he was one of the only Christians who had an office on each side of the 'iron curtain', and spent part of his time in the Russian and part in the Western section of Berlin. In each area he heard continually the same tale of a peace-loving population striving to establish security and better social conditions, but compelled to live in fear and on guard against the intrigues and aggression of its war-mongering and imperialistic rival. The stories were the same, even to details; the principal characters were reversed.[1] From one view of the chessboard America was white and Russia black; from the other, the black pieces were American, the white Russian. Every action by the other side was a threat and must be countered accordingly. The world is split into two camps in true Miltonic fashion, Satan and his angels against the armies of the living God. The tragedy is enhanced by the evident fact that in consequence the mentality and actions of both parties are becoming increasingly identical. Fear, not faith; despair, not hope; hatred, not love, are becoming the cardinal qualities even of Christendom.

Under such conditions—the phobias of the last thirty years, Germans, Jews, Bolsheviks, Fascists, Hitler, Stalin, besetting an already war-damaged world have distracted us all—there is a tendency to repeat the defence set up by Christians when they first faced the downfall of a civilization, and to take refuge in the modern equivalents of the desert, in hermitage or cloister. To preserve the treasures of our religious inheritance, to build up reserves of spiritual power, to establish camps of refuge or cells of influence, this can best be done by deliberate withdrawal from the world. Let there be set up communities in areas free from the threat of destruction where beauty and learning and brotherly

[1] Cf. report of his speech of 1 March circulated by the British Council of Churches.

love may find a home till the storms have spent their force. Then from the monasteries may go out a Christian mission to recall and restore. Meanwhile their inmates will not be idle or self-seeking. They will live as intercessors, simply, strenuously, loyally, waiting upon God, and ministering so far as they may to man.

No one who knows the devotion and effort that has been put into the establishment of such communities, or who realizes the strength of their appeal and the seeming hopelessness of any other course, will wish to condemn those for whom this is the chosen way. There is too strong a testimony to the value of seasoning the everyday life with the salt of prayer and contemplation to justify any condemnation of such a principle applied on a larger scale. But it cannot be denied that such a way accepts the division of life into this world and the next, that it is hard if not impossible to reconcile with the method of Jesus or with an incarnational philosophy, and that it goes far to justifying the charge that religion is an escape from fact to fantasy. There may be occasions and individuals that require such a policy. But Jesus, who lived in a time of oppression and a member of a subject people, rejected both the way of the Zealots and the way of the Essenes: He would neither fight nor flee. If we are to see life steadily and whole in God, if we are to live eternally, His way may have to be ours. We, too, must go down among 'the people of the land', and share their lives and sufferings, and walk that way with them.

That way is, as St Paul argued and the Fourth Evangelist proclaimed, to live here and now 'in the heavenlies', in the new age, in the realm of ends; to behave in this work-a-day world as if the Kingdom of Heaven was already here, as in some sense indeed it is. We must be content to take short views, facing each situation as it arises, not allowing ourselves to be frightened into compromises or evasions by fear of the possible consequences of our actions, nor determining our course by precedent or precept without regard to the particular circumstances of the case. It is plainly our business to study the issue as carefully and objectively as we can. We are rational beings and must not mistake prejudice for insight or the uprush of repressed emotion for inspiration. But equally plainly it is not our concern, nor is it in our power to forecast the future like a gambler on the stock exchange and to decide our duty by a carefully calculated table of profit and loss. We are living with God in God's world. His Christ is our example, His Spirit is our guide. To argue, for example, that if we refuse to use atomic weapons civilization will be destroyed, is to assume a knowledge which we cannot possess, as well as a right to do evil that good may come. Jesus for less than this said to Simon Peter 'Get thee behind me, Satan'.

The issue is so important and so much has been written and spoken about 'guidance' that it is perhaps advisable to treat the subject more fully. To live eternally must first involve the constant practice of the presence of God, the attempt to become more sensitive to it over a widening range of our experience. The traditional means of grace have a value attested by generations of believers and may not lightly be set aside. But they should be treated as representatively and not exclusively sacred. A church is consecrated as a house of God not in order to confine worship to it but that every home of man may be similarly honoured. The eucharist has a unique sanctity in order that every common meal and all human fellowship may disclose Christ in its midst. We are bidden to pray without ceasing because by specific prayers we may make all life a communion. So we shall come to particular decisions with a measure of expectancy and of confidence. In these decisions the facts of the case must be scrutinized, analysed, and studied in their context and with all available resources of sympathy, knowledge and experience. We must also study our own attitude to them, with the deliberate effort to make full allowance for and to discount our personal wishes and fears, conscious and subconscious. If the problem is difficult we must be prepared to take time and if needful to agonize over it; not otherwise have we the right to lay it before God and ask for guidance. When we are able to say with sincerity 'Thy will be done', when, that is, we have got away from the selfish outlook and become conscious only of the eternal realities, our course is made plain. A constraint is laid upon us and other alternatives become impossible. We know what we have to do.

To explain the matter thus may be to suggest that the practice of the presence of God involves merely a purification of our sense of values, and that living eternally is equivalent to entry into a realm in which beauty, truth and goodness are seen and followed. We have laid such stress upon the teaching of the Christian Platonists, whether of the third or of the seventeenth century, that this danger must be specially noted. For the Platonist is always exposed to the temptation to identify the Kingdom of Heaven with such a realm, to subordinate persons to values and assume that, only as persons express and embody the valuable, can they be of permanent importance. To Plato himself the Good, the καλὸν κἀγαθόν, was the synonym of deity, and the ideas which constituted reality were abstractions or qualities rather than persons. The Christian, like the author of the Fourth Gospel, is by contrast one for whom the Kingdom is essentially a family, a nexus of personal relationships, and its members are of worth in themselves to God and to one another. If they display value, this is a proper indication of their fuller life: it does not establish a claim to special favour or any right to 'bargain for God's love and stand Paying a price at his right hand'. Man's obsession with 'things', his greed of possession and lust for power, have given him so deep-seated an esteem for what he reckons valuable that to attain a true estimate of people and of personal relationships is enormously hard. Yet to do so is obviously a necessary element in this business of living eternally. For every real communion with God is inevitably linked up with a new relatedness to our neighbours. The practice of His presence can never for the Christian be only a flight of the alone to the Alone.

A proof of this may be derived from the apocalyptic experience which follows the shock of sudden bereavement. When the familiar security is smashed and the whole setting of life lies in ruins, out of the almost intolerable pain there comes, to many at least, an assurance that though the medium through which the relationship has found expression can no longer convey it, the relationship itself remains essentially unaffected and persistent and this conviction is accompanied by the discovery that it is as a means for the initiation, development and perfecting of personal relationships that the world of things serves its true end. Manifest as are the beauty and order, the worth and usefulness of the details of our physical environment, it is as the scene and occasion and enhancement of our relationships rather than for their own sake that they exist and are valued. So we verify the fact that we can live eternally under the conditions of earth. So we take courage to affirm that this planet which has been capable of receiving the Christ is also capable of realizing and co-operating with the fulfilment of His prayer for the coming of His Kingdom and the doing of His will.

That this quality of life *sub specie eternitatis* is immortal is the conviction which arises both from the evidence of those who have known it and from the character of the experience itself. We have already considered the testimony of the great mystics, and of a multitude of others who make no claim to greatness, that in his moments of ecstasy and communion man enters into an eternal relationship. Here and now, in and through his earthly environment he makes contact with that which abides. He is assured that this contact is 'a possession forever'. By it and at least to that extent he is seised of immortality. To those of us who are still dominated by the dualism of soul and body, spirit and matter, such a conviction will inevitably seem strange. But for those of us who discover that the physical universe, as our senses register and interpret it, is, if not in itself but as thus interpreted, a mode of our own experience, the dualism ceases to be axiomatic. Rather we accept existence not as the imprisonment of an immortal soul within an ephemeral body but as an encounter between persons, the experiences of which come to them through various modes and at differing levels, but in such fashion as to suggest the different facets of a single reality which the experiencing subject can integrate into a coherent whole. The universe apprehended by us in our moments of clearest insight as a unity is split up by our perception into a multitude of impacts and impressions which we can define, analyse, compare and combine. Our lives and thoughts become coherent and intelligible in proportion as 'broken bits of being' are fitted together into a consistent pattern. To enlarge the extent of his perception and at the same time to increase its integration is the two-fold task of the individual. In proportion to his sensitiveness to this personal encounter and to the value, the beauty and truth and goodness of the universe, and to the range and wholeness of the resultant experience will be his ability to realize the eternal in and through the ephemeral. If he is content to live on the surface and in bits and pieces he will in consequence cut himself off from abiding relationships and disintegrate his personality, even to the extent of becoming insensitive to real values and a creature of selfish and wholly transitory desires. For such, it may be, there is eventually no contact with the eternal, no relationship that abides, no end but destruction.[1] But if we are honest and have any wide acquaintance with mankind, we shall find it difficult to discover anyone thus entirely self-enclosed. We shall feel a proper doubt about our own eternity, but increasingly recognize the eternal in our neighbours. In any case, and mercifully, it is not our business to judge any except ourselves.

In this interpretation it is clear that 'an immortal soul' is not a permanent element nor is immortality the birthright of any son of man.[2] We are what we love; we abide so far as we love what is real and abiding; our survival is conditional upon the quality of our relationships; and that quality is revealed and, as we follow Him, imparted to us by Jesus Christ.

But as we come to discover how deeply our life in this world is permeated by and dependent upon the eternal and to realize that ultimately our transient thoughts and acts even in their most self-centred form are nevertheless fragmented and distorted refractions of the one abiding reality, as we develop awareness of the presence

[1] Gehenna is a rubbish-destructor not a torture chamber; to read back the ideas of the *Inferno* into the Gospels is bad theology and worse religion.

[2] In Friedrich von Hügel's book, *Eternal Life*, the summary of which, pp. 381–96, is the richest recent exposition of the subject, the tradition of hell and the acceptance of a real duality of matter and spirit makes 'conditional immortality' unacceptable; cf. p. 370. His sense of the importance of matter and the value of the natural order go far to modify the body-soul antithesis.

of God, consciousness of the measure 'of the stature of the fulness of Christ', and the ability to see all things as consummated in Him, and as in consequence we cease to criticize and condemn and learn instead to appreciate and to suffer, we shall find the fundamental experience of adoration and penitence, humility and joy, repeating itself in the complexities and the activities of our concrete situations; and shall begin to glimpse a meaning in the claim that our life here and now can be and should be all of a piece and all in God.

St Paul in what may perhaps be his last authentic epistle, that to the Philippians, when he had come to his fullest interpretation of the cosmic Christ as 'the mystery of God,...in whom are all the treasures of wisdom and knowledge hidden',[1] turned back to the Jesus who had emptied Himself of His glory and, living among us as a servant, had been obedient unto the death of the Cross. His mind must be in us; we must know Him both in the power of His resurrection and in the fellowship of His sufferings; we must be a colony of heaven planted here on earth. Then in his final paragraphs he summed up the practical conclusion: that we rejoice[2] in the Lord; that we behave with poise and spontaneity;[3] that we be free from anxiety and worry, opening our lives to God so that His peace which is beyond the world of speculation and argument may keep us emotionally and intellectually in Christ Jesus. So can we encourage one another in dwelling upon the things that are true and honest and just and pure and lovely and of good report; and God will supply our every need. The man who could write such a letter from prison and under the threat of death had won his freedom and was living eternally.

Yet for him, as in fuller measure for us all, these apprehensions of eternity are at best partial and transitory, conditional upon the response that we in the totality of our personality can make to them. In art and literature, music and mathematics, science and

---

[1] Col. ii. 2, 3.

[2] That we 'fare well' is perhaps a better rendering: but cf. I Thess. v. 17.

[3] The word is untranslatable: Matthew Arnold called it 'sweet reasonableness'; 'moderation' (A.V.), 'forbearance' (R.V., Moffatt, etc.) are too negative and colourless; 'courtesy' (R. A. Knox) perhaps too external.

philosophy, as in life itself, there are moments in which the eternal illuminates, transfigures and is manifested by the ephemeral. There are particular achievements which for some of us at least are in this sense revelatory: in them the quality of a sacrament is fulfilled and the outward and visible becomes the symbol and instrument of the inward and spiritual. We partake and are satisfied. But though we accept such revelation as 'light for the day', we cannot but acknowledge how insensitive we are to its presence, how blind to its character, how ready to obscure, distort and misuse its meaning. Those of us who live chiefly in the dark, conscious of our own selfishness and sin and oppressed by a constant sense of dereliction, may well expect to be condemned for an exaggerated appreciation of such flashes of insight and enlightenment as we receive, and perhaps are guilty of believing that what we see, fragmentary and spasmodic as it is, has a more obvious and universal significance than, if we were more accustomed to it, we should dare to claim.

Plainly the whole process with which these lectures have been concerned is still in the making; the New Reformation is incomplete; we can only see a fraction of one act in the drama, a yard or two of the road to the horizon. That we are justified in making any guess at the meaning of the whole; that we, being what we are, can claim any knowledge of its real nature; that for us any ultimate reality can be revealed; to such doubts we may rightly hesitate to reply. Yet whatever our insufficiencies, life for individual and community depends upon the refusal to abandon the quest. Now abide faith, hope, love; by these we can go forward; and the apostolic expansion of them into the terms of the familiar 'grace'[1] may for some at least make the way plain. We can walk it in the faith expressed in one of St Paul's greatest affirmations: 'for we know that the Universe itself co-operates for good to those that love God.'[2]

[1] II Cor. xiii. 14.
[2] 'And we know that all things work together for good to them that love God', Rom. viii. 28. In spite of Professor Dodd, *Moffatt Commentary*, pp. 137–9, this seems the plain meaning of the text. It is tempting to adopt the reading suggested by W. L. Knox, *St Paul and the Church of the Gentiles*, p. 105, n. 2.

NOTES

It is worth noting that so far as English universities were concerned the attempt to treat theology as an exact science was fostered by the general and almost axiomatic belief in the difference between academic and vocational training.[2] That true learning was, if not useless, at least of no professional value was a conviction deeply ingrained and still not wholly abandoned.[3] Arising out of the distinction between the gentleman who had no need to work for his living and the professional classes whose livelihood depended on their earning capacity, it gave a prestige to the 'useless' accomplishments, mathematics and classics, and prevented for a long time the recognition of the vocational subjects, even medicine and law, as qualifying for a first degree. The view that any special training which would lead directly to a 'business' career or even to immediate professional status could not properly be provided at Oxford or Cambridge survived until after the First World War. In consequence any proposal to frame the theological curriculum so as to train men for the ministry of the Churches or even to present its contents in such a way as to promote discipleship met, until lately, with serious opposition. 'Theology', it was often said, 'has nothing to do with religion.'

Such a remark, however mistaken, could only have arisen from a belief that theology if it were to maintain its position as a genuinely academic subject must accept and employ the scientific method as then

---

[1] The account of Oxford, at the time to which this note refers, in R. G. Collingwood's *Autobiography* and Bishop F. R. Barry's *Recovery of Man* seems to me over-severe.

[2] Thus in 1870 at Cambridge, Professor W. Selwyn had defeated the proposed Voluntary Theological Examination 'on the ground that it seemed to be meant as a relief to the Bishops in examining candidates for Holy Orders'. Cf. D. A. Winstanley, *Later Victorian Cambridge*, p. 162.

[3] Thus, for example, Dr E. Brunner in his Gifford Lectures, *Christianity and Civilisation*, II, pp. 16, 17, tries to draw the distinction between science which has no practical aim and technology whose aim is strictly utilitarian, and G. H. Hardy, *A Mathematician's Apology*, especially §§ 16 and 21, defends pure mathematics on the ground of its uselessness.

understood. As we have seen, this method involved restricting the scope of science to such problems as were amenable to factual and quantitative treatment; it was also at this time contrasted with the practical and technological disciplines of the engineer and the electrician, the surgeon and the agriculturist; nor did it willingly include any use of the imagination or any appreciation of value since these belonged to the realm not of fact but of fancy. Historians, in spite of the protests of the author of *Clio a Muse*, had been ready to adopt this method, even though they distinguished themselves from the scientists by their belief that science was concerned always with the general while they dealt only with the particular. It was natural under the circumstances that theologians should follow their lead. A factual record of those events with which the development of man's knowledge of God was associated, and from which the system of belief and cultus has been derived, was the theologian's primary aim. That an objective account of them could be obtained by the techniques already familiar to the historian and the philosopher was not to be doubted. When T. R. Glover in 1920 published *The Jesus of History* he was followed by a large number of others who from their several standpoints claimed to give an authentic and impartial exposition of the facts. These were generally sincere and often learned; they were based upon evidence in the New Testament; yet they not only differed very widely but reflected their author's ideas and ideals. This is proof not only of the many-sidedness of their subject but of the impossibility of escaping subjectivity in history.

The breakdown of the confident belief in an objective and academic education as contrasted with a personal and practical has had far-reaching consequences, the full effects of which are still obscure. In the arts and to some degree also in history and theology the result has been an extravagant subjectivity almost anarchic in its relativism; and a consequent reassertion of the contrast between the scientific and the literary cultures. It is no doubt well to declare that we are educating people not propagating ideas: but if this leads to a renewed segregation of the academic from the vocational and technical, it may well become a thoroughly retrograde step: we do not want to see a B.Tech. set over against a B.A. But at present the effort to avoid such a cleavage, and to prevent the specialization that accentuates it, is coming from the scientists rather than from the supposedly more liberal and humane disciplines—though the recent response in many universities to the plans for cross-faculty teaching and for the provision of 'general' and 'background' lectures may indicate a greater measure of co-operation in the future.

II. ON THE YOUNG AND THE CONCEPT OF FREEDOM

As a result of a number of conferences with students and other young people in recent months as well as from wider ranges of evidence, it seems to me clear that one chief cause of the present restlessness and mass-hysteria is the degradation of the idea of freedom. Under Christian influence and against any religious background, freedom is seen to involve service to an ideal[1] and what Augustine called 'the blessed constraint of not doing wrong'. Deprived of its religious reference it easily becomes a mere exercise of anarchic self-will, 'freedom to do what I like and to possess what I can pay for'. In Britain and still more in America this is its almost universal significance. When parents are exhorted to 'give the kiddies a good time: they'll never have it again'; and educators inveigh against rules or any imposed discipline; and psychologists denounce inhibitions as the source of nearly all our ills, it scarcely needs the modern cult of glamour with its pornographic novels and strip-tease acts to give the younger generation an unnecessarily rough passage to maturity.

The young are not now prepared to follow Dr Margaret Mead and take their sexual ethics[2] from Bali, and do not in Britain accept Dr A. C. Kinsey's evidence as universal or conclusive. The best of them are in revolt against a liberty identical with licentiousness, but having no clear idea of freedom and disliking both American individualism and Russian regimentation are liable either to follow casual enthusiasms or to surrender to the claims of medievalism. The message of neo-orthodoxy, that on earth no progress is possible and conduct only a choice of two evils, is not giving them much encouragement in their aspirations.

III. ON MYSTICISM AND DUALISM

It will be evident that the treatment of mysticism here briefly stated differs widely from that in Evelyn Underhill's great book on the subject. To it and to her my own debt is deep and long-standing. In the days

[1] Cf. the collect 'whose service is perfect freedom'.

[2] She recognizes that 'the biological needs of our mammalian nature' (*Male and Female*, p. 18) even when satisfied leave life 'flat' but does not easily get her readers off flatlands—or Freudianism.

when she and her husband stayed with me in Blechingley we debated in a long series of letters the fundamental issue of her dualism—a discussion starting from a Soldanella flowering in my garden and the consequent question whether the 'grace' which we both acknowledged in it differed in kind or in degree from that in the Eucharist. Then, as now, it was impossible for me to accept her 'two-step philosophy'[1] and a two-story universe, or her treatment of magic and mysticism with its contrast between 'the outward and visible' and 'the inward and spiritual' or her insistence upon the 'way of unknowing'. It seemed to me then, and it seems still, that on her premises she was bound in the last resort to identify the mystic way with negation and to accept so sharp a cleavage between natural and supernatural as to endanger any fully incarnational philosophy. That she protested against this conclusion, and never willingly accepted it, is clear enough. But in fact, like Dionysius the Areopagite and all his school, she was forced into a dualist philosophy and a monophysite Christology. To me the antithesis which occasions this duality is not inherent in the nature of things or in reality but in the difference between our experience and our ability to interpret. As individuals we split up the unity which in our moments of integration we apprehend into a diversity of private worlds.

It seems clear that a fresh survey of the whole subject in the light of a less Cartesian background and of recent psychological researches would be timely.

IV. ON INTERCESSORY PRAYER

It is obvious that any such incarnational philosophy as we have been advocating is committed to a belief in what Charles Kingsley called 'a living, immanent, ever-working God'[2]—a God who is and acts. His action is manifest, to those who have eyes to see, in the processes of nature ('the things that are made' of Romans i. 20) and the events of history which, as we have claimed, can properly be regarded as the Acts of the Holy Spirit. It is manifest also in the Scriptures, the effective symbol and instrument of the Logos or Word of God, and in the dramatic liturgy of the Eucharist and other special sacraments. One of the most evident spheres and examples of such divine action is in the practice of intercession.

[1] *Mysticism*, p. 43; and compare with this, chapter VI on symbolism and chapter VII on magic.

[2] In the famous letter about the *Origin of Species* in *Life*, II, p. 171.

As we argue later it is here as always difficult, if not impossible, for our analytical insight to determine precisely the point at which God's inspiration and our human co-operation can be segregated. We can recognize, after the event and in all humility, that at such a time we were sustained and guided by a power not our own; that our whole sufficiency is of God; that in us, apart from Him, dwells no good thing. But, however complete our dependence, there is yet a moment of obedience and submission in which we must actively co-operate, and for which, because we are persons not things, sons and not slaves, we cannot abrogate responsibility.

Yet hard as it is to draw the line, broadly speaking, in this matter of prayer, the distinction is clear. Prayer, however poignant its appeal, can never be merely the cry of our own human need, the outpouring of our own heart-break or aspiration. Such petition will doubtless exert power: the passion of yearning for another's safety, the whole-hearted plea for his success, may well have their influence upon their object. But such effect as they produce comes, it would seem, from us alone: it is born of our agony and draws upon our strength.

But in intercession the power is not ours but of God, and it becomes available in proportion as we place ourselves in His presence, submit ourselves to His will, and let His Spirit have free course in us. That is why all prayer begins with an act of worship and is wholly conditioned by the clause 'not my will but thine be done'.

The Cambridge Platonists to whom we have been much indebted have given us a metaphor which will explain in the simplest terms the working of the intercessory power. If the soul is, as they declared, the mirror of the Lord, then the first moment of prayer is to lift the mirror till the light of God falls upon it. The act of contrition and confession that follows represents the cleansing from the glass of the stains revealed by the light. In intercession the light reflected from the soul is directed towards those for whom we wish to pray. It is not our light but God's that streams out towards them. Just as in Scripture the prophet reflects and transmits the vision of God, and we still feel its illuminative and healing power, so in intercession as we lose ourselves in our consciousness of God and of those for whom we pray, His presence and power become effective in them to fulfil the purpose of God's love. Of its reality and influence there is a mass of evidence which no one who has experience of it will easily dismiss.

V. ON THE CHRISTIAN AND THE BUDDHIST CONCEPTION
OF SUFFERING

It is important to attempt to make plain where the interpretation here presented differs from that of the syncretistic and neo-Buddhist philosophy put forward by Mr Aldous Huxley[1] and more persuasively by Mr H. I. Fausset. Interesting and important as it is to see the extent to which recent studies of Buddhism have rejected its manifest elements of world-negation and escapism and have assimilated the Buddhist non-attachment to the Christian agapé, there still remains in such restatements a conviction that in the last resort process is incompatible with deity, and suffering an element which belongs to the creature not to the Creator.[2]

This appears very clearly in Mr Fausset's criticism of the Christian acceptance of the Cross as the redemptive act—the symbol and instrument of creative love. Mr Fausett rejects the divinity of Jesus precisely at the point in which most Christians find it supremely manifested—at the cry 'My God, my God, why hast thou forsaken me'. He cannot admit the possibility of such self-emptying in the deity.[3] To my mind at least he reveals at this point his failure to enter into the full significance of suffering: it is akin to his lack of humour and to his ultimate nostalgia for the womb. One feels at the end of his very searching and honest book that he regards creation as a mistake, the process of history as a tragedy, and the perfecting of a small aristocracy of spiritual genius as its only value.

If there is not a real self-giving of the Creator in His creativity, if a detached compassion is the fullest response that man (or God) can achieve, if all our love, with its ecstasy and agony, is to end in this Olympian calm—then for me at least the adventure of the Universe loses its significance. The contemplation of one's own navel and even the Lotus-eaters' dreams are not far off.

In spite of the beautiful insistences in his prologue, Mr Fausset, like Mr Aldous Huxley—and Gautama—has never really been 'earthed'. For them no real incarnation, no real unity of divine and human is attainable; and if so, then the process of nature and history can only be regarded from the religious standpoint as an illusion.

A fuller and more scholarly appreciation of Buddhism is presented

[1] In *Ends and Means* and *The Perennial Philosophy*.
[2] Cf. *The Perennial Philosophy*, pp. 260–7.   [3] Cf. *Towards Fidelity*, p. 108.

by Professor R. H. L. Slater in *Paradox and Nirvana* (Chicago, 1951) which is an acknowledgment of the positive value of Nirvana and of Buddhism as a religion but does not fall into the error of arguing that non-attachment and love, the impersonal and the super-personal, the Buddhist and the Christian, are basically similar. Moreover, Slater discloses the source of the difference when he draws attention to the absence of any such personal union, between the Buddha and his followers, as exists between the Christian and Jesus Christ and is developed and interpreted in the doctrine of the Holy Spirit. The succession of Buddhas and Boddhisatvas, the belief in the Atman or emancipated self, and even the development of a stress upon emotion in Mahayana Buddhism do not bridge the gulf between Nirvana and this world or give a full meaning to the concept of redemption or to the words of the Lord's Prayer, 'Thy Kingdom come, Thy will be done, in earth as it is in heaven'. For the Buddhist, God, if there be a God, remains in the heavenlies: we ascend as we escape.

VI. ON THE FORM-CRITICISM

Dr R. H. Lightfoot's volume of Bampton Lectures, *History and Interpretation in the Gospels*, is certainly one of the most interesting and important of the English works which accept the main principle of the *Formgeschichte* school. He agrees with the school that, in the long period during which the things concerning Jesus were preserved orally, they gradually took the shapes supposedly familiar in contemporary story-telling; that the earliest and indeed all the Gospels were made up of little units of sayings or traditions; that with the exception of the passion narrative there is no continuous record of events; and that to the authors alone is due the arrangement of all the rest of the material.

In thus breaking away from the exaggeratedly literary concepts that have dominated the great period of Synoptic study in Britain which had its first-fruits in Sir John Hawkins's *Horae Synopticae* and its fullest harvest in B. H. Streeter's *The Four Gospels*, Dr Lightfoot has done valuable service. Whether or no we agree in detail with the 'form' hypothesis, it is important that the relationship of the gospel material to the early Christian communities and the consequent evidence that the tradition goes back behind its committal to writing and perhaps to the beginnings of the Church should be emphasized. Those of us who know the tenacity of memory of men and races who do not rely on the written word, the speed with which stories take a fixed form and the accuracy with which they are repeated and preserved, will not agree that such an oral period need involve a time of myth-making.

But Lightfoot's work, learned and detailed as it is, has not commended itself to all scholars. The reason is mainly twofold. First, while admitting a sequence of events in the passion narrative he quite arbitrarily assumes that no such arrangement linked together the little units ('pericopae') which constitute the rest of the Gospel. This seems a plain exaggeration. The stories, whether originally told by eye-witnesses or by hearsay, were not isolated from the subject which they were intended to illustrate—be this an aspect of Christian conduct or a reminiscence of the teaching and works of Jesus. They took form in a sequence; there is a strong probability that in origin this, like the Passion narration, was historical. Plainly the sequence could be altered to suit the subject to be illustrated; but in the early times actual memories would check dislocations. Thus there are sections in St Mark which consist manifestly of disconnected episodes; but in the main a coherent scheme is evident; and in many details this is plainly not due to the author's ingenuity but to the survival of authentic reminiscences that indicate the occasion and place of the event. No one will wish to reaffirm H. B. Swete's belief in a regular consecutive itinerary for the Galilean ministry[1] or even to accept all the details of F. C. Burkitt's reconstruction;[2] but to sweep this aside unexamined for the sake of an arbitrary hypothesis, which even so is not applied to all the material, is a serious critical weakness.

So too in his denigration of St Luke and his references to the scholars who are not prepared to accept the recent strictures upon his Gospel and Acts, there is evidence of the same failure to look at the evidence fully and in perspective.

The fact is that the reaction against the textual scholarship which gave us such monumental work on the Synoptic Gospels has gone too far and has now accomplished its one valuable result—the reminder that behind them lie a period of oral tradition and the catechetical needs of the infant churches. All the elaborate classification of paradigms can be dismissed as an example of ingenuity and subjectivism; and with it go, first, the belief that the stories are 'stylized' and imaginary, and secondly the suggestion that the Gospels are myth, not history.

---

[1] Cf. his commentary, pp. lviii–lx and lxxxi–lxxxiv, and maps.
[2] Cf. *The Gospel History and its Transmission*, pp. 79–95.

I may perhaps be allowed, as one who in the days before the First World War lectured on the Synoptists and urged that they contained plain signs of oral tradition, to repeat the remark that it is as absurd to suppose that the Gospels were composed by groups of anonymous Levantines who had no first-hand knowledge of Jesus as to suppose that Napoleon's battle orders were composed and issued by the camp-followers of the Grand Army. The world was not changed by the myth of a Christian Mithra but by men like the Greeks who came to Philip saying 'Sir, we would see Jesus'.

VII. ON OBSERVATION AND MIRACLE, LEGEND AND HISTORY

The extent to which the description and indeed the actual observation of any event is conditioned by the presuppositions of the observer is familiar to every student of nature. Those who like myself were brought up on Victorian anecdotes of bird and animal life, on Kipling's Jungle Books, on Thompson Seton and 'the School of the Woods' will know that all their own earlier records of behaviour were suspect. My own contact with Professor Lloyd Morgan warned me of the need to reject most of my previous observations; for I could not be sure how far the details were suggested and coloured by my expectations and by human analogies. To become a trained and competent observer involves a definite discipline.

Yet when this warning is applied to the records of miracle in an age that believed as fully in demons as we do in bacteria, it must not be forgotten that such presuppositions though they affect and even distort the interpretation of events do not necessarily impair the substantial actuality of their occurrence. To assume as too many critics have done that the appearance of miracle in itself reduces the status of the record from history to legend and justifies us in rejecting the whole as fictitious is totally illogical. Because, for example, Tacitus describes the prodigies which proclaim public calamities (e.g. *Annales* xiv 64; xv 47) or Shakespeare declares that 'The heavens themselves blaze forth the death of princes' or Waterton ascribes the descent of vultures upon a corpse to their sense of smell, or Dr J. B. Watson interprets mental activity in terms of imperceptible movements of the larynx, the absurdity of the explanation does not disprove or even discredit their testimony in other respects. If, for example, in the current

histories of science the prevalence of mechanistic concepts has introduced misinterpretation of evidence and mistakes of omission and
commission, this does not mean that such histories can be dismissed as
legendary and valueless.

VIII. ON F. D. MAURICE

Though it is becoming a platitude to say that of all English Christians
of the nineteenth century F. D. Maurice was the most important and
the most prophetic,[1] it is strange that of the many books that have
lately been devoted to him so few realize the basic simplicity of his
message. He was one of those very rare men who habitually lived and
thought against an eternal background, *sub specie eternitatis*. All his
experience was conditioned by his conviction of the universality of
Christ and of the unity of all men, whether they know it or not, in Him.
This did not mean that he was misty or unpractical (as superficial
observers supposed): to have founded the first college for the higher
education of women, presided over the Christian Socialists and played
a chief part in the establishment of the Co-operative movement, to
have been Principal of the first Working Men's College, and the
inspiration of the most vital social and religious pioneers of the next
generation—these are sufficient achievements to silence such criticism.
It did mean that his own confession, 'the desire for unity both in the
nation and in the Church has haunted me all my days',[2] was profoundly
true. For those who liked neat dissections and analytical logic as for
those to whom his background was invisible, he seemed heretical and
futile: they are going to oblivion.[3] For those like J. M. Ludlow and
Charles Kingsley, Tom Hughes and Alexander Macmillan, F. J. A.
Hort and later B. F. Westcott who knew the secret of his quality, he
was the prophet; their work, like his, lives. He might on occasion fail
to interpret the eternal accurately; he might hesitate intolerably until
he saw what he must do; but in the hungry forties when Church and
State were alike helplessly bewildered he had a compass by which to
set his course.

[1] Cf., for example, N. Annan, *Leslie Stephen*, pp. 179–84, which appreciates his greatness but does not seem to understand its quality.
[2] Sir J. F. Maurice's *Life of Maurice*, II, p. 632.
[3] A list of some of his critics is given in my *Christian Socialism, 1848–1854*, pp. 78–81;
others are cited by H. G. Wood, *Frederick Denison Maurice* (Cambridge, 1950), pp. 3–10.

So in this matter of the Atonement he paid small heed to the traditional metaphors which by this time were irrelevant and dangerously misleading, but penetrated to the real experience of which they had once been effective explanations and disclosed in new and poignant terms the essential significance and scale of what Christ had done and is doing for mankind.[1]

IX. ON SUFFERING AND SIN

The ancient belief that suffering is always the consequence of sin, even if not the proof of God's punishment of the sinner, is still so widely accepted[2] as to need fuller consideration. In these lectures suffering is used in its original meaning of sensitiveness and sympathy, the sharing of experience with others, the self-giving of love. As such it is plainly an eternal element in the nature of God.

To those who condemned Patripassianism (the suffering of God) as a heresy, suffering meant concrete pain and this involved 'changeableness' or transience. The belief that God the Father suffered with His Son on Calvary was condemned in order to prevent confusion between the Godhead and the manhood of Christ, and to maintain the changelessness of the divine.

As is (I hope) evident, I do not regard suffering as equivalent to pain, although at the human level and in an imperfect and sinful world it normally includes it. I believe this distinction to be in agreement with the teaching of the New Testament and of the richest thought of the Second Isaiah,[3] where suffering is the redemptive energy of love in action.

In the Gospels the *locus classicus* is perhaps not John ix. 2–3 (of the man born blind, 'neither hath this man sinned nor his parents'), though this is at least proof that Jesus was not regarded as accepting the simple sin-suffering tradition, but Mark ii. 5, where Jesus says to the palsied 'Son, thy sins be forgiven thee'. Commentators, surprised that there is no reference to the man's repentance or to the connexion between sin and disease, have been puzzled by this even to the extent of suggesting a fusion of two stories, the forgiveness of a penitent and the cure of a paralytic. To anyone who realizes two points, the sense of guilt which

---

[1] Cf. A. M. Ramsey, *F. D. Maurice and the Conflicts of Modern Theology* (Cambridge, 1951), pp. 58–71.

[2] It is disappointing to find that so valuable a book as F. C. Grant, *An Introduction to New Testament Thought* constantly equates suffering with sin, e.g. 'sin, suffering, Satan, death', pp. 185 etc.   [3] Cf. Isai. liii and lxiii. 9.

the traditional belief imposed upon the sufferer, and the concept of God as wrathful and estranged which this belief involved, the utterance of Jesus is both intensely relevant and in full accord with His primary message. He says in effect 'God is not what you suppose: He is not vindictive but loving and merciful: be freed from your sin-obsession'. His subsequent words demonstrate that forgiveness (restoration of a loving relationship)[1] has taken place, and brought with it the possibility of restored health.

X. ON AGAMIC COMPLEXES IN PLANTS

There would seem to be a strong case for discounting the conclusions reached by Babcock and Stebbins in their study of *Crepis* (p. 63) and endorsed in a less definite form by Stebbins, *Variation and Evolution in Plants*, pp. 396–419, that agamic complexes, such as *Hieracium* and *Rubus*, represent relatively unimportant and 'doomed' stocks. This contention seems to rest on the argument that 'the life expectancy of agamic complexes is shorter than that of sexual groups' since 'sexual species may give rise to entirely new types by means of progressive mutation and gene re-combination but agamic complexes can produce only new variations on an old theme' (pp. 4–17); and to be supported by the case of *Houttuynia cordata*, an apomict which may be the last survivor of an ancient agamic stock.

In view of the great advantage, in a changing environment, of the apomict's ability to perpetuate its variation over the tendency of the sexed form to return to its norm, and in view of the obvious adaptability and vigour of *Hieracium, Crepis, Rubus* and the like, it may well be doubted whether agamic reproduction should be written off as racially disastrous. We know little of the cause of mutations and certainly cannot assume as Stebbins does that they are a potent source of novelty in the sexed but cannot produce similar effects in apomicts.[2] There is no evidence (so far as I am aware) that agamic complexes represent a 'dead end' except the theory that their method of reproduction cannot be so effective as the sexual—a theory of which no proof is offered.

[1] This is the basic meaning of forgiveness in the teaching of Jesus as in the Lord's Prayer and in Matt. xviii. 21–2, Luke xv. 17–24; and on its negative side Mark iii. 28–30, where deliberate insensitiveness to goodness renders such relationship impossible.

[2] C. H. Ostenfeld, *Journal of Genetics*, xi, 117–22 (1921), has discovered the existence of apogamic mutation in *Hieracium* (*vulgatum* agg.).

It is perhaps worth while to suggest that here in Britain where our variety of climate, altitude and geology favours a wide adaptability, and where we have, in addition to the agamic groups already named, many superficially similar complexes, e.g. in *Ranunculus* (*aquaticus* agg.), *Viola*, *Alchemilla*, *Rosa* (*canina* agg.), *Euphrasia*, *Orchis* and the Grasses, especially *Alopecurus*, *Bromus* (*secalinus* agg.), *Festuca*, *Poa*, *Calamagrostis* and *Agropyrum*, a thorough investigation of the whole problem should be undertaken. At present while we pay tribute to the work not only of cytologists like J. Clausen, Gustafsson, Müntzing and C. D. Darlington, but of taxonomists like Pugsley and Drabble, it seems to an on-looker tolerably plain that speculation has outrun demonstration and that we here are very favourably placed for a cytological, genetic, and ecological survey of the whole question. Enquiries might be directed to the following points:

1. What is the precise character and the probable cause of apomixis in the various agamic groups?

2. Is it demonstrable that apomictic varieties are more numerous and adaptable than varieties in sexual complexes, e.g. *Euphrasia*?

3. If so, is such variability less advantageous to the species than sexual reproduction? And if so on what genetic and physiological grounds can this be established?

4. Are mutations less likely to produce new types in agamic than in sexual groups? If so, why so?

It is easy to guess the answers to most of these questions: the subject has had enough of guess-work.

XI. ON CONTROLLED ADAPTATION

I am allowed by the kindness of my brother-in-law to print the two following from his observations:

I.

'Many years ago, when resident naturalist at a little biological station at Larne Harbour in Ireland, I observed an interesting case of immediate and continuous adaptation to an environment by very young specimens of the Tunicate, *Ascidiella aspersa*. This species is sessile and normally attached to rocks, piles, oyster-shells and so on by nearly the whole of one side of the test. I have seen many thousands of the species and have never come across one which had not a large area of attachment.

'While at Larne Harbour I fertilized some eggs of *aspersa*, eggs and milt being taken from fully sessile specimens. Embryos and larvae in successive stages of development were drawn from the jar in which the organisms were kept alive and the remainder attached themselves to the sides and bottom of the jar. A certain amount of a rather flocculent substance became deposited on the bottom of the jar, gradually rising to a depth of over a centimetre. It was interesting to find that, although the young tunicates on the sides of the jar were attached, in the normal way, by the greater part of one side of the test, those on the bottom were at first attached by a very small area at one end. These then produced very thin and hardly visible stalks which gradually increased in length as the deposit in the jar became deeper, so that the animals, apart from their stalks, were always in the clear water above the deposit. The stalks were so thin and flexible that the animals "waved about" on the slightest movement of the jar.'

2.

'When I was a boy I kept many marine animals alive in shallow pie-dishes through which a constant but very small stream of sea water flowed. Of the sea-anemones I found that the Daisy Anemone (*Sagartia bellis*) was the easiest to keep alive and in health. These remain fully expanded nearly always, feed well and grow very fast, if regularly fed. At first I used to feed them on limpets cut into fairly large pieces. Later, however, I found a bed of mussels and started to feed the anemones on mussels. The anemones swallowed these considerably faster than they had swallowed the limpets, in fact, they seemed to prefer them—to use ordinary English. Once or twice I tried limpets again, but, on placing these on the discs of the anemones, they were immediately rejected, without any attempt on the part of the anemones to swallow them; usually a single outer tentacle was passed inwards under the food, and this was then, quite rapidly and without the slightest hesitation, thrown off the disc. Mussels fed to the anemones were always readily taken, even immediately after they had rejected limpets. If overfed on mussels, further mussels were never readily rejected, the anemones always attempted to swallow them, even if parts were left protruding from the mouth.'

H. J. BUCHANAN-WOLLASTON
Formerly Principal Naturalist, Ministry of
Agriculture and Fisheries

XII. ON THE EVIDENCE OF SIR CHARLES SHERRINGTON

That we must learn to abandon the body-mind antithesis at least in the dualistic form proposed by Descartes, the 'ghost in the machine' as Professor G. Ryle calls it, was made evident to many of us by the appearance of one of the most attractive and profound of the last attempts to accept it, the late Sir Charles Sherrington's Gifford Lectures. Few men have been better qualified to interpret the physiology and philosophy of the mechanism of the living creature; no one has done it with greater wealth of illustration or range of presentation. Yet his work could not but convince a careful reader of the total inadequacy of the Cartesian dichotomy. Committed, as he felt himself to be, to maintaining the complete separation of the machine and the psyche, and in consequence to rejecting any idea of concomitance,[1] he was driven to a doctrine of parallelism, and to a manifest bewilderment as to the recognition or explanation of purpose, and to a multitude of attempts to define which actions belonged to the 'energy-system' and which to the 'mind'. He could not bring himself to associate mechanism with purpose[2] or assign to Nature any element of design or value: she was not even immoral, but only a-moral.[3] Yet he could not merge mental phenomena in physics and chemistry or represent them as in any sense derivable from energy. With an almost passionate desire for unity of interpretation, but with an honesty that refused to gloss over inconvenient facts or to ignore his own valuation of the suffering and frustration of the evolutionary process he could only set out his hesitations and leave us with the conviction that, granted his postulates, the problem was insoluble.

XIII. ON THE HOLISM OF GENERAL SMUTS

It is obvious that the general outline of the creative process to which we are looking has much in common with what J. C. Smuts has called holism—the tendency inherent in all entities, physical, organic and human, to enter into combination and form 'wholes'. His book

[1] Even in the living organism he insisted that 'mind' was only intermittently present, *Man on His Nature*, pp. 317–19.

[2] I am afraid that he like most mechanists was exposed to A. N. Whitehead's expostulation, 'What is the sense of talking about a mechanical explanation when you do not know what you mean by mechanics?' (*Science and the Modern World*, p. 24).

[3] *Op. cit.* p. 383.

Holism and Evolution, published in 1926, took up ideas already developed by S. Alexander and C. Lloyd Morgan[1] in their Gifford Lectures, but set them in a wider context and with a more definite emphasis. The unique combination in him of an almost universal range of interest, a wide knowledge in many fields of science and learning, an alert and creative mind, and a swift and penetrating insight made him not only a statesman striving to bring his country into an international order, but a philosopher well qualified to formulate a large and appropriate schema of integration. For nearly twenty years, from 1930 when he spoke for me in Liverpool Cathedral till his death, we were in correspondence over these matters; and on his last visit to Cambridge he was looking forward to getting back to them and to rewriting the last chapter of *Holism* so as to demonstrate that the holistic process had its proper culmination in the integrative energy of the deity.[2] It is to be hoped that when his papers are fully studied material for this chapter will be found among them.

XIV. ON THE DOCTRINE OF THE TRINITY

Any full treatment of the subject must needs be lengthy and would probably fall outside the field proper to these lectures. The difference noted in Chapter VII is of course ancient, and the confusion over the precise meaning of hypostasis in the Nicene Creed is familiar to all students of Jerome. It is permissible to say in criticism of Dr Hodgson's appeal to experience that there are in fact and among Christians of unquestionable sincerity and ability two distinct types, those whose religion centres in thought and devotion upon Christ, and who see God (as it has been quaintly said) as 'just Jesus everywhere', and for whom there is little distinction between the indwelling Christ and the Holy Spirit, and those whose worship is primarily directed to God, God as revealed in and interpreted by Christ, God who is active in the incarnate Word and the indwelling Spirit, but who is essentially one. To the first it is natural to think of the Trinity in terms of the analogy of three men; to the second the Augustinian analogy of three elements in the personality is more satisfying.

---

[1] Only the first volume *Emergent Evolution* (1923) of his Gifford lectures had appeared in time for Smuts to see; cf. *Holism and Evolution*, p. 321. Their thought is strikingly similar.

[2] This was in fact the obvious conclusion of the book as first published; but in 1926 he still associated religion with a supernatural and biblical cosmology.

It is probably sufficient to say that each of these types can show both arguments and 'fruit' to rebut any suggestion of heresy, and that the attempt made by C. C. J. Webb and others to argue from the quality of human personality to that of the Godhead is dangerously anthropomorphic. But for me at least, it is a great comfort to find Dr Karl Barth, whose characteristic doctrines seem to me gravely exaggerated and almost heretical in their transcendentalism, proposing that, in view of the modern meaning of 'person' as centre of self-consciousness and of the consequent danger of tritheism, we should drop the term and speak of 'three modes of existence'.[1] This is certainly nearer to the Nicene theology and does not prohibit either of the two types of experience.

XV. ON DR W. D. DAVIES'S CRITICISM

Dr W. D. Davies in his long and careful review of St Paul's doctrine of the Holy Spirit castigates me for associating the Holy Spirit with the cosmic process, and quotes my books, *The Creator Spirit*, p. 23, and *Science, Religion and the Future*, p. 73. He states in criticism that 'The Spirit in Paul is not "the manifestation of the Godhead in the cosmic process"; it is on the contrary, however unsatisfactory such language must be, a gift poured forth from on high; it is supernatural; it retains the sense in Paul as in the Old Testament of "a specially given energy"'.[2] It is only fair to say that in the passages quoted I did not connect the cosmic activity of the Spirit with St Paul; and that in criticizing my *Creator Spirit* Dr W. Temple stated that he would prefer to assign the cosmic activity of the Godhead to the Logos.[3] But I had of course worked thoroughly over the Pauline use of the Spirit, and in other parts of his book found Dr Davies expressing my own conclusions, namely (i) that it is difficult to distinguish the Stoic from the Rabbinic ideas of Spirit in St Paul;[4] (ii) that 'there is no consistency in St Paul's use of the term πνεῦμα: sometimes he employs it to denote a normal element in human nature (e.g. Gal. vi. 18; I Cor. ii. 11; Rom. viii. 16)';[5] (iii) that, though he claims that Paul sharply distinguishes the spirit of man from the Holy Spirit, this claim is very hard to reconcile with (ii) or with e.g. Gal. v and vi (how can love, joy, peace, etc. be sharply

[1] Cf. *The Doctrine of the Word of God*, p. 400.
[2] *St Paul and Rabbinic Judaism*, p. 190. He quotes this from H. Wheeler Robinson.
[3] I have discussed the confusion of Logos and Spirit above, pp. 85–6.
[4] *Op. cit.* pp. 181–3.   [5] *Ibid.* p. 185.

distinguished as divine or human?); (iv) that he seems to accept Paul's speech at Athens (Acts xvii. 27–9), which is irreconcilable with his criticism of me.

The plain fact is that like many recent students he exaggerates the contrast between Hellenic and Jewish ideas in St Paul and first-century Judaism, ignores the extent to which the Logos doctrine is a legitimate development of New Testament theology, and tends to ascribe to the Pauline vocabulary a technical precision which is not in fact discoverable in it.

XVI. ON ESCHATOLOGY AND THE SECOND ADVENT

In the usual tradition of Protestantism and in most modern references, eschatology is not interpreted as the realm of ends or eternal life but as the last day, the end of the world; and this is commonly identified with the Second Advent of Christ. The present phase, since the first coming of the Lord, is an interim, in which all progress is illusory; the prayer for the coming of the Kingdom refers only to the final catastrophe; salvation is attainable by individuals, it is meaningless for society; the length of this phase is wholly unknowable; and at its close Christ will come in triumph and for judgment; and history will be finished.[1]

It is characteristic of this conception that the Second Advent is sharply contrasted with the First. Jesus was born in a stable, lived the friend of sinners, went about doing good, and was betrayed and slain. Christ will come again in glory; every eye will see Him; His wrath will fill the world with terror; His vengeance will cast the wicked into hell; His kingdom will be established in power.

There is no doubt evidence for such a contrast in a few passages of the New Testament; and in one or two in St Matthew it is impossible to reconcile the eschatology with the Johannine or 'realized'. It is difficult to believe that the consequences of such a contrast have been appreciated. If true it means that the first coming is a mere preliminary, incomplete in its effects, alike in its picture of God and in its message to men. For in it the last word is to be spoken not by the victory of suffering love but by the vengeance of an impatient despot. Love will have been proven impotent; power and wrath will replace it.

Such a culmination could only be tolerable if, as the Apostles

[1] So, for example, R. Niebuhr, *The Nature and Destiny of Man*, II, pp. 49–54. Niebuhr, like Schweitzer, relies almost entirely on St Matthew for his biblical authority.

(according to Schweitzer) believed, the interval were short—if in fact the second coming followed immediately as part of a single drama. If the first coming is neither final nor effective, and the second is indefinitely postponed, then the claim that Christ is the image of the invisible, or the Gospel the power of God unto salvation, becomes untenable; and the whole ethos of Apocalyptic is changed.

For in the first century men could regard a sudden irruption of the divine and the end of the world as a possible and eagerly awaited event. It might happen tomorrow—literally as predicted. The possibility gave a zest to life and for the Christian a vivid hope. To us with our knowledge of geological time and astronomical space such an event can only be taken seriously in terms of the hydrogen bomb—and this would be human and diabolic, not supernatural and divine. No one but a criminal lunatic could look forward to it with enthusiasm; and if it came it would not be the end of history but only of humanity or our planet.

Moreover a God who behaves after the fashion of the *Dies irae* is not of one substance with the Crucified nor a deity with strong claim to our worship. Judgment (as defined in John iii. 19) [1] is a terrible reality: so is the austerity of love (as Jesus reveals). But this second adventism, which suggests an experiment that can at any moment be replaced by something radically different from it, is calculated to destroy all confidence in the sufficiency of Jesus or of the Church.

[1] The A.V. rendering of which is misleading!

INDEX

Abelard, 93, 95
Acts of the Apostles as history, 17, 169
Adam, J., 4
Adler, A., 26 n.
Agar, W. E., 17, 141–2; quoted, 168
Alexander, S., 219
Al-Hallâj, 59
Allport, G. W., 28 n.; quoted, 30–1
Allshorn, F., 164 n.
Annan, N., 213 n.
Anselm, St, 93
Anti-rationalism, 52–3
Apollinarius, 87, 98 n., 99 n.
Apollonius of Tyana, 74
Aquinas, St Thomas, 185
Arber, A., 139 n.
Arberry, A. J., 59 n.
Arianism, 98
Aristotle, 186 n.
Arnold, M., 202 n.
Athanasius, St, 88, 98 n.
Atonement, doctrines of, 92–7
Augustine, St, 24, 25, 124 n., 127 n., 156;
    his great omission, 164; quoted, 206
Aulen, G., 92

Babcock, E. B., 133 n., 215
Bacon, F., quoted, 155
Baillie, D. M., 72 n., 75 n., 102 n., 128 n.,
    147 n.
Baillie, J., 75 n., 129 n.
Baldwin, J. M., 132 n.
Barnes, E. W., 6, 128 n.
Barry, F. R., 189 n.
Barth, K., 42, 46 n., 152, 220
Barton, B., 71 n.
Beausobre, J. de, 115 n.
Bennett, G. T., 136
Benson, M., 186 n.
Bergson, H., 153–4
Bernal, J. D., 142
Bethune-Baker, J. F., 6, 98 n.

Birds, behaviour of, 11; evolution of,
    134
Blake, W., 13 n., 195
Bonnet, P., 136 n.
Bosanquet, B., quoted, 179
Bowman, A. A., 4, 23 n.
Boycott, A. E., 141 n.
Boycott, B. B., 143 n.
Boyle, R. 129
Bridges, R., 112
Browne, T., 32 n.
Browning, R., quoted, 2, 108, 178
Brunner, E., 35 n., 42, 52 n., 120 n.,
    204 n.
Buber, M., 33 n.
Buchanan-Wollaston, H. J., 136 n., 216–17
Buddhism, 55, 209–10
Bultmann, R., 7 n.
Burdet, A., 138 n.
Burkitt, F. C., 74 n., 188 n., 211
Burnaby, J., 164 n.
Butler, S., 129 n.

Cadoux, C. J., 71 n.
Cairns, D., 4
Caldecott, A., 36 n.
Calvin, J., 156
Canonization, conditions of, 100, 127
Capek, K., 117
Carington, W., 136 n.
Carlyle, T., 12
Cartesianism challenged, 14
Chadwick, H., 89 n.
Chalcedon, creed of, 88
Chesterton, G. K., 25
Christ, impact of, 62–3; portraits of, 69, 70;
    lives of, 71; significance today, 80–1
Christology in New Testament, 73–4; in
    early Church, 82–3, 86–7; in modern
    times, 101–4
Clausen, J., 216
Clement of Alexandria, 19, 83

223